The

CONFIDENTIAL

Guide to

Golf Courses

Volume 3 - The Americas (Summer Destinations)

by

Tom Doak

with

Ran Morrissett
Masa Nishijima
Darius Oliver

PHOTOGRAPHIC CREDITS

Unless otherwise noted, all photographs in this book are by the author, Tom Doak.
Additional photo credits, see page 288.

Renaissance Golf Publishing, LLC
530 E. 8th St.
Traverse City, MI 49686
email: confguidegolf@gmail.com

Printed in Canada

10 9 8 7 6 5 4 3 2 1

ACKNOWLEDGMENTS

The information in this book is the product of many years of days and nights away from home. It wouldn't have happened unless each of us had the support of a family who have forgiven our curiosity about the world and its golf courses.

Nor would any of us have been able to travel so much except for the generosity of other golfers, who have hosted us at their clubs and occasionally let us sleep on their couch, helping to defray the costs of travel. Some readers might see this as a potential conflict of interest, but no one could have seen as much as we've seen while paying full freight … we are all golf bums, plain and simple. As you'll see, we've overcompensated for any potential conflicts of interest by being blunt about our opinions, for better or for worse. We apologize to our hosts if we did not find their course as appealing as their company.

Volume 3 is a home game for yours truly. I grew up in Connecticut, not far from the great courses of Westchester County and Long Island, NY, where I started trespassing as soon as I got my driver's license. For the last thirty years, I've spent the bulk of my time in northern Michigan, which is why there are so many courses reviewed from the Midwest. And I've been fortunate in my design career to have worked on nineteen courses reviewed in Volume 3, not to mention a couple that no longer exist, and many older courses where we are retained as consulting architects.

So, for starters, in this book I need to thank my mom and dad for feeding my childhood interest in golf course architecture at a time when it was a really odd obsession. Neither was more than an occasional golfer, but they loved the outdoors, and they were happy that I wound up working at something I loved, even though both passed away too soon to see the best of my work.

I visited many of the most famous courses in this volume while I was in college, studying to be a designer: in fact, the very first famous course that responded to one of my letters was The Country Club, in Massachusetts, which I went to play as a freshman at M.I.T., courtesy of their green chairman, the late Charlie Pyle. I'm still amazed that places like the National Golf Links of America and Merion were so accommodating to a 19-year-old with a dream. I saw many others [including a couple of them in the dirt] while serving my apprenticeship with Pete and Alice Dye. And it's been lovely in the past couple of years to walk unannounced into pro shops from coast to coast, and be warmly received and sometimes invited to play.

Thanks among others to club pros like Fred Muller, Bill Kittleman and Alan Carter for hosting me at their clubs and sharing their other favorite venues; to local experts like Bill Shean in Chicago, Lorne Rubenstein in Toronto, Larry Lambrecht in Rhode Island, Brad Klein in Connecticut, and Michael Moore in Maine for sharing their secrets; and to restoration architects like Ian Andrew, Ron Forse, and my own associates Bruce Hepner and Brian Schneider for pointing me to their discoveries.

For the maps and illustrations herein, full credit goes to my European associate Angela Moser, who did all the drawings and helped get me comfortable with the software to put the book together. The cover art is the third in a series from the talented Josh Smith, who is also the superintendent at Orinda Country Club in California.

Most of all, to my wife, Jennifer, thanks for helping me with the graphic design and layout of the book, for supporting me in making time for the things I love to do, and for feeding Zenzi when I'm away.

Pacific NW

The Mountain
West

New
England
& The
Maritimes

The Great
Lakes

Vancouver

The Great Plains

NYC Metro

Washington D.C.

The Appalachians

Mid Atlantic States

TABLE OF CONTENTS

INTRODUCTION

Welcome back to The Confidential Guide.

If you're new to the series, a quick overview: the main purpose of this book is to serve as a travel guide, to steer you to fun courses you may never have heard of, and to save you from paying hundreds of dollars to play courses that we feel are overrated. To that end, herein we have provided our honest reviews of each course we've visited over four lifetimes of golf travel.

When I wrote the first version of this book 27 years ago, I was only 27 myself, and it was circulated strictly among friends, so I didn't think twice about writing a negative or even outrageous review of a course where I felt it was warranted. That's what made the book infamous, and sought-after. Nowadays, I am all too aware that any negative review generates controversy, and even speculation as to my motives.

If anyone thinks I enjoy the controversy, they are mistaken. I get no kicks being vilified for putting my opinions into print, and often wonder whether my wife was right to say that it would be a really great book if it weren't for the numbers!

Undoubtedly, it would be much easier and more politically correct to just pretend we never saw certain courses, or to pull punches and give a lukewarm review to a course to which you couldn't drag us back. But this book demands nothing less than our honesty. You are paying to hear our real opinions, to help decide if you want to make the effort to see a far-away course. If we don't think you should go, we'll say so, and hopefully offer several better alternatives, no matter how much it may offend some architect or developer.

Lost in all this is that the magazines focus on our negative reviews, and pay scant attention to our positive reviews of the many courses that we've enjoyed. Though some of our lowest ratings have been given to modern courses, we've also awarded high marks to many courses by those very same architects, and I've included three other opinions alongside my own to be sure I'm being as fair as possible. There aren't many architects working today who have written more good things about others' work than I have.

Amazingly, this book covers almost as many courses [675] in this one region as my original Confidential Guide covered in the entire world. That makes it the biggest book in our series, and probably the best, judging by the number of 7's and 8's and 10's we've passed out.

Volume 3 is also a great testament to the volume of quality work done over the last 25 years, both in the creation of new courses and the restoration of older gems. One fair criticism of Volume 2 was that there are several courses that have been markedly improved since we last saw them 10 or 20 years ago, and in fact there are several courses I've seen recently where I was amazed how much better they looked than when I first saw them. But, our resources are not unlimited -- especially the most precious of them, our time -- so all we can do regarding this flaw is to say that the more dated our review, the more chance there is that we may have missed on our review of a course. Just remember: it could go either way!

INTRODUCING MY CO-AUTHORS

When I chose to embark on a new edition of The Confidential Guide, I knew that I could not do it all by myself, if it was to be anywhere near as thorough as the previous editions. More than three thousand new courses were built around the world in the boom between 1995 and 2008, and though I've gone out of my way to see the best of them, my day job has limited my time for seeing the work of other designers. To do the last twenty years of design any justice, I would need help; but for the book to be coherent, those helpers had to share a similar viewpoint and the same high standards, so our reviews would be compatible. Three potential collaborators stood out for me, and when I wrote them at Christmas of 2012 to see if they would be interested, I had them all signed up in a day.

I will introduce them alphabetically – which is also the order in which their reviews and grades of courses are included in the book.

I first came to know Ran Morrissett directly as a result of The Confidential Guide. The very last entry in the collector's edition was in the "gossip" section for New Zealand, where I mentioned a course in the far north of the North Island, near Ninety Mile Beach, and offered brownie points to any of my readers who would go to check it out. A year later, I heard from Ran, who had gone to play the course, Kaitaia, and recommended it to me. A few years later, Ran and his brother John founded the web site Golf Club Atlas.com, with in-depth reviews of their favorite courses and a discussion group where I am a regular participant. He is a first class writer and analyst of golf courses, and I'm happy that the resurrection of this book, like that of The World Atlas of Golf, has drawn him to put his words into print. More recently, Ran partnered with Ben Cowan-Dewar in the development of Cabot Links, featured prominently in the Gourmet's Choice here.

I have known Masa Nishijima longer than Ran or Darius, since the days when we were both skinny young men who traveled the world to see as many golf courses as we could. In addition to writing about golf and baseball for the major Japanese magazines, Masa conducted VIP international golf tours for the Japan Travel Bureau. In between tours, he did research for JTB, checking out all the cities of Europe and Asia to find the places where international travelers would be comfortable and welcome. His research included visits to more than 1400 courses, though for Volume 3, I've seen almost 600 of the courses reviewed, double the number of any of my co-authors.

It was Masa who introduced me to Darius Oliver, the young Australian who completes our foursome. After growing up in Melbourne, and starting to write about golf courses for Australian Golf Digest, Darius set out on a world tour in 2005 to produce his two large-format books, Planet Golf and Planet Golf USA. Since we started our project, he has also been involved in the creation of the new Cape Wickham course in King Island, Australia.

The four of us got together in New Zealand in February 2016 at the opening of Tara Iti -- one benefit to this undertaking is getting to spend time together with my friends and playing some golf. I was even a witness to Ran making the first hole-in-one at Cabot Cliffs, and am amazed at his restraint not to nominate it as his favorite 16th anywhere!

All of our reviews are written in my voice, for consistency, though the number ratings show that there are some courses where I rely entirely on my co-authors' views, as I haven't been there.

WHAT WE LIKE

If you're going out of your way to play a course that's new to you, you deserve to know whether the trip is worth the effort. Value for money is different for each observer, but time is a precious commodity for every one of us.

The four of us don't think exactly alike, as you'll see from the disagreements on ratings for some courses; criticism [and indeed, golf course architecture itself] is a matter of opinion rather than a science. But we generally agree on what we're looking for:

We believe good golf comes in all shapes and sizes – as you'll see with one of my selections for The Gourmet's Choice, the nine-hole Hooper Golf Club in New Hampshire.

We prefer interesting designs that make the golfer think first and then execute, if he or she wants to score well.

We believe the best courses are fun to play – striking the right balance between challenging the good player, and allowing the higher handicapper to get around the course with a minimum of delay.

We prefer golf holes where the last two or three shots [on the greens and recovery play around the greens] are just as interesting as the first two or three shots.

We believe golf courses were meant to be walked, and we have a hard time thinking highly of a course that is so tough to walk as to make a buggy essential or even desirable. Luckily, Volume 3 does not require us to bend this rule, as the weather in the northern U.S. and Canada is more conducive to golf, and many of the best courses have caddy programs.

We love a golf course where the playing surface is well presented -- which is not the same thing as perfectly green, or perfectly uniform. Golf is part of Nature and Nature is full of variety and randomness that we should embrace. [Indeed, the uniform conditions presented at many modern courses are a turn-off.] However, since course conditions change from day to day and year to year, and it's impossible for us to stay current in this area, conditioning has only a minor role in our ratings of courses.

We love a course that has a character of its own, and isn't quite like anywhere else. Why would you lug your clubs through the airport [or subject them to the rigors of baggage claim] to play a course that's just like home?

We don't care whether a course has hosted tournaments, but we recognize the value of a course that has stood the test of time.

We hate designs that punish the same golfer hole after hole, whether that golfer is the 30-handicap man or the Tour professional.

As Bobby Jones once professed, we don't mind playing with other golfers as long as we don't have to look for their golf balls -- although the potential for lost balls causes strong divergences of opinion on certain courses, depending on our own experience there.

We believe what the Dalai Lama told Carl Spackler the day he caddied for him in Tibet * [big hitter, the Lama - long] – that the purpose of life is to be happy, and the more we care for the happiness of others, the greater our own sense of well-being becomes. So here we are to share our happy experiences of golf and travel with you, in the hope that you may come to have more of them yourself.

(* and a note to the reader of Volume 1 who questioned me on this: it's a *Caddyshack* reference. His Holiness The Dalai Lama has never played golf. Just think how happy he could be if he did!)

AGREEING TO DISAGREE

Everything in golf course design is a matter of opinion, and everyone's opinion [including ours] is based on their own limited experience of a golf course – how well they played, whether their hosts were generous or rude, the condition of the course and even what the weather was like.

The most we can do is try to put our own biases aside, and confine our comments to what we liked or disliked about the course and why. That's one reason I've asked three other people to collaborate with me.

Our ratings for each course are based on the Doak Scale, introduced in the first edition of The Confidential Guide back in 1988 -- a numerical 0-10 rating for each course we've seen, according to the definitions on the next page. The original intent of the numbers was to balance what I wrote, so I could criticize a course without the reader mistaking that emphasis as my overall view. Now (alas) people pay more attention to the numbers than anything else, but it's what we *write* that matters.

Every course reviewed will have a series of one to four ratings that follow it, plus [in brackets] the year in which one of us last saw the course. The ratings are always listed in the same order -- alphabetical by last name -- with my rating first, then Ran, Masa and Darius; there are dashes in place of numbers when we haven't seen the course. So, for example:

7 8 7 7 means that Ran rates the course a bit higher than the rest of us, while
- 8 7 - means that I haven't seen it, and neither has Darius.

Note that the ratings above are functionally the same ... the grades are the same, though you have only two opinions, instead of four. If you are doing the math to average our grades, you're missing the point.

It is inevitable that readers will disagree with some opinions expressed here; as you can see on pp. 272-279, my co-authors only concur with my own rating of courses about half the time. These disagreements may come in one of four ways:

If you think that we have underrated a course that you personally enjoy, that could well be true, since we have probably only played it once or twice ourselves, and it might have been ages ago -- that's why every review includes the year we last saw the course, right after the ratings. Hopefully you will allow us some room to be fallible, if our opinions of other courses align with your own.

If you think that we have overrated a course, consider that perhaps you have only played it once or twice, and your own experience might have been biased by other factors on the day.

If you think that we are generally stingy with our praise, and that we rate many courses too harshly across the board, consider that our scale may just be different than your own, but relativity is what matters. If your "6" is our "4", then all you need to take away is that you would be happy to play any of the other courses we have rated a 4 or higher -- as we would, too.

If our "4" is your "7", but our "7" is your "4", then we just have different tastes -- and you are welcome to return the book for a full refund.

However, if you are one of those people, as Gary Player professes to be, who believes that all courses are good and that no one should criticize a man's golf course, we can only apologize that this book is not for you. For us, one of the greatest appeals of the game is that every golf course is different. To pretend they are all equals is to deny their essential quality.

THE DOAK SCALE

0 – A course so contrived and unnatural that it may poison your mind, which I cannot recommend under any circumstances. Reserved for courses that wasted ridiculous sums of money in their construction, and probably shouldn't have been built in the first place. [Note that a 0 is not one less than a 1 … it's a special rating for a certain type of course which offends my sensibilities. If I hadn't given it a 0, it would probably be a 4 or 5, and some people might even like it.]

1 – A very basic golf course, with clear architectural malpractice and/or poor maintenance. Avoid even if you're desperate for a game.

2 – A mediocre golf course with little or no architectural interest, but nothing really horrible. As my friend Dave Richards summed one up: "Play it in a scramble, and drink a lot of beer."

3 – About the level of the average golf course in the world. [Since we don't go out of our way to see average courses, the Doak scale is deliberately skewed to split hairs among the good, the better, and the best.]

4 – A modestly interesting course, with a couple of distinctive holes among the 18, or at least some scenic interest on top of decent golf. We would enjoy playing here.

5 – Well above the average golf course, but probably about the average among courses covered by this book. A good course to play if you're in the vicinity and looking for a game, but we wouldn't spend another day away from home for it.

6 – A very good course, definitely worth a game if you're in town, but not necessarily worth a special trip to see. It won't disappoint you, because we haven't over-promised. [Some 6's are courses we love, but we're not sure you would like; others are courses you may love, but won't appeal to others.]

7 – An excellent course, worth checking out if you get anywhere within 100 miles. You can expect to find soundly designed, interesting holes, good course conditioning, and a pretty setting, if not necessarily anything unique to the world of golf.

8 – One of the very best courses in its region [although there are more 8's in some places, and none in others], and worth a special trip to see.

9 – An outstanding course – certainly one of the best in the world – with no weaknesses. You should see this course sometime in your life.

10 – Nearly perfect; if you skipped even one hole, you would miss something worth seeing. If you haven't seen all the courses in this category, you don't know how good golf architecture can get. Drop the book and call your travel agent, immediately.

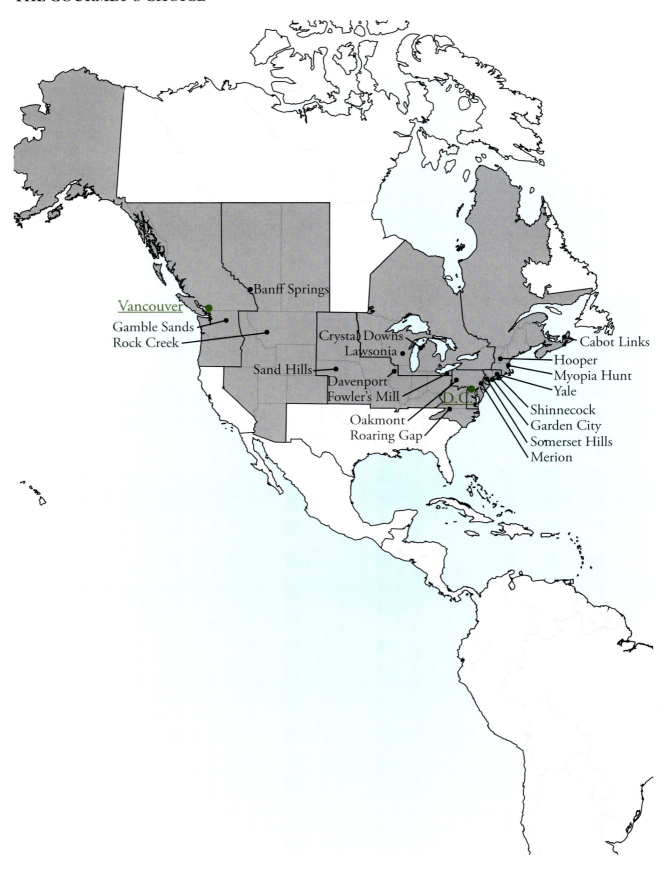

Banff Springs

Vancouver

Gamble Sands
Rock Creek

Crystal Downs
Lawsonia

Sand Hills

Davenport
Fowler's Mill

D.C.

Oakmont
Roaring Gap

Cabot Links

Hooper
Myopia Hunt
Yale

Shinnecock
Garden City
Somerset Hills
Merion

Although we envision this book being used mostly as a quick reference check to decide what courses to see in your travels, we cannot resist the temptation to break out a few of our favorite courses and write a bit more about what makes them special to us.

Instead of producing yet another list of "greatest" courses that includes all the usual suspects, The Gourmet's Choice highlights some of our favorite courses: the places that stir our souls, and will reward the visitor with something out of the ordinary. In the original world-wide edition of *The Confidential Guide*, there were 31 flavors, in honor of the wisdom of ice cream makers Baskin and Robbins. A dozen of my original selections are within the territory covered by this volume of the book, though for variety's sake, I have only reprised four of them for this version of The Gourmet's Choice: Crystal Downs, Garden City, Merion and Sand Hills.

In choosing our favorites, we've tried to maximize variety, and spread the praise around to all parts of the U.S. and Canada. There are links courses and mountain courses; top 100 mainstays and courses you've probably never heard of; and courses that opened in 1893 and 2012. There are three U.S. Open sites, and six courses that are open to public play. Each course is the work of a different architect, to ensure that we don't play favorites, even if we have them.

One thing I forgot to mention in the previous edition of the book is that the ! and ? marks on the scorecards are chess notation: ! is a great hole, !! or !!! are among the best holes in the world, ? is an odd or questionable hole, and ?! is an odd hole that turned out brilliant, in our view.

Here, then, are the 18 courses we've selected -- the courses we would take a good friend to play:

Banff Springs, Banff, Alberta, Canada
Cabot Links, Inverness, Nova Scotia, Canada
Crystal Downs, Frankfort, MI

Davenport CC, Pleasant Valley, IA
Fowler's Mill, Chesterland, OH
Gamble Sands, Brewster, WA

Garden City Golf Club, NY
Hooper, Walpole, NH
Lawsonia (Links), Green Lake, WI

Merion (East), Ardmore, PA
Myopia Hunt Club, South Hamilton, MA
Oakmont CC, PA

Roaring Gap, NC
Rock Creek Cattle Company, Deer Lodge, MT
Sand Hills, Mullen, NE

Shinnecock Hills, Southampton, NY
Somerset Hills, Bernardsville, NJ
Yale, New Haven, CT

Banff Springs

Banff, Alberta, CANADA

Laid out along the white water of the Bow River, with wooded mountains looming on three sides and pinching the middle of the course, Stanley Thompson's Banff Springs is one of the great achievements of golf design. The most expensive course ever built when it was completed in the 1920's -- the Yale University course, the bookend to our Gourmet's Choice selection, was its only competitor -- every last feature of the design had to be created with imported fill spread out over either rocky or marshy ground.

Though the dramatic scenery that surrounds the course is what makes it a beautiful place to visit, what makes the golf is Thompson's bold fairway bunkering. At par-5 holes like the 7th and 18th, you have to make long carries over bunkers defining the three-shot route, if you want to attack the greens in two or even get close to them. At par-4's like the 14th and 16th, the bunkers eat into the sides of the fairway to create an S-shape to many holes, as if they are par-5 holes in miniature. On others, like the 12th, there is plenty of fairway to drive into, but a bunker on the left gives you a gentle shove over toward the treeline on the right; only a bold drive over the end of the bunker opens up the approach to the green. There are only two short par-4 holes at Banff; no "holiday" golfer could fail to notice how many stout two-shotters they must face.

Stanley Thompson's par-3 holes are always a focal point of his work, and the five one-shotters at Banff are no exception. The fourth hole, the famed Devil's Cauldron, plays across a small glacial pond to a steep green set in a bowl on the opposite bank, with the mountains looming behind. But the short 8th and long 10th along the river are a great one-two punch, and the uphill iron shot to the 2nd is underrated because it comes so early in the round.

For years, the unpredictable condition of the course held it back in the rankings, as one could never be sure whether a rough winter or herds of elk would leave their mark on the greens. [On Tom's visit in 2015, the course was in remarkably good condition]. But in 1988, management made a conscious decision that haunts the design to this day, by moving the starting point to the middle of the course when the new Tunnel Mountain nine [a great addition for occasional golfers on holiday] was brought online.

Playing the holes in the sequence presented today is like starting a novel on Chapter 5, and then reading the prologue at the end. The flow is just wrong. Thompson's breathtaking opening tee shot from the foot of the hotel across the Spray River is the 15th today, but now you've got to climb way up the hill from the old Home green, so you are out of breath before you see it. The two gentle par-4's after this made much more sense early

The gargantuan Banff Springs Hotel looms over the former finishing hole, today's 14th.

in the round than at the end, and the Devil's Cauldron, which you used to anticipate all the way out, now comes much earlier in the round. Three of the par-5's are now in the outward half, and then there's not another until the 18th, when originally they were spaced more evenly as the 4th, 7th, 11th and 13th. Most of all, Thompson's magnificent home hole, finishing at the confluence of the Bow and Spray Rivers underneath the monolithic Banff Springs Hotel, is now the 14th, rather than the climax to the round, with the former pro shop now a restaurant for the hotel.

If the owners were to return the sequence of Thompson's routing, I believe there is a good chance the course would be a fixture in lists of the world's top 100. By making their decision based on business and ease of operation, they have failed to honor a magnificent history. - *MN*

SCORECARD

1.	Prettie	414 !	10.	Little Bow	210 !
2.	Rundle	171 !!	11.	Magpie	417
3.	Gibraltar	513 !	12.	Big Bow	442 !
4.	Devil's Cauldron	175 !!	13.	Sulphur	225 !!
5.	Trough	424 !	14.	Wampum	440 !!
6.	Fairholm	373	15.	Spray	475 !
7.	Hoodoo	602 !	16.	Goat	414 !
8.	Papoose	138	17.	Sarcee	376
9.	Jinx	501 !	18.	Windy	570 !!

6938 Yards - Par 71

Cabot Links

Inverness, Nova Scotia, CANADA

Many moons ago, when I was just starting out in the golf course construction business for the Dye family, I spent a bit of time sharing an apartment with Rod Whitman. He came across as a supremely talented guy, who was so quiet about it all that I wondered if he would ever be able to find work on his own, even though he had already done one solo design, Wolf Creek near his home in Alberta.

By 2007, Rod had a half-dozen design credits to his name, and his minimalist sensibility seemed perfect to the young developer trying to put together a new resort in Nova Scotia, Ben Cowan-Dewar. The site was a former mining site along the water right in the town of Inverness, with more than a mile of frontage along the Gulf of St. Lawrence. The provincial government was offering to help finance the project in order to create tourism opportunities in this town on the back side of the famous Cabot Trail.

Their timing was bad, but ultimately fortuitous; the economic slowdown of 2008 made the project more appealing than ever to the government, so Rod forged ahead that first year almost by himself, doing much of the preliminary shaping to turn the reclaimed site into something more resembling a real links. The fact that he didn't have an army of shapers behind him gives the course a much different look than most of today's modern masterpieces: the bunkering, in particular, is effective but not eye-catching, so that the course serves up its strategy without making it so obvious. Much of the best shaping work is found in the contours of the fairways, which have a wrinkly, unpredictable quality to them. But there are also some steeper side-slopes that can take a good drive into a difficult position, such as the hollow up the right side of the par-5 opening hole, or another similar hollow in the 12th fairway.

The sequencing of the holes was changed after the course had been open for two years; I'm lucky to have visited just after the change so it doesn't confuse me in writing about it. After the getaway opener [best played conservatively] and a long par-3 2nd with a Biarritz-style green, the course really comes to life with its next two par-4's. The bunkerless 3rd is just 330 yards from an elevated tee, but there is a wetland down the right side to the green, and a six-foot dune at the front left of the green so that players who bail away from the right side will have a difficult semi-blind pitch to a green that doesn't hold well. [Longer hitters may even find themselves playing uncomfortably back toward the wetland with their second shot.] The longer 4th, playing back uphill away from the sea, has a sharp and well-bunkered slope defending the right front flank of its green, so the best approach is given to those who take on the bunkers down the left side on the tee shot.

The second shot to the par-5 11th plays dramatically uphill to a landing area on a bluff.

The next two holes are set across a small road from the rest of the course, and at the 6th you discover the reason for this crossing, as the Cape-type par-4 plays around the water toward the town's small marina behind the green. The long 8th is the first hole right along the main shoreline, playing to a remarkably wide green, the left half of a double green with the par-4 13th, at the base of a huge dune at the center of the property.

The 9th through 11th loop up to the clubhouse and back to a green high on the dune, and the 12th and 13th are two excellent par-4's off the dune and back to its base, before one plays the short 14th from the dune top down to a green with the sea behind -- this is supposed to be akin to the 7th at Pebble Beach, but the steep slope at the back is unforgiving to the weaker player who may not be able to hold the rock-hard green from above. The 15th and 16th play dramatically down the shoreline, and the finishing hole returns right beneath the windows of the resort's fine restaurant ... the only clue in eighteen holes that you're in the new Scotland, and not the old one.   - *TD*

SCORECARD

1. 540 !	7. 141	13. 440 !
2. 247 !	8. 580	14. 102 !?
3. 330 !	9. 360 !	15. 413 !
4. 450 !	10. 385	16. 457 !
5. 178	11. 620 !	17. 170
6. 465 !	12. 450 !	18. 475 !

6803 Yards - Par 70

Crystal Downs

Frankfort, Michigan, U.S.A.

Most people who know me have heard of Crystal Downs, the Alister MacKenzie course that lured me to northern Michigan as a college student in 1982, so it's hard to explain how unknown the course was back then. The only person on the *GOLF Magazine* rating panel to have played the course was Jack Nicklaus, who visited on a summer trip with his parents as a young teen; even in Detroit, the most that you could find anyone to say about it was that they'd heard it was very good. I decided to investigate, and fell in love with the course and the region.

Of course, I travel year-round, and the club is just far enough from my house that it's hard to make time for golf when I'm home, so I only play it about ten times a year -- but every round is still a thrill. Like all of Dr. MacKenzie's work, it makes the absolute most out of the landscape, with bunkers placed to highlight the drama of the terrain and the shots required. It is also one of the most challenging courses I know: though it's only 6,500 yards, par is 70, the rating almost 74, and the combination of windy days, gnarly native roughs, and heavily contoured greens ensure that there are only one or two scores a year below par.

I'm not a good enough golfer anymore to expect to break 80 on such a tough course, and I surely don't want to get beaten up when I play, but the Downs doesn't beat you up. There are a handful of holes that are very dif-

ficult, but there are plenty of others where two good shots will leave even the average golfer a chance at a birdie, so you never feel like you're out of the game. Its short par-4 holes, in particular, are captivating. There's the 5th, where you play over a ridge [and possibly over the crown of a large oak in the valley in between], and then along the back side of the ridge to a green tilted away from the tee. The 7th has its boomerang-shaped green nestled in a half-blind dell. The 15th, which I didn't identify at first as a great hole, is one of my favorites now, because it's so tricky to find a level spot to drive the ball for the short pitch to the green. And the polarizing 17th, with its narrow downhill tee shot through the trees, and deep pit to the left of the green, is a potential card-wrecker on any day when you are playing well and dare to think you might post a good score.

Few courses have four holes as good as that, but that's just the short par-4's. The long par-4 opener is one of the toughest, but most inviting, in the game. The short 11th, with its wicked three-tiered green, is a beauty hidden in the trees breaking up the long climb to the heart of the back nine. And the 8th [diagrammed on page 157] is one of great par-5 holes in all of golf, where the important strategy is to try and find level lies for your second shot and approach.

There isn't a green that doesn't command your full attention: on my second visit,

The tee shot over a ridge at the 5th kicks off a stretch of five holes like you have not seen anywhere else.

I remarked to the pro, Fred Muller, that the 2nd green was more severe than I had remembered, and he replied casually, "Oh, I've seen members putt off every green on the golf course." By now, so have I.

While I have given Dr. MacKenzie credit for the design, it is only fair to mention that the course was built by his partner at the time, Perry Maxwell, so it is no coincidence that the only course that bears any resemblance is Maxwell's Prairie Dunes, built a few years later. It's impossible to divide the credit properly between the two; MacKenzie was only on site twice, which is why he never wrote much about it, but that's more time than he spent on any of his work in Australia, or at Lahinch or Augusta. His two great skills were in routing a course to find interesting green sites, and in enlisting talented associates to build his designs after he moved on to the next property. I've tried to emulate those two skills myself; the only difference is that when I land a project as good as Crystal Downs, I keep going back.   - *TD*

SCORECARD

1. 460 !	7. 335 !!	13. 442 !
2. 429	8. 550 !!!	14. 147 !
3. 191 !	9. 175 !	15. 327 !
4. 409 !	10. 395	16. 588
5. 353 !!	11. 196 !	17. 311 !?
6. 384 !	12. 430	18. 400

6518 Yards - Par 70

Davenport

Davenport Country Club, Pleasant Valley, Iowa, U.S.A.

Golf course architects are quickly typecast in the modern era, and find themselves working on similar pieces of land across the country that are offered as good "fits" for their style. What's amazing is how often the same thing happened back in the Golden Age, when travel (and comparison) was far more difficult. Charles "Hugh" Alison wound up with several similar sites during his residence in Detroit in the 1920's while running the U.S. office of Colt, Alison and MacKenzie [until the latter was replaced by John Morrison]. Three of Alison's best-known works -- Milwaukee Country Club, Kirtland in Cleveland, and The Park Club in Buffalo -- are built over parkland terrain with a river looping the site and a couple of holes set on the other side.

Little did I know that there was a fourth such course, Davenport Country Club, in the heretofore underrated golfing state of Iowa. The course hides in plain sight just a couple of miles from where Interstate 80 crosses the Mississippi River, in the Quad Cities region. It's hard to fathom how such a course was overlooked for so long, but until a recent restoration by Ron Forse and company it was only 6,400 yards, and probably dismissed by the magazine rankings with their emphasis on "resistance to scoring." Though the renovation drew my attention, I certainly did not expect it to be better than Alison's more famous tracks. But, you learn something new with every trip.

The whole course lies within a mile of the Mississippi, but you never see the river as many holes are built around a deep stream valley as it works its way downhill, and the clubhouse faces north, into the stream valley, with its back to the river. The downhill opener features the stream prominently in view, across the 9th fairway, but then the par-5 2nd plays across the stream on its second shot, from a plunging downhill/sidehill lie. The 4th through 6th holes make a nice little loop of their own, before one of the best holes on the course at the par-4 7th: a high fairway on the left runs out about 240 yards from the tee, forcing long hitters to choose between laying up for a level second shot, or driving farther down into a valley and having to play a stoutly uphill second from closer range.

The 9th, played through a narrow valley with the stream just to the right of the fairway its whole length, returns the golfer underneath the clubhouse; the long par-3 10th, reminiscent of Bel-Air in California, plays across the creek from high to high.

The par-4 11th is one of those old-fashioned holes you don't see anymore, tilting sharply from left to right its whole length, so that you have to control your trajectory while playing from a hanging lie; the 13th and 14th, playing back toward the clubhouse, both run right along the top of a ridge.

The 16th at Davenport is the start of a remarkable finishing run.

Cementing the quality of the course are three dramatic finishing holes, set at the far western end of the stream valley, where a second, larger creek loops in to join the main creek. From the tee at the all-American 423-yard 16th, sixty feet above, you have to carry 220 yards to clear the new creek, with the fairway set between the continuing creek along the left and a rocky bluff to the right.   The strong par-3 17th plays back across the creek, uphill to a green carved into a wooded slope.

Last, but certainly not least, the big finishing hole plays back upstream on the main creek, with a fairway bunker eating into the line of play from the right, and its green set across the creek, at the base of a bluff, almost underneath the bridge to the 10th green. It is such a natural hole that I was startled to learn that they'd had it backwards for many years before the restoration, with the fairway running along the bank on the right, and the big oaks to the right of the green essentially blocking the line home. It's a great lesson in how one important change can make such a huge difference in one's lasting impression of a course.   *- TD*

SCORECARD

1. 466	7. 424 !!	13. 529 !
2. 546 !	8. 162 !	14. 456 !
3. 401 !	9. 520 !	15. 168
4. 406 !	10. 210 !	16. 423 !!
5. 228	11. 387 !	17. 181 !
6. 357	12. 468	18. 427 !!

6759 Yards - Par 71

Fowler's Mill

Chesterland, Ohio, U.S.A.

More than any architect in history, Pete Dye's career is tied to the game's growth and popularity on television, especially the period from 1986 through 2006. His courses from southern California to Oklahoma to Wisconsin to those in South Carolina's Low Country and Florida produced indelible, televised moments.

Mr. Dye frequently manufactured courses from nothing that made the professionals gnash their teeth while creating a television spectacle. Sometimes the drama was augmented by a splendid setting (The Ocean Course at Kiawah) while other times (PGA Stadium) Mr. Dye reached so far as to yield a course that would not be fun to play on a regular basis. With each passing decade, his courses became more feature laden. In some ways, Mr. Dye became a prisoner of his own success with clients clamoring for … what else? A 'Pete Dye course'!

Yet, it was his pre-1985 work that was truly revolutionary. What he produced was unlike any other architect, before or since. Design tenets were borrowed from the great links in Scotland, hazards were imaginative and on a scale never seen before (a few even featured railroad ties), and greens varied wildly in size and configuration. Variety, variety, variety is what he preached.

One of Dye's earliest works is also one of his least heralded. Today's Fowler's Mill was developed in 1971 as a private course by TRW corporation, keen to have its own golf facility of similar stature to Firestone's and NCR's to the south in the state. To accomplish that, TRW secured 1500 acres (!) in the rolling suburbs thirty minutes east of Cleveland. Visions of a 54 hole facility were eventually reduced to today's 27 hole one but the fact remains: Pete and his brother Roy had a block of choice land from which to design the main 18 when they arrived here in 1969.

As such, Fowler's Mill represents one of Dye's best canvases. Unlike many of his more famous, manufactured works, this one stemmed from his (underappreciated) ability to route holes across land replete with natural features. Highlights include the mighty 461-yard 4th that boomerangs around a scenic lake and the 455-yard 6th which doglegs right over tumbling ground before concluding at a green expertly located on a natural hillock. The 7th green benched into the hillside and the 13th on top of a ledge are both inspired, bunkerless one shotters. Blind tee shots were unheard of at the time but that's what the golfer confronts at the 11th, where the tee ball must scale a steep embankment.

His periodic use of the Chagrin River that runs through the middle of the property is scintillating, too. No homes intrude on play. One might wish for sandier soil (and some better placed cart paths on the second nine) but otherwise, this inland course has

At the 9th, the golfer who takes on the carry off the tee has an easier angle of approach down the length of the green, while those who opt not to cross water off the tee face a much tougher angle of approach.

ideal topographic interest.

What's especially shocking is to find three multi-route holes on a 1970's design. The first is the par 5 8th where the long hitter can take a short cut across broken ground and a nest of bunkers to reach the green in two. More impressive are the 9th (pictured above) and the 12th where the day's hole location, easily visible from the elevated tee, dictates whether to play one's tee ball right or left of the river that again is put to optimum use.

Compare this kind of option filled golf to the more straightforward offerings of the 1970's and hindsight makes it easy to pick Mr. Dye as a standout talent. It also provides a glimpse as to how the man who built such massive earth-work courses as French Lick

and Whistling Straits fostered so many of today's minimalists. On such fine property, Mr. Dye's touch was soft upon the land.

TRW exited the golf space in 1986 and today's course is public. Go play it: you don't need television to tell you this is a special design – and a special architect. - *RM*

SCORECARD

1. 429	7. 197	13. 184 !
2. 375	8. 588 !	14. 521
3. 211	9. 388 !!	15. 429
4. 461 !	10. 428 !	16. 374
5. 502	11. 369	17. 191 !
6. 455 !!	12. 350 !!	18. 550

7002 Yards - Par 72

Gamble Sands

Brewster, Washington, U.S.A.

When the first volume of the new *Confidential Guide* was released, *GOLF Magazine* did its best to stir up controversy from my review of David Kidd's Castle Course at St. Andrews, with much speculation as to my motives. In fact, my motivation for that review was no different than for this one: to help you decide where to go, and where not to.

North-central Washington state is much farther off the beaten path of the golf establishment than St. Andrews [and that's too bad for David], but nearly every golfer who makes the trip to Gamble Sands will be glad he did. For starters, it's a spectacular setting for the game, with most of the course set on the edge of a plateau 500 feet above the Columbia River in the distance below. But what most golfers will appreciate is that David has renounced any intention of challenging Rory McIlroy, and refocused on building an exciting course that's playable for everyone.

The early reviews of the course that I'd heard suggested he might have tilted too far toward playability -- in one group, five of eight golfers reportedly shot their career lowest rounds! -- but on my visit with Ran Morrissett in the fall of 2015, neither of us found the course unchallenging in the least. It would certainly be more interesting with a bit more contour in and around the greens -- say, one-third of the way from flat to The Castle Course, instead of one-tenth -- but from tee to green it's so well routed and so pretty that not many golfers will mind, especially if they are sinking those straight putts.

Contrary to conventional wisdom, Gamble Sands uses the most dramatic parts of the terrain early in the round, instead of saving it for the finish, with much of the first nine playing along the outer edge of the plateau to the player's right. Some architects might avoid having so much trouble on the "slice side," but letting such golfing biases dominate the design leads to repetitive work. David's decision is based more on artistry and borrowed views: working counter-clockwise makes the off-course views much better than when they are at the golfer's back, and he just provides enough width that no golfer is forced over the edge. Holes like the 2nd, 3rd, 5th, 7th, and 9th put the view right in the golfer's face every time he looks up, and that is a big part of their appeal. From the big uphill tee shot at the 3rd to the diagonal tee shot at the 17th, to the massive, Mike Strantz-ian scale of its hazards, Gamble Sands is all about visual drama.

In spite of its wide fairways, the course is full of interest from the tee. Many of the bigger holes tempt you to play close to a big waste bunker along the direct line to the green, while the long par-4 5th rewards a wide-left play with a speed slot and a better angle of approach. The 8th, 12th and 14th each have one of more bunkers dividing the fairway left and right, forcing you to choose a line.

Ted Sturges and Tom Doak walk toward their tee shots on the drivable par-4 2nd hole, with the Columbia River far below in the background.

Gamble's other secret is that it's full of half-par holes, many of which have the fraction in the golfer's favor. After a straightforward opening hole to get you in position, the drivable par-4 2nd is set up to maximize the views from its hilltop tee; the 8th and 12th are also just 300 yards from the main tee. With the 7th and 18th being invitingly reachable par-5's, it's possible that the long hitter will have multiple chances for an eagle, and what golfer wouldn't enjoy that? [It has always been part of the secret appeal of Augusta National.]

The long par-3 6th, a Redan-ish hole with a gathering green in a bowl, and the short 10th with its multi-tiered green, are two of the rare occasions where there is more jazz in the greens contouring; and the 225-yard 16th is the only one where the contouring gets carried away.

The critical success of Gamble Sands has put David Kidd back in the limelight, and back on the radar of developers around the world. It seems that he has found a winning formula, and the results will be exciting to see.
  - *TD*

SCORECARD

1. 422	7. 514 !	13. 562
2. 301 !!	8. 313 !	14. 437 !
3. 633 !	9. 429	15. 467 !
4. 166	10. 155 !	16. 225 ?
5. 517 !	11. 436 !	17. 428 !
6. 265 !	12. 333	18. 566

7169 Yards - Par 72

Garden City

Garden City Golf Club, Garden City, New York, U.S.A.

The politics of an all-men's golf club are hard to defend in the modern world, as any man with daughters could tell you. But for a young designer, being engaged as the consultant to this particular course was the greatest of blessings. Whenever I needed a reminder to keep my designs simple and let Nature rule the day, all I had to do was think about Garden City.

It only makes sense that the best of our early American courses owed much of their quality to the ground where they were laid out. A first look at the relatively flat plain in back of the low-slung clubhouse might cause questions for you -- the par-3 2nd, pictured at right, has the most elevation change of any hole on the course. The superior nature of this course starts not with topography, but with the soil ... a beautiful layer of sandy loam topsoil, with coarse gravel underneath to ensure it drains well. The playing surface is always good here, and the rough can get really rough in a wet year.

After the rough, what golfers tend to remember most are the fairway bunkers, small deep pits seldom seen in the American landscape. Most of these bunkers were placed around the course by Walter Travis, who adopted the club as his second home fresh on the heels of victory in the 1904 Amateur Championship. For a couple of years, I puzzled over their random depth; some are three feet deep and others six, and it seemed to have little correlation to the nature of the next shot. Once we got into the dirt to start rebuilding them, I realized how they came about ... they dug down only until they hit the gravel layer underneath, because anything deeper would leave spoils that had to be carted away instead of spread out in the fairway!

Many of these bunkers are inescapable with any club but a wedge, but Travis understood that such hazards aren't as unfair or boring as some golfers complain: their value increases dramatically on holes of certain lengths. At any of the par-5's, for example, the bunkered golfer will be tempted to try for a bit more yardage so as to get home with his next shot. On the shorter par-4's he will think about trying to advance within chipping distance, and in so doing, risk leaving the ball in the bunker. Garden City bristles with holes of such length, making it a superb match play venue.

There are only three par-3 holes on this par-73 course, but they present as much variety as any set of short holes I can summon. The 2nd is a tiny pitch over an old quarry, to a long and narrow green on a bias; the 12th a big shot over a cross-bunker to a squarish green guarded by two huge mounds *in* the green, to either side of the pin; and the 18th is Walter Travis' ode to the Eden hole at St. Andrews, with the far right of the green transitioning into a practice green on the back patio of the clubhouse.

The short 2nd hole plays over some old quarry works, with the town close by.

But what has really allowed Garden City to appeal to all players is the equitable simplicity of Devereux Emmet's original green sites. Nearly all are just a ground-level extension of the fairway, as on many Scottish courses; but nearly all of them tilt slightly to the back and to one side. The combination of speed and tilt has ensured that it remains difficult to get the ball close to the hole with an approach shot, because you have to allow for the ball to bounce and roll away after it lands, even when approached with much more lofted clubs than Emmet could have envisioned. At the same time, the oldest member always has his chance to get the ball close with a 3-wood approach, if only it is straight enough and the weight perfectly judged. For many years, the club maintained only one teeing ground per hole, and if the wind is blowing in your face on a long par-4 on a given day, you just have to accept that the hole is going to be especially hard. In other words, here they play a game the Scots would still recognize.

The lesson of Garden City is that giving the golfers some leeway -- *not* making it harder -- is what's enabled the course to stand the test of time. - *TD*

SCORECARD

1. 302 !!	7. 550 !	13. 538 !
2. 137 !	8. 418	14. 343
3. 407	9. 323	15. 447 !
4. 523 !	10. 414 !	16. 405 !
5. 360	11. 416 !	17. 495
6. 440	12. 193 !?	18. 190 !!

6911 Yards - Par 73

Hooper

Walpole, New Hampshire, U.S.A.

I was not very familiar with the work of designer Wayne Stiles, until my visit to New England last summer. Then it seemed like everywhere I went there was another unheralded course designed by Stiles: Prouts Neck in Maine, Rutland in Vermont, and above all the nine-hole Hooper course, straight north up I-91 from Hartford and Springfield.

I'd heard of the course many years ago from the late Bob Labbance, who wrote Stiles' biography, but it wasn't enough to have any idea what to expect. So, imagine my excitement to get out of the car and walk to the pro shop, and spy the inviting opening hole pictured at right! It is the shortest of par-5's -- even I managed to get home with two good shots -- but trouble lurks to the left for its entire length, and the steeply sloped green does not give up a two-putt birdie easily.

When the long par-4 2nd hole turned out to be just as enticing -- albeit quite a bit tighter, due to trees and a gravel road [marked out of bounds] on the right -- I was hooked. The landing area for the fairway is crowned, and the green has a neat hole location at the back left, with a shoulder protruding into the green to defend it. I racked my brain trying to think if I'd ever seen a better pair of opening holes, and in the moment, anyway, I could think of none.

More, you say? The 3rd is a very short par-4 with a difficult pitch to a green defended by sand across the front. The two par-3's are both excellent holes, with the 4th green playing uphill and the boundary road again threatening a lost shot to the right, and the 6th playing strongly across a valley, reminiscent of the 7th at Whitinsville with bunkers stacked up on the steep slope to its right.

The finishing run is surely a bit of a letdown compared to the strong start, with none of the three par-4's exceeding 400 yards. However, they fill the gaps in the scorecard nicely: the five par-4's list off at 285, 311, 350, 381, and 427 yards, plus the two par-5's at 456 and 474. And though birdies can be found, it's also easy to trip oneself coming home: the 7th green has a nasty tilt from left to right, and the semi-blind tee shot at the 8th lures one dangerously close to the out-of-bounds road.

The par-4 9th runs back up alongside the 1st toward a beautiful, small clubhouse, which has sadly been shuttered for a few years now. The club failed financially and is now owned in trust by the town of Walpole, where some of the trustees don't understand what they have, and wonder aloud about selling off the land. That would be a crime, since discussion of the best nine-hole courses in America comes down to Mike Keiser's Dunes Club in Michigan, Culver in Indiana, Donald Ross's Whitinsville, and Stiles' Hooper. My choice is Whitinsville, but it's a close call.

Hooper's short par-5 1st is one of the most inspiring openers in golf.

Still, comparisons of nine-hole courses are hard to relate to, if you've never seen
a great one. To put it in clearer perspective,
let's imagine we had an 18-hole course with
the front nine of Hooper and the back nine
of Whitinsville. I'd rate the composite course
one of the top fifty courses in America.
Hooper is super.   - *TD*

SCORECARD

1. 456 !!	4. 155 !	7. 311
2. 427 !!	5. 474 !	8. 381 !
3. 285	6. 194 !	9. 350

3033 Yards - Par 36

Lawsonia

The Golf Courses at Lawsonia (Links course), Green Lake, Wisconsin, U.S.A.

It wouldn't have been right to do a book about Midwestern courses without an example from the work of William Langford, the unheralded Chicago-based designer who worked from the 1920's to 1950's, for much of that time in partnership with fellow engineer Theodore Moreau. The large-scale, muscular earthworks of his designs were a precursor of the modern era, and a major influence on Pete and Alice Dye, the latter having spent her summers on the nine-hole Langford design at Lake Maxinkuckee, Indiana.

Langford and Moreau built many fine courses in their trademark style all over the midwest, but without question their best-preserved design is Lawsonia, developed just before the Depression from the 1,000-acre Victor Lawson estate overlooking Green Lake, in central Wisconsin. The scale of the property and its undulations are a perfect match for their style. After the Depression, the property was purchased by the Northern Baptist Assembly as a conference center and retreat, and for many years the maintenance suffered because golf was not a high priority for its owner; but a few years back the church hired an outside firm who cherished the course to manage it, and since then it has been in fine shape.

You might not think that an architect known for major earthworks would need to be good at routing golf holes, but Langford's

design at Lawsonia proves this to be a lie. Of course, it's important to locate bold features in the right setting, but it is the juxtaposition of features which makes Lawsonia so captivating. Often, a bunker or ridge on a hole in the background works together with the bunkers with the bunkers in the foreground to complete the picture -- as, for example, the fairway bunker at the 2nd forms the left side of a trough with the bunker left of the 4th green, or how the steep bank off the left side of the first fits together with the large cross-bunker left-center of the 5th fairway.

These juxtapositions are especially prevalent on the front nine, where the routing changes directions brilliantly and unpredictably. The two starting holes are unusual, both of them curving right nearly ninety degrees until the 2nd green winds up by the entrance gate. The opening hole isn't noteworthy until you get to the green, with a 15-foot drop to its left and rear, and all of the putting surface tilting off to the right front. The 2nd is a great hole in many aspects: a blind tee shot is framed by two bunkers on the horizon, and when you crest the hill between them you are staring straight on at the massive Guernsey Barn and its two silos that dominate the original farm property. From there, two big grass bunkers on the right and a greenside bunker left turn the downhill approach into a right-to-left shot, even as the fairway sweeps in from left to right.

The par-3 7th epitomizes the outsized, man-made featuring of Langford and Moreau's work.

The best stretch of holes on the course is from the par-5 5th, with its tight tee shot and diagonal cross-bunkers on the second, to the sweeping downhill 6th and the scary pitch at the 7th, hidden in a corner to the right. The par-5 9th, with its blind second shot, gives the short hitter a narrow ridge to play for in order to make the green visible for his approach.

Though roundly praised by other visitors, I find the back nine a bit less exciting than the front half, mostly because the tighter boundaries forced all the longer holes to be played in parallel, north and south. The difficult par-5 13th is many good players' favorite, but those incapable of two big shots are left with no good place to play their second ... the 11th and 18th are both better holes in my book, and this *is* my book.

Most of all, Lawsonia is an exhilirating venue for the game, and a wonderful example of how earthwork can sometimes be more appealing than Nature.   - *TD*

SCORECARD

1. 418	7. 161 !	13. 568 !?
2. 431 !	8. 339 !	14. 154
3. 386	9. 535 !	15. 394 !
4. 203 !	10. 239 !	16. 443 !
5. 487 !!	11. 510 !	17. 383
6. 439 !!	12. 183 !	18. 580 !

6853 Yards - Par 72

Merion

Merion Golf Club (East course), Ardmore, Pennsylvania, U.S.A.

Jack Nicklaus has said that, "Acre for acre, Merion is the best test of golf in the world." For all the preoccupation by outsiders over how short it is, first-time visitors are generally shocked to find how hard it can be!

Set on just 126 acres, the East course at Merion is perhaps the world's most perfect example of routing, with its first hole and last six packed tightly around the clubhouse, and the other eleven on a long and narrow parcel running beside Ardmore Avenue. However, it's not well known that the plan was done in two steps. Designer Hugh Wilson's original 1912 plan played across the road at the 2nd, 10th, 11th and 12th holes; when traffic on the road multiplied in the automobile age, Wilson's protege, William Flynn, came in to modify it. At Flynn's suggestion, the club purchased the small low corner of land for the 11th green, where only a few years later the great Bobby Jones clinched his match against Eugene Homans in the final of the 1930 U.S. Amateur, to complete the Grand Slam.

Though his fellow Merion members sent Wilson to the U.K. to study the best courses before completing his design, Merion has fewer prototype holes of the classic era than its contemporary rival, the National Golf Links of America. Aside from a nod to the Redan at the long par-3 3rd, and the short 13th, it is a distinctly American design, with its large white-faced bunkers prominent in the landscape.

The opening hole, doglegging to the right, is a perfect prelude of what is to come; it's nothing more than a drive and pitch, but the angle of the green and its guarding bunkers make it very difficult for those who miss their tee shot to the right, no matter how far they drive. Once the road is crossed, two of the next three holes are par-5's -- the only two on the course -- with the boundary lurking along the right side of the 2nd from tee to green, and a small stream cutting just in front of the green of the long 4th, making for a difficult pitch from a downhill lie. These two holes loop to either side of the long par-4 5th [see diagram, p. 106], the toughest hole on the course and, along with the long par-4 6th, the culmination of a very rude awakening.

Merion's second act is made up of very short holes; of the next seven holes only the 12th exceeds 400 yards. It's a stretch that gives the members hope of a few pars, but the best players feel acute pressure to make birdies, knowing what lies ahead. Though there are four short par-4's in quick succession, each of them has a different character. The narrow target of the 7th green contrasts with the deep bunker guarding the front of the shallow 8th; the generous fairway to the right of the 10th makes the "Baffling Brook" right up against the 11th green all the more intimidating, with almost no chance of holding the green if one has driven into the rough. In between, the long tee ball to the kidney-shaped 9th green is one of the most difficult shots on the course.

The famous quarry first comes into play on the long approach to the par-4 16th.

Crossing the road again, the very short 13th is a respite before the five closing holes, although the shallow green leaves little margin for error, as Phil Mickelson found out in the last U.S. Open here.

The three finishing holes, played around the remains of a rock quarry some forty feet deep, are like nowhere else. The second-shot carry at the par-4 16th is beyond the ability of many players, but Wilson's three-shot route around the rim of the quarry has been restored. The downhill par-3 17th is made by the sharp terrace at the front of the green; and no golfer can fail to be inspired by the plaque in the 18th fairway honoring Ben Hogan's famous shot to clinch a spot in the playoff for the 1950 U.S. Open, especially once they see how tough it is to hold that green.

For me, though, no visit to Merion is complete without a stop afterward in the library room. It is a cool space that allows reflection on the course and on all the golf history that has happened on this small piece of real estate.   - *MN*

SCORECARD

1. 350 !	7. 360	13. 115 !
2. 556 !	8. 359 !	14. 464 !
3. 256 !	9. 236 !	15. 411 !
4. 628 !	10. 303 !	16. 430 !!
5. 504 !!	11. 367 !	17. 246 !!
6. 487	12. 403	18. 521 !?

6996 Yards - Par 70

Myopia Hunt Club

South Hamilton, Massachusetts, U.S.A.

Supposedly founded by a group of bespectacled men from Boston, Myopia Hunt Club is an old-fashioned golf, horse and hunting establishment located in the village of South Hamilton, north of the city. The golf course was designed by member Herbert Leeds, whose first nine holes were in play for the staging of the 1898 US Open, and his full 18 ready by the time the championship returned in 1901. That tournament was won with what remains a record-high winning score of 331. No player in the field broke 80.

Obviously golf changed plenty post-1901, but so too did Myopia. Like Hotchkin at Woodhall Spa and Fownes at Oakmont, Leeds continually tweaked and refined his design, altering features and adding bunkers right through until his passing in 1930. Famously he was said to watch good players at the club closely, and build bunkers whenever and wherever he felt their poor shots had not been sufficiently punished. He also dug his existing traps deeper if escape became too simple and mixed irregularly shaped trench-like bunkers with smaller, narrow pits where it was difficult to take a proper swing at the ball. The Leeds greens at Myopia are also severe, a number so steeply pitched that there are only a handful of pin positions.

Dominated by rumpled ground and a series of unspoiled hills and small ridges, the routing at Myopia continually changes direction and is refreshingly free from the burdens of modern convention. It opens with a drivable par four, has a stack of other half-par holes and only three short holes, if the 250+ yard 3rd can indeed be called short. Plus you don't return to the clubhouse until the 16th hole.

Among the highlights here are the short opener, played along the shoulder of a hill to a nasty green set on the horizon, and the plunging par five 2nd. Fast starts are certainly possible, but so too are major stumbles immediately thereafter. The 3rd is a monster one-shotter across a large bunker to a reasonably small green, and the 4th a mid-length hole that bends around a marsh toward one of the most acutely angled targets on the course. In the previous edition of this Guide Tom Doak heralded the 4th as perhaps 'the best hole of its length in the free world.'

Other notable holes at Myopia include the beautifully undulating 7th and impossibly narrow par three 9th, its green only a few yards wide and surrounded almost entirely by sand. The blind drive on the 10th and meandering fairway and small green on the 12th are also memorable. As is the brutal approach back up the ridge on the 13th and wonderfully unforgiving targets at the par three 16th and par four 18th.

The wicked tilt of Myopia's 4th green makes a spinning approach shot a liability.

Arguably the most memorable aspect of Myopia Hunt Club, however, is the experience itself. The club oozes old-world ambience and charm, from the winding entrance drive along an old polo field to the secluded golfing grounds, complete with the occasional wandering horse, and unpretentious canary colored weatherboard clubhouse. Fortunately, apparent insecurities about the course's modest length have abated in recent times and the Myopia fairways are slowly being expanded out to recapture the playing features – and grandeur – of Leeds's masterpiece.   - *DO*

SCORECARD

1. 274 !	7. 404 !	13. 349 !
2. 487 !	8. 472	14. 392
3. 253 !	9. 136 !!	15. 525
4. 392 !!	10. 406 !	16. 192 !
5. 417	11. 339	17. 391
6. 260	12. 446 !	18. 404 !

6539 Yards - Par 72

Oakmont

Oakmont, Pennsylvania, U.S.A.

Like Carnoustie and Muirfield, Oakmont is a course universally respected but not often loved. Its relentless difficulty is beyond the ability of most golfers to appreciate.

While other "most challenging" courses have receded into history, Oakmont hasn't gotten any easier for the best players in the world. Well, that's a bit of a stretch -- the course isn't as hard as it was in 1927 or 1935, when William Fownes had the bunkers raked in furrows to make recovery harder on his father's holes, and only one player [a member!] broke 300 over two U.S. Opens. But there's not a player alive who wouldn't take even par as his score for an upcoming championship, and have a few beers watching his peers try to best it.

As at Garden City, Oakmont's ability to hold up so well over time is because its greens follow the general tilt of the ground, and that means a bunch of them fall away from the line of play, often at some of the most difficult holes [such as the 1st, 10th, 12th, and 15th]. You have to avoid the rough on these holes off the tee, and hit good solid shots so you can be past the flag in regulation, and putting back up the slope. Players who try to sneak one on the front of the green to get close to the hole don't realize the risk they are taking if the ball gets caught up in the collar in front, until their first putt goes toddling past the hole, and doesn't stop until it gets to the back fringe.

Oh, did I forget to mention green speed? From time immemorial, Oakmont has always been reputed to have the slickest putting greens on the planet, and few memberships would put up with such conditions long enough to argue the point. It's probably not true that they slow down the greens to host a major championship there, but they don't speed them up like they do for club events. Indeed, the club's masochistic bent toward green speeds was always the one reason I hesitated to place the course among my favorites ... I always thought it indicated they had something to hide.

Three things helped soften my view of the course. First, over the forty-plus years that I've watched golf, Oakmont is the least changed design of any of the championship venues, save The Old Course at St. Andrews, and I have great respect for the test of time. Second, though they are never the holes the media focuses on, the course provides a good helping of short par-4's and par-5's mixed well into the flow of the round, so that the average golfer is never far from having a chance to get back into the match. And third, the elimination of thousands of trees over the past 20 years has returned the course to its original, unique character -- a stark landscape with deep bunkers and open trenches for hazards, that looks like it might have been a battlefield in a long-ago war.

Architect Fownes's deep trench hazards are particularly in evidence on the approach to the 5th.

I seem to favor different holes than the legions of golf writers who have reviewed the course before me. The first and tenth, plunging downhill to fallaway greens, are a great introduction to each nine, where pars are not earned with a normal "green in regulation," but usually with a bit of scrambling. I don't have much love for the steeply pitched 2nd green, or the Church Pew bunkers at the 3rd [imitated in copy-cat style on courses all across China], the ridiculously long par-3 8th, or the driveable but blind short par-4 17th. But I am smitten with the elusive contours of the 4th and 13th greens, the downhill pitch to the par-4 5th, the wild contours of the 9th green with the practice putting clock incorporated in the back, and the classic par-4 finisher with its unheralded severe green.

Paradoxically, the product of Oakmont's short-game challenge is a course that consistently identifies the game's best ball-strikers, including Jones and Snead and Hogan and Nicklaus and Johnny Miller and Ernie Els, and now Dustin Johnson, too.

 - *TD*

SCORECARD

1. 482 !	7. 479	13. 183 !
2. 340	8. 288	14. 358
3. 428 !	9. 477 !	15. 499 !!
4. 609 !	10. 462 !	16. 231
5. 382 !	11. 379	17. 313 ?
6. 194	12. 667 !!	18. 484 !!

7255 Yards - Par 71

Roaring Gap

Roaring Gap, North Carolina, U.S.A.

The subject of golf course rankings is interesting and polarizing. It started in the 1960s when *Golf Digest* published a list of the "Toughest Courses in America". Realizing the inane mistake of excluding the sub-6500 yard Cypress Point Club, *Golf Digest* quickly pivoted and rebranded the list as the "100 Greatest," but still included the idea of "resistance to scoring" as an important aspect of greatness.

Today, with panelists armed with titanium 460cc heads, the tendency remains to sniff at courses that measure under 6500 yards. Look no farther than Roaring Gap to understand what a huge disservice this is to a course's perceived merit – as well as the game itself. In the United Kingdom, quick walking courses of such length that require thoughtful golf are cherished, further highlighting just how much higher their golf I.Q. is than ours.

Prior to the advent of air conditioning, the Tar Heel state wasn't a pleasant bargain through the summer months and early autumn. Thus, several prominent families in Elkin, Winston-Salem and Pinehurst elected to pursue a summer retreat in the nearby Blue Ridge Mountains. The low humidity and cool evenings were ideal in many respects, including the ability to have grasses that were conducive to good golf through the summer months.

At an altitude of 3200 feet, the property which Donald Ross was given in 1925 had appeal, but what he accomplished with this tableland was extraordinary. Tom Doak in the first edition of *The Confidential Guide* listed – shrewdly – the par 5s as being one of the best sets in the country. The bunker-less 7th hole meanders within its own valley with a brook threatening down the left, while the bunker-less 11th plays to a supremely dramatic plateau green. Best of all might well be the last one whereby the 16th features a wonderful punchbowl green whose right to left canted putting surface has vexed even the longest hitters for decades. And guess what? Since Tom last saw the course, the holes have been immeasurably improved thanks to one of the most detail-oriented restoration projects undertaken on a Ross course.

Holes of alarming excellence populate the design. In addition to the aforementioned par 5s, the Volcano one shot 6th hole exemplifies how the 6,455-yard Roaring Gap challenges the best. Precision is at a premium when approaching this (hugely) underestimated set of Ross green complexes. Take the 12th as another example. It traverses the property's most tumbling landforms, culminating at the course's most severely back-to-front tilted putting surface. Sloppy positioning of one's ball above the hole is tantamount to strokes mounting.

The 17th at Roaring Gap offers one of the most expansive views anywhere in the golf world.

The course builds all the way in with the highlight for many surely being the one-of-a-kind skyline green found at the 17th (seen above). The joy of playing this sub-350 yard hole highlights the fallacy of golf course rankings that routinely overvalue power at the expense of craftiness. Here, a premium is placed on driving right (closer to the out of bounds) as a serpentine bunker extends from the left front of the green. The 50-mile views over the valley toward Pilot Mountain and Hanging Rock invigorate the spirit.

The Home hole requires a 230-yard thump to a two-tiered green located in front of the charmingly low-slung golf house. A review of the scorecard might not dazzle, but the hole character, the isolated environment on an escarpment made all the more impressive by the historic Graystone Inn as a backdrop to the 4th green, and overall playing experience never fail to 'wow.'

There are thousands of courses longer and tougher in this country, but if there are a hundred places that one would rather have a game in the United States than Roaring Gap, the author hasn't seen them.
- *RM*

SCORECARD

1. 461	7. 519 !	13. 155
2. 160	8. 398 !	14. 385
3. 364	9. 301	15. 411 !!
4. 386	10. 371	16. 539 !!
5. 393 !	11. 515 !	17. 347 !!
6. 146 !!	12. 371 !	18. 233

6455 Yards - Par 72

Rock Creek

Deer Lodge, Montana, U.S.A.

The 'ideal' of a course built on sandy soil near the sea predetermines many rankings. Yet, the world is full of wonders and to narrowly define what makes for perfect golf is to disregard the game's ultimate advantage: its diverse playing fields.

Authors from Zane Grey to Wallace Stegner have waxed lyrically about the American West. For splendor in the great outdoors, Montana is second to none with Yellowstone to the south and Glacier Park to the north. Yet, from a golf perspective, it has long been barren: its boulders and rocky soil are as far removed from the game's sand-based origins along the North Sea as can be imagined. And yet … every now and then, the right confluence of resources and talent are brought to bear so a stereotype can be shattered. Such is what happened at Rock Creek.

With Tom Doak's career in high gear, Bill Foley contacted him to build a course on a 32,000 acre ranch owned by his partners and him. Always interested in doing something different, Doak was intrigued though aware of the limitations. Indeed, the heart of the project ultimately became the arduous task of removing boulders while preserving the three to five foot land contours so well suited to golf.

Several site visits produced a lazy loop with holes that meander up one side of Rock Creek and down the other via a routing that provides an unmistakable sense of place. The 2nd through 5th climb toward distant peaks. The 7th swings left and the golfer might think he was at Ballybunion so big and powerful are the landforms. The roaring Rock Creek diagonally crosses the one shot 8th and expresses the authenticity of the golf (and the place) in sharp contrast to the measly recycling brooks found in the lower states.

If the view from the tee on the half par 10th doesn't take your breath away, the spirit of the American West must not resonate within you. For the rest of us, we are dully encouraged by one of the widest fairways in golf to take a full and glorious swing at the ball. As with so many of the holes here, by flirting with a hazard, the golfer can gain an advantage, this time perhaps reaching the green in two with an heroic, gambling second shot. The rest of us enjoy plenty of short grass to bumble our way along.

Features similar to the best links courses are found throughout, starting with a central bunker cursedly placed precisely where you would like to hit the opening tee ball. Occasional blind tee shots, the back left punchbowl in the 2nd green, the saddle green at the 4th, the false front at the 6th, the sunken 9th green, the billowing 11th fairway, the horizon 13th green with the valley stretching out behind, time and time again, the classic design tenets are no different than in Scotland. Courtesy of the inspired selection of Kentucky

At the 5th, you choose which mountain to aim at from the tee: carrying the bunkers to the right opens up the green, while a lay-up to the left leaves a semi-blind pitch to the short par-4.

Bluegrass, the course plays firm but balls hang on the fairway contours. Flighting the ball through the wind from an uneven lie across a fearsome hazard is all of a sudden the same in Montana as it is in Scotland.

The thrill ride continues at the 11th with its lumpy fairway. The out of position golfer faces a blind approach from the depressed right fairway bowl while the drive that tightropes high left along a spine affords a fine view of a green silhouetted by evergreens. The one shot 13th and two shot 14th are among the longest pars that Doak has ever built and match the grandeur of the state; no cramped golf in Big Sky country! Importantly, they are followed by the drivable par 4 15th, highlighting the course's immaculate ebb and flow and pacing of its holes. The variety within the golf wants for nothing and is found in a most

unlikely, rugged setting.

Off the course, the cabins and low key facilities embody rustic luxury. In my personal rankings, I have the course one notch higher (i.e. a perfect Doak 10), acknowledging a personal bias whereby the American West holds as much visceral appeal as any place in the world with this design capturing those attributes. - *RM*

SCORECARD

1. 435	7. 486 !!	13. 265 !
2. 471 !	8. 193 !	14. 548 !!
3. 577	9. 403 !	15. 352 !!
4. 457 !	10. 632 !!!	16. 467
5. 354 !	11. 439 !	17. 191 !
6. 443	12. 155	18. 598

7466 Yards - Par 71

Sand Hills

Mullen, Nebraska, U.S.A.

"Build it and they will come!" That's what the voice in his head told Kevin Costner in the movie *Field of Dreams*, and it was also the rallying cry for the development of Sand Hills Golf Club, in western Nebraska. Only a handful of investors were willing to believe, but because the land was so perfect for golf, they were able to get the project into the ground.

The Sand Hills are no less than one of the great wonders of the golf world -- a region of sand dunes fully 60 miles north to south and 150 miles east to west, with endlessly rolling contours. Until twenty years ago, though, few golfers had ever heard of the place, because no one traveled this way -- most of the land between Omaha and Denver was "flyover country," and of course the highways had avoided the region because of all the sand and hills! Only the people of Nebraska spoke of this unique landscape before architect Dick Youngscap parlayed his successful development of a Pete Dye course and housing tract in Lincoln into a chance to build a club out in what Ben Crenshaw has called "the promised land" for golf.

Some would say that designers Bill Coore and Crenshaw had it easy, because everything you would want in golf holes existed all across the land, ready to be used; but coming up with the perfect routing on a site teeming with options is never as easy as a good architect makes it look. The first time I visited, in the spring of 1993, the only thing that had been done was to flag out the margins of the fairways on the ground and mow down the prairie grasses, yet when we reached the turn we got out our golf clubs and hit balls around the back nine, and had a real sense of playing every hole. It cost some money to put in the irrigation system and grass the place, but it cost practially nothing to shape, other than digging bunkers and losing the material that had been excavated. Thirteen of the greens looked to me like they were ready to grass without shaping anything at all, and some of the ones that needed work [the 2nd, 4th, and 8th] turned out to be among the best of the bunch.

Even at that, developing a golf course in a location with a four-and-a-half-month golf season is no sure thing, and the club would never have thrived unless the finished product was so good ... and unless Dick Youngscap kept the cost of all the infrastructure within reason, whether it was using a retired railroad tank car as the pressure tank for his irrigation system, or getting his overnight cottages and clubhouse [located out of sight from the course, down by the Dismal River] built for an affordable cost. In the twenty years since Sand Hills opened, I've had at least a half-dozen clients who said their model for a course was "like Sand Hills, but with better lodging," not realizing until the 2008 recession that the affordable cottages were the other reason Sand Hills had succeeded.

The 4th is the only artificial green at Sand Hills, tacked onto a slope to bring a ferocious natural bunker into play.

Playing at Sand Hills is an emotional experience right from the very first tee, perched on a knob with a diagonal carry to make over a big open expanse of sand, and the green beckoning from a ridge in the distance. On a calm day, low scores are there for the taking, but there aren't too many calm days! The first five holes invite you to hit away freely, and get used to the wind. The twin short par-4's at the 7th and 8th, played in opposite directions, are holes that can make your round, or ruin it. The back nine is the stronger of the two, particularly when the wind is from the west, and the first three par-4's [plus the 9th and 14th] play into its teeth.

Like Pine Valley, the course is so good that it's become a bit of a sacred cow -- no one is allowed to challenge it as the best of modern courses, not even Bill and Ben! But none of us can protest too loudly, because if it hadn't been for Sand Hills proving the business model, it's likely that few of the other great courses of the past 20 years would ever have been built. It really is a dream come true. - *TD*

SCORECARD

1. 549 !!	7. 283 !	13. 216 !
2. 458 !	8. 367 !	14. 508 !!
3. 216 !	9. 402	15. 469 !
4. 485 !	10. 472 !	16. 612 !
5. 412	11. 408 !	17. 150 !
6. 198 !	12. 417	18. 467 !

7089 Yards - Par 71

Shinnecock Hills

Southampton, New York, U.S.A.

The large clubhouse at the top of a hill is a cliche of American golf, but nowhere has it been done better than at Shinnecock Hills. From its wrap-around porch, arriving golfers and those who have just finished playing can look over 14 of the 18 holes stretched out below, and past them, the National Golf Links of America, running away toward its signature windmill and Peconic Bay beyond.

When Americans come to Tokyo to visit Kasumigaseki Golf Club, I tell them its history is similar to Shinnecock Hills; in both cases it took quite a few years before the course evolved to its final form. At Kasumigaseki, it was C. H. Alison who refined the work of several earlier designers; at Shinnecock, it was William Flynn and his partner Howard Toomey, who in 1930 created a dozen new holes over the top of the course's previous incarnations, by Willie Davis, Willie Dunn, and C.B. Macdonald.

The treeless, undulating course is fully exposed to the wind, and the wind can change direction and strength quite rapidly here on the eastern end of Long Island. Flynn's routing is up to the task. The layout is a series of smaller loops and triangles, so that nearly every tee shot attacks the wind at a different angle than the hole before, and you never go for more than two or three holes without seeing the wind in your face.

The opening hole "Westward Ho!" is one of the shortest two-shot holes on the course, but no pushover: after a downhill tee shot, its green is domed and falls away to both sides and to the back. The par-3 2nd is one of the toughest in the game, with three bunkers short left of the green that can quickly ruin one's card; many players would be wise to follow my caddie's advice to play it like a bit of dogleg and hope that the ball runs up.

After the strong par-4 3rd, played to one of Macdonald's original greens, the 4th and 7th tees are side by side, and the next three holes are a difficult loop, with the pond near the 6th green of particular trouble to anyone who misses that fairway. In addition, the par-5 5th is a fine hole: the shallow diagonal line of the fairway is defended by seven bunkers on either side, and though the green is reachable in two, it is elevated and crowned. Certainly, this hole is overshadowed by the course's only other par-5, the famous 16th, which sits right beside it playing in the other direction, straight toward the clubhouse looming on the horizon.

The front nine ends with "Ben Nevis," named after the highest mountain in the U.K., with a semi-blind approach up the steepest hill on any top-ranked course. After a snack in the screened porch at the corner of the clubhouse, it's off to a wonderful four-hole loop on the east end of the clubhouse, cut off from the rest by a small public road that actually crosses the 12th and 13th fairways.

The par-5 16th is one of William Flynn's best three-shotters, and an iconic view of Shinnecock.

The roller-coaster 10th fairway and its steep approach have caused tears among the world's best players in the last three U.S. Opens, but even that is not as difficult as the short 11th, Hill Head, played uphill to a shallow green guarded by four bunkers at the front and sides, and a steep drop-off behind. Dubbed the "world's shortest par five," it is the shortest of the par-3 holes at Shinnecock, which display a great balance of different yardages.

The finishing holes at Shinnecock are not all as fierce as we commonly see on championship courses -- of course, it was not designed for championships. However, the dogleg 14th, with its second shot up a long valley, and the long finishing hole, with its fairway leaning right just when you need to go left, are both bruising holes even for the best golfers.

Best of all, the 18th avoids the cliché by finishing in a bowl well below the clubhouse. It's a perfect amphitheater for a tournament finish, and you don't have to climb back up to the clubhouse until after you've putted out.
- *MN*

SCORECARD

1. 393 !	7. 189	13. 370 !
2. 226 !	8. 398 !	14. 443 !
3. 478 !	9. 443 !!	15. 403 !
4. 435	10. 412 !	16. 540 !!
5. 537 !	11. 158 !!	17. 179
6. 474 !	12. 468 !	18. 450 !

6996 Yards - Par 70

Somerset Hills

Bernardsville, New Jersey, U.S.A.

A quiet old-money club just ten minutes from the USGA headquarters, Somerset Hills was founded as a 9-hole course in 1899, beside Ravine Lake in north-central New Jersey. Members moved to a larger estate in Bernardsville in 1916, and a full 18-hole layout designed by A.W. Tillinghast. This is a very early example of Tillinghast's fine design work, where every fold of a tight property has been well used. His front nine is built across a softly moving meadow that once housed a racetrack while the back occupies more heavily wooded and undulating ground. The course is short by modern standards, but the greens are quite treacherous and among the region's most inspiring. We are told they were the gold standard for greens difficulty when the USGA developed its Slope System for handicapping.

Not only was Somerset Hills one of Tillinghast's earliest designs, it was also one of his most creative. The course tests almost every club in your bag and offers golfers endless variety with some unique hazard arrangements and a range of approach shot challenges. The use of droplet mounds, whether grassed over or part of a bunker complex, is particularly intriguing as are some of the experimental putting contours, which are often difficult to decipher. A number of targets, for example, are cleverly angled one way but look like they lean the other. Some that appear quite flat are actually rather steep.

Less obviously dramatic than the back nine, the front retains remnants of the old racetrack and is more spacious and easier to walk. It's also full of tremendous holes. Tillie's fearsome Redan-style 2nd is something to behold, as are green complexes on par fours like the 5th and 7th. Most pleasing, however is the variety of green sites and green settings across the nine. Some are perched; others are set down on the ground. Some demand an all-carry approach, either uphill or down, while others are open to a bouncing shot and lean one way or the other.

Enjoying the pick of the golf terrain, the homeward nine starts with the only hole modified significantly from the Tillinghast design, its green pushed back up an incline and par extended from four to five. This green site feels out of place on a course of such quality, and it's not surprising there is a plan to rethink it to make it fit better with the rest of the course. It's quickly forgotten, anyway, as the 11th and 12th are both fine holes set down alongside a dam, followed by a brilliant series of mid-length par fours atop a higher ledge, each with outstanding green complexes. The 13th and 14th greens, in particular, need to be seen to be believed.

Aside from extending the 10th years ago, Somerset Hills has diligently preserved its great layout and thankfully resisted the urge to modify holes or soften their wonderful green shapes. As with many clubs of this

The 12th green at Somerset Hills juts into a large lake, after the par-4 11th sweeps around a wood.

vintage, they did go through a dark period between the 1960's and 2000's where greens and fairways shrunk in size and trees were planted inappropriately across the property. Consultant Brian Slawnik deserves great credit for guiding the club through a recent restoration project, patiently and carefully working hole-by-hole to return much of the layout to the original Tillinghast plan.

What's cool about Somerset Hills are not necessarily the things that Tillinghast experimented with here and then took onto later projects, but rather the unique design features that he rarely tried anywhere else. There are dozens of Tillinghast courses across America, but none other quite like this one.   - *DO*

SCORECARD

1. 448	7. 484 !	13. 409 !
2. 205 !!	8. 230	14. 416 !
3. 376	9. 529 !?	15. 407 !
4. 457 !	10. 496	16. 170 !
5. 343 !	11. 412 !	17. 387
6. 501	12. 151 !	18. 335

6756 Yards - Par 71

Yale

New Haven, Connecticut, U.S.A.

For a state blessed with strong land-forms, and where plenty of money has always been in residence, Connecticut has fewer great golf courses than one would hope and expect.

Our Puritan heritage might have had something to do with it -- even when I was growing up in the 1960's, there were plenty of "Blue laws" restricting activity on Sundays -- but the other restraining force was the gift of the glaciers, leaving so much rock right under the surface of the ground. Golf course construction in Connecticut has always been much more expensive than in neighboring states, and the further one gets from New York City, the harder it is to justify such costs.

Cost was not a deterrent for Yale University in the 1920's, when the widow of former football captain Ray Tompkins donated the 700-acre Greist estate for the purpose of developing a golf course and nature reserve. They turned to Charles Blair Macdonald for advice, and Macdonald advised them to hire his protégé Seth Raynor for the job, and to be ready to spend a king's ransom to transform the hilly, rocky site. Upon its opening in 1926, the Ray Tompkins Memorial Course at Yale was reputedly the most expensive course ever built, at a cost of $400,000.

What's most impressive about the course is the huge scale of it all. From the very first tee, perched high above Greist Pond,

there is a formidable carry to start the round, and the long first green with a plateau along the right side and a punchbowl on the left, well guarded by sand, is more than 10,000 square feet. The second hole, playing back alongside the first, reveals its character on the approach, where the bunkers guarding the left side of the green are close to twenty feet deep.

Those deep bunkers, as others on the course, are the work of Yale alum Charles Banks, who was the headmaster of the nearby Hotchkiss School when Raynor came to build nine holes there, and subsequently hired Banks to help supervise other projects. Banks's bold featuring and Raynor's bold routing paired perfectly on the university's dramatic site. At the short 5th, deep trench bunkers surrounding the green. At the par-4 8th, the long green has a pronounced right-to-left tilt due to a shoulder at the right edge, so the 14-foot deep bunker on the left is a better miss than the 12-foot deep bunker on the right! And at the par-4 10th, the near-vertical approach to the green is fronted by deep cross bunkers, although the audacious four-foot tier in the green likely adds more strokes to the daily aggregate.

What's most noteworthy about the Yale course is that Raynor's usual template holes are less prominent than normal. The 3rd and 4th holes, for example, are loosely based on the Sahara and the Road hole, but with a big pond in between them, most observers

A much younger Tom Doak putts out of the swale in Yale's 9th green. The elevated tee lurks above.

would never recognize the templates. The aforementioned 8th hole is a beauty without a name, while one of the most stunning holes is the par-5 18th, zigzagging its way back to the clubhouse over or around a steep ridge 150 yards short of the green.

The exceptions are the par-3 holes, where Raynor's templates are in force, but at a much larger scale than normal. The Redan 13th, from its high tee, is less interesting than most versions of the hole, because the approach is much easier to stop on the green after its steep descent. The same might be said of the Biarritz 9th, where a long approach is almost impossible to bounce through the swale, but the length of the hole and the great front hole location between the swale and the pond in front put this Biarritz in a class of its own.

As with the whole course, no education in golf architecture can be complete if you haven't played it.   - *TD*

SCORECARD

1. 410 !	7. 377	13. 212 !
2. 374 !	8. 406 !	14. 365
3. 411 !	9. 213 !!!	15. 190
4. 437 !	10. 396 !	16. 553
5. 147	11. 379	17. 437 !
6. 421	12. 400	18. 621 !?!

6749 Yards - Par 70

NEW ENGLAND, QUEBEC AND THE MARITIMES

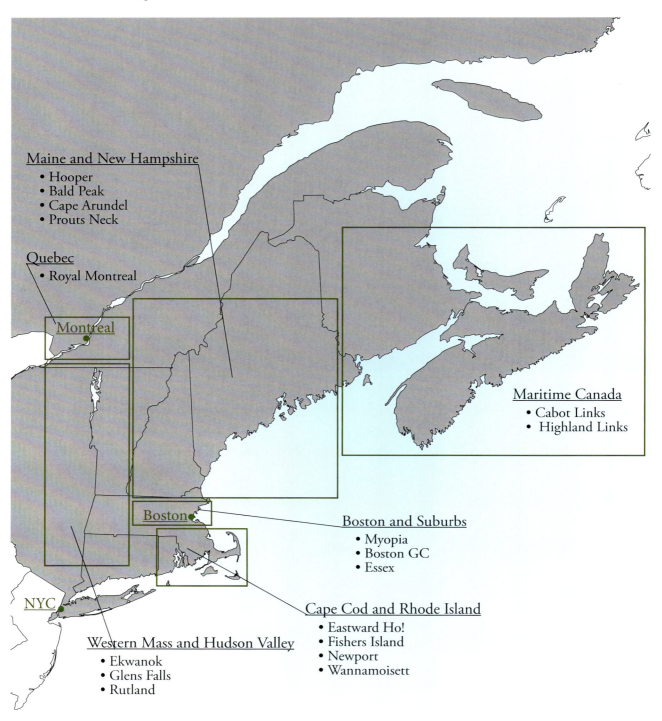

Maine and New Hampshire
- Hooper
- Bald Peak
- Cape Arundel
- Prouts Neck

Quebec
- Royal Montreal

Montreal

Maritime Canada
- Cabot Links
- Highland Links

Boston

Boston and Suburbs
- Myopia
- Boston GC
- Essex

NYC

Western Mass and Hudson Valley
- Ekwanok
- Glens Falls
- Rutland

Cape Cod and Rhode Island
- Eastward Ho!
- Fishers Island
- Newport
- Wannamoisett

The only place in America you'll find golf with the quirk and charm of courses in England, is in our own New England. This is not coincidence, but congruency: in both areas the development of new courses was driven by unusual parcels of land and topography, and by frugal golfers who saw the game as a pastime, not a business.

The prime mover was the Scotsman Donald Ross, who lays credit to no less than 29 of the courses in the New England section of our book. From Essex County, Massachusetts, where he was the professional for several years after 1910, to Sakonnet in Rhode Island, where he and his second wife spent their summers later in life, Ross was the dominant figure in New England golf from the turn of the century right up until the Depression, and received the lion's share of great commissions here.

Ross's local legend status kept most of his famous rivals from even trying to get work in the region, so the rest of the work in New England went to underrated designers like Deveruex Emmet, Wayne Stiles, and Walter Travis, with the occasional outlier like Herbert Fowler at Eastward Ho! Their small rolls in the greens and "chocolate drop" mounds in the roughs are not just a practical solution to ridding the site of rocks and debris; they are also the sort of human-scale features that make short game play interesting, and the only scale of earthworks that it made any sense to try and introduce to the landscape before the boom years of the late 1920's.

There would be few more enjoyable golf trips than one could make lazily driving from the Boston area up into Maine, or down toward Rhode Island and Cape Cod. The only problem is that of access, as nearly all of the courses we write about in the New England states are private clubs, few of which welcome unsponsored guests except in the off-season: you have to "know people" to play here.

Quite a contrast, then, is Maritime Canada, where all of the courses we cover are resort venues for whom visitors are their bread and butter. From Ross's course at St. Andrews, New Brunswick up to Stanley Thompson's Highlands Links and the new Cabot Cliffs [10th hole below], the Canadian courses are one of golf's hottest new destinations. The irony: the courses are spaced surprisingly far apart for those of us who don't know our Canadian geography so well.

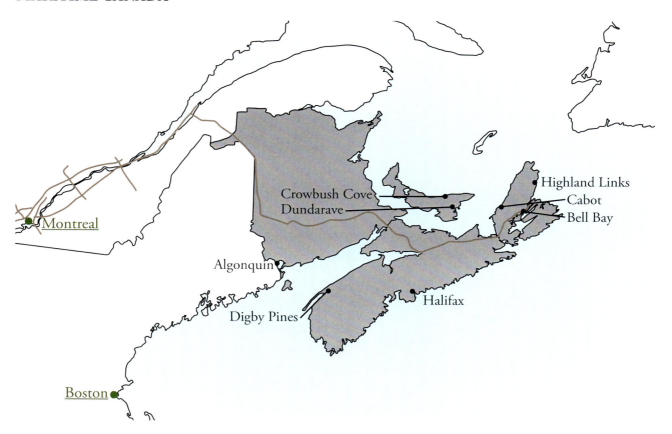

Algnoquin Hotel GC, St. Andrews-by-the-Sea, NB. Donald Ross, 1926, remodeled by Tom McBroom.

I haven't seen the course since the remodeling, but except for five decent holes that overlook Passamaquoddy Bay, there wasn't much to work with here. It's certainly not a destination for Donald Ross fanatics, though the hotel is a lovely stopover if you take the time to drive up to Nova Scotia. 4 – 5 - [1989]

Bell Bay GC, Baddeck, NS. Tom McBroom, 1997.

This was the first modern course built on Cape Breton since Stanley Thompson's time, but it's never great when the best view on the course is off the back of a tee [the 18th]. Some of the land is over-shaped for such a rustic setting but the contrast of native grasses and the pines give the course a handsome appearance. Don't skip the charming town. - 4 3 4 [2007]

Cabot Cliffs, Inverness, NS. Bill Coore and Ben Crenshaw, 2015.

We go to press as Cabot Cliffs is barely a season old, and already being compared to Cypress Point and Sand Hills. With several holes along the clifftops it seems to me the comparisons should be made with Pebble Beach: there is no other place on the Atlantic coast worthy of the comparison. As a big fan of two-shot holes, finding only six of them here [the longest of which is 404 yards] left me feeling a bit hollow, though I'm sure some of the six par-5's will play like long par-4's in certain wind conditions. We look forward to seeing how this beautiful collection of golf holes work together as the course matures. 8 8 - 8 [2015]

Cabot Links, Inverness, NS. Rod Whitman, 2011.

See the "Gourmet's Choice," pp. 10-11. 8 9 - 7 [2015]

Links at Crowbush Cove, West St. Peter's, PEI. Tom McBroom, 1994.

It's a good rule of thumb that a course with the word "links" in its name, is almost never a true links, as Crowbush is not. Though the par-4 16th and the tiny par-3 17th play among the dunes on the shoreline, the rest of the course feels more like a TPC, with pot bunkers, heavy mounding, artificial ponds, and greens that favor aerial approaches. It's hard to look further along the beach and not think about what might have been. - - - 5 [2005]

Digby Pines Resort, Digby, NS. Stanley Thompson, 1926.

Set in the woods a mile from the waterfront hotel, Digby is a well-done resort course with plenty of room to swing the club. A deep ravine / stream cutting through the property provides a splash of drama at the par-3 6th. 4 - - - [1989]

Dundarave GC, Georgetown, PEI. Michael Hurdzan and Dana Fry, 1999.

A pleasant woodland golf course by the Brudenell River, Dundarave is noteworthy for the large, reddish-tinted bunkers that are employed liberally throughout. The best hole is the par-4 8th, bending around a string of diagonal bunkers before heading toward the lake. You'll need a cart, though, due to several long breaks between holes. - - - 5 [2005]

Halifax G&CC, NS. Old Ashburn course by Stanley Thompson, 1922.

Though the club also owns a newer, regulation-length course on the outskirts of town, this old-school, par-66 layout is the one you want to play. The cramped, sloping property made for a difficult routing exercise, yet the variety of lengths in the par-3's and two-shotters gives ample opportunity to employ all the clubs in your bag. The par-4 16th with its approach from a downhill lie over a rushing stream is a terrific hole. 4 4 - - [2015]

Highlands Links, Ingonish, Cape Breton, NS. Stanley Thompson, 1935.

Certainly one of the most remote of great courses, I drove to Cape Breton from my parents' home in Connecticut and was startled to find it was just as far as Florida! Most of the course lies within Cape Breton Highlands National Park, and the routing is a real trek from the shore up a river valley into the mountains, and back down, covering six miles in all. Where the terrain was too steep for golf, there are no holes, making for green-to-tee walks as long as 400 yards along the river between the 12th and 13th. It's a lovely experience, as long as you pack a picnic lunch and a full can of mosquito repellent.

The variety of golf holes is excellent, coming in all lengths from the 164-yard 5th over an undulating bowl of fairway, to the 570-yard 7th, named Killiecrankie, after the glen north of Pitlochry that saw one of the bloodiest battles in the Scottish war for independence. Thompson's greens are largely untouched, so you can readily appreciate his genius at creating interesting internal contours at the 2nd and 18th. However, being located within a national park has hampered the necessary tree removal required for proper light and air movement that would promote proper playing conditions. 8 8 8 7 [2011]

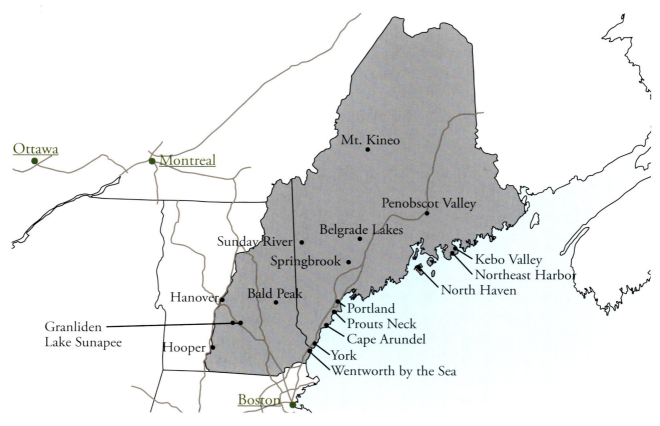

Bald Peak Colony Club, Melvin Village, NH. Donald Ross, 1922.

Few places I've seen radiate as strong a character of their own as Bald Peak, from its front gate to the clubhouse and pro shop set among a cluster of cottages on a ridge, to the course itself. The front nine plays down close to the shore of Lake Winnipesaukee at the short 5th hole with its punchbowl green, and then climbs sharply back up at the par-5 9th, while the second nine plays back toward the gate house and looks out toward the forested mountains to the north. The course tips out at 6300 yards, and is defended by only twenty bunkers. Yet so many of the greens sit up behind false fronts before sliding away to trouble that the approach shots will give golfers fits no matter the club in their hands. The three short holes on the back nine are especially good: the drop shot 12th is named "Battleship" for its small elevated green which looks like the prow of a big ship from the 14th fairway below and behind it, the right-to-left 15th requires two extra clubs as it climbs sideways up the slope, and the 17th green with its high right plateau is one of the wonders of the golf world. 7 - - - [2015]

Belgrade Lakes GC. Clive Clark, 1998.

Many of Maine's courses are semi-private, but unfortunately for our readers, hard to access in the prime summer season. An exception is Belgrade, a strictly daily fee course always open to visitors. The view from the putting green and first tee out northward to the lakes is phenomenal; take time to savor it, because you don't get it again. Built on a steep, rocky site, many holes are benched in to soften the slopes, yielding a lot of green-to-tee climbs. You've probably seen pictures of the course showing a lot of rock in play, mostly excess material from the construction process, stacked up to make a feature of it after they got tired of hauling it away; it's a practical solution that actually gives the course a different look. Overall, not a bad course, but it's all quite modern in a spot where you're not looking for that. 5 - - - [2015]

Cape Arundel GC, Kennebunkport, ME. Walter Travis, 1922, from an earlier layout.

Two miles from the Bush family compound, the short and quirky Cape Arundel has some truly wild Travis greens that make it worth the trip. With only two holes of over 400 yards, you'd think it would be too short to hold the interest of strong players, but Tour players like Fred Couples and Davis Love enjoyed their games with the President, and Deane Beman is a member. It's a bit of a hodgepodge – many of the holes are crammed together like a turn-of-the-century municipal course – but the 1st, 13th, 14th, and 18th along the Kennebunk River are very picturesque. 6 - - - [2000]

Granliden on Sunapee GC, Sunapee, NH. Walter Travis, 1925.

Wheeee! This unknown nine-hole course for a private residential community is laid out a bit like a toboggan run … you climb up a steep hill for four holes, play one across the top in the shadows of a modern condo community, and then run steeply back down the hill on a couple of the wildest golf holes I've ever seen. It's only 2200 yards, with five par-3's and a 200-yard par-4, but it looked like loads of fun, and Travis's tiny, undulating greens are somehow well preserved even though the course has had years of being barely functional. 3 - - - [2015]

Hanover CC, NH. Orrin Smith, 1922, with revisions by Ron Prichard.

Dartmouth's course provides a tight, hilly test for the faculty and students. The most interesting holes are four "practice holes" that are all that's left from a nine-hole addition

The short 12th at Bald Peak needs no sand to defend its embankments.

by Dartmouth alum Ralph Barton, on hillier land at the far end of the main course. 4 - - - [2002]

Hooper GC, Walpole, NH. Wayne Stiles, 1927.
        See the "Gourmet's Choice," pp. 22-23. 7 - - - [2015]

Kebo Valley GC, Bar Harbor, ME. Herbert Leeds, 1891, extended by Waldron Bates and Andrew Liscomb.
        Near the entrance to Acadia National Park, this woodsy, hilly course has been confounding golfers since the turn of the century, when President Taft took a great many strokes to escape the deep sand pit at the par-4 17th. 5 - - - [2015]

Lake Sunapee CC, New London, NH. Donald Ross, 1928.
        I knew nothing about this course until a friend scheduled a game here, but by the turn I was wondering where are all these "mailed in" Donald Ross designs; even his less celebrated courses are consistently good. Highlights were the wild green of the par-5 6th and the strong par-4 that follows it, and the three big finishing holes. In contrast to most of the older courses in New Hampshire and Maine, this is a more testing course at 6700 yards, but it is wanting for a couple of those short par-4's with character that make others in the region so much fun. 5 - - - [2015]

Mt. Kineo GC, ME. Architect unknown, 1890.
        A short ferry ride from Rockwood across a narrow neck of Moosehead Lake, these modest nine holes were part of a huge resort hotel built in the 1880's at the foot of Mt. Kineo, with its 700-foot cliff face looming directly behind the 4th green. Henry David Thoreau made the mountain famous after visiting in 1846, and recounting how the mountain was sacred to many Native American tribes, who used the stone to make arrowheads. The mountain's place in golf is not as fascinating, but any golfer on a moose safari should make the boat ride over to have a hit. 3 - - - [2015]

North Haven GC. Wayne Stiles, 1916.
        If your idea of heaven is a big summer cottage with a sailboat and lots of privacy, North Haven might be the place for you. It's where Charles Lindbergh got away from the limelight, but I don't think he came for the golf. The nine-hole course is set along a broad ridge, with all the fairways tilting strongly to one side or the other; only the 130-yard 6th along the water's edge, and the 230-yard finishing hole, are relatively flat. The course has its moments, especially when it gets dried out and bouncy, but if you come here with too many expectations it'll be a long ferry trip back. 4 - - - [2015]

Northeast Harbor GC. Club from 1895; present course by Arthur Lockwood, 1916, extended to 18 holes by Herbert Strong.
        Set at the foot of Acadia National Park, here is an old-money enclave par excellance. Its wonderful clubhouse is like Burning Tree brought to Maine, with Adirondack chairs on the covered porch. For many years the course was only 15 holes, after being reduced from nine during the Depression; the Ford family put up the money to clear and restore the last three holes about twenty years ago. At 5606 yards from the tips, the par of 70 is within range of single-digit handicaps, if they can stay on the straight and narrow, but the beautiful fescue roughs and native areas usually take their toll. Best holes include the par-5 4th around small knobs; the 316-yard 5th uphill across a small stream dividing the fairway; the 181-yard 12th with ridge and steep fall-off at left, and the downhill 13th at 352 yards. 5 - - - [2015]

Penobscot Valley CC, Orono. Donald Ross, 1924.

Here is a classic Ross routing that puts a lot of beautiful undulation to good use. It fits the property like a glove, but unfortunately the golf ball has outgrown it: the many 380- to 410-yard par-4's ain't what they used to be. Greens are relatively tame for Ross, with small lumpy contours, but some interesting hole locations on the wings. 6 - - - [2015]

Portland GC, Falmouth Foreside, ME. Donald Ross, 1921.

With the clubhouse commanding a fine view down across the golf course to the Atlantic shore, Portland is a magnificent setting for golf. The course is a tale of two parts: the open ground below the clubhouse includes two fine par-3 holes at the 4th and 7th, but the most difficult stretch is from the 10th to 15th holes, set in a spinney of pines on the highest ground. 6 - 5 - [2000]

Prouts Neck CC, Scarborough. Wayne Stiles, from a 1907 layout.

Low-key and low-lying, this under the radar club occupies a lovely setting at the end of the road south of Portland. The pro shop and 1st tee overlook the beach; the low dune ridge that runs alongside the opener is also in play at the 2nd green, 3rd tee, 14th green and 15th tee. Though there isn't much elevation to work with here, the small undulations in the fairways and lots of native-fringed bunkers give it real character. 6 - - - [2015]

Springbrook GC, Leeds. Al Biondi, 1966.

A sharp contrast to the old-money Maine courses profiled here, Springbrook is a do-it-yourself daily-fee design by golf professional Al Biondi, a few miles west of Augusta [Maine, that is]. It's a great piece of ground for golf, with big crowns and dips in the fairways, but it's not too hilly to walk as many of the holes abut low drainage areas. The heaving

fairway on the par-4 opener and the dramatic second shot at the short par-5 17th are moments to remember. 5 - - - [2015]

Sunday River GC, Newry. Robert Trent Jones, Jr., 2004.

Most ski resort courses are in the valley at the bottom of the hill; Sunday River sits on the hillside, affording great views to the north. The routing prioritized the visuals and drama of a handful of signature holes, including the par-3 4th, the long 11th and the par-4 finisher, leaving the rest of the supporting cast to fight the slopes to get you to the next good hole. At least it's wider and more playable than its older cousin at Sugarloaf, which none of my friends in Maine were keen for me to see. 5 - - - [2015]

Wentworth by the Sea CC, Rye, NH. George Wright, 1897, with revisions by Donald Ross and Geoffrey Cornish, 1964.

Wright and Ross had the right idea stopping at nine holes; there really wasn't enough land or enough dirt to make eighteen. Many of the newer holes are characterized by abrupt contours, rock outcroppings, and swampy roughs. 3 - - - [1986]

York Golf & Tennis Club. Donald Ross, 1923, from an 1897 layout.

York is a bit of a grab bag: the long par-3 opener with its green hard against an out-of-bounds public road and the Alps-like 3rd hole must be left over from the original design here. Added to Ross's wonderful 300-yard 5th and the short 7th with their greens down by the river, the sum total is a course full of character. Though not long, the course is quite difficult for the lesser player, with forced carries over water on the approaches to the 4th and 12th, and also on the second shot to the par-5 13th with its ultra-difficult hilltop green. 5 - - - [2015]

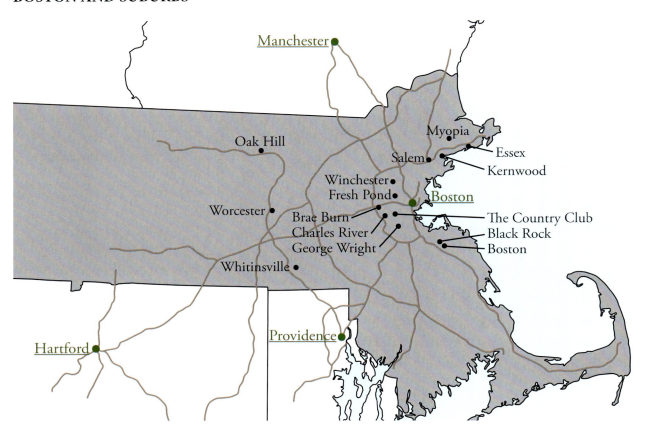

Black Rock CC, Hingham. Brian Silva, 2002.

No dead architect has enjoyed a greater surge in recognition over the past 20 years than Seth Raynor. As his brand of template holes gained in popularity, several modern architects took notice and became incorporating them into their own designs. Brian Silva is a prime beneficiary as his original designs here and at Black Creek in Tennessee are laced with Raynor's favorite design features. Examples here include a monster 12,000 sq.ft. punchbowl green at the end of the reachable par five fourth, the Redan green at the 9th, and a Biarritz type swale through the 11th. As with Raynor's own work, some of the best holes are true originals such as the short 7th with a tricky pitch to its narrow green, and the switch back sixteenth played beside a quarry wall. – 6 - -   [2006]

Boston GC, Hingham. Gil Hanse, 2005.

This may be the hardest course that Gil Hanse will ever build. A bit of an homage to Pine Valley, it would be tough sledding for a 15-handicap, and indeed, on this steep terrain, sledding might be more fun than golf if you don't have an "A" game to bring. But the golf is first-rate. There is a fantastic set of green complexes in all shapes and sizes – narrowest of all at the short par-4 5th – and those greens are consistently more difficult to approach the safer you drive from the tee. The only real detraction from the golf is the difficulty of the walk – the course is arranged on either side of an arterial road, and the walk between nines is as tough as any of the golf holes. - 6 7 7 [2007]

Brae Burn CC, Newton. Donald Ross, 1912.

A wonderful layout in the west suburbs of Boston, Brae Burn features small and severe greens and a variety of hilly holes. Did they really play the 255-yard 17th as a par three when Walter Hagen won the U.S. Open here in 1919? They did. 6 - - - [1999]

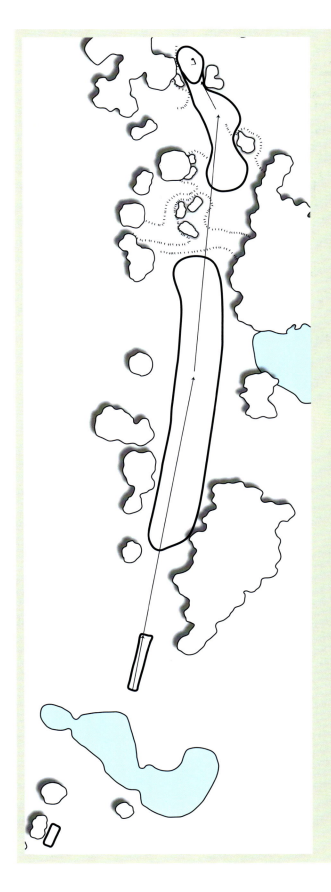

The Country Club, Brookline, MA
12th hole, Composite course - 625 yards
[also the 8th hole, Primrose nine]

The recent renovation by Gil Hanse at Brookline is outstanding, most of all for transformation of this long par-4. While it was always a difficult hole with a somewhat awkward blind second shot, today's longer hitters were driving to the end of the fairway, right up underneath the steep bank 150 yards before the green ... leaving themselves blind shots home after a good drive.

What to do? Hanse added a tee 125 yards back [and conveniently, closer to the previous green] and turned the hole into a par-5. Today, it takes two *very* good shots to get up the hill with your second shot for a good look at the green, and not leave the blind 150-yard pitch for your third.

Charles River CC, Newton. Donald Ross, 1921.

Here in the golf rich suburbs of Boston, this private course doesn't receive the attention it merits. The routing takes the golfer on a fine tour of some exhilarating New England topography -- and some wickedly contoured greens invariably found on high spots around the property. Highlights include the four-foot drop from back to front at the fifth green, the ubiquitous driver par 3 hole found at seemingly all his northeast courses (here it is the 11th with a neat kick slope in from the left) , a charming pair of back to back short par fours (the 12th and 13th) showing that Ross did indeed follow nature's lead, and one of the finest finishing holes in New England. Also, the 8th played down into a valley before climbing back uphill is one of Ross's most photographed holes for good reason. The fact that Ross was a dues-paying member here for many years should tell you something. - 7 6 - [2002]

The Country Club, Brookline. Old course by Willie Campbell, 1894, with revisions by Geoffrey Cornish, Rees Jones and Gil Hanse. Primrose nine by William Flynn, 1927.

This fine, old-fashioned New England course has hosted two of the great moments in American golf: Francis Ouimet's playoff victory over Harry Vardon and Ted Ray in the 1913 U.S. Open, and the U.S.A.'s comeback victory in the 1999 Ryder Cup. Its greens are some of the smallest of any famous championship course, and there are outcroppings of rock prominently in play on two of the best holes – the par-4 3rd, which people somehow forget in those lists of the best 18 holes in the U.S., and the par-5 11th (the 9th on the Composite course). Modern designers shy away from features like the cross bunker that guards the home green, but more is the pity because we've yet to meet the golfer who doesn't appreciate an old-fashioned challenge. 8 9 7 7 [2013]

The 3rd at Brookline is an old-fashioned hole that still packs a punch.

Essex County Club, Manchester. Donald Ross, 1910.

When I wrote the original version of *The Confidential Guide*, Essex wasn't thought of as one of the more prominent Boston layouts, but it has ascended over time with just a bit of fine-tuning. Donald Ross was the professional here for several summers – his old home sits by the second green – and his course incorporates some unique, small features left over from its early days, such as the bowl within the 3rd green. It is also a good routing across interesting property, with a fairly flat front nine giving way to more of a roller-coaster ride on the back. The 11th is now often cited as among Ross's best one shot holes but it is the collection of memorably diverse two shot holes on the back that make this course worthy of comparison with his other first-tier designs. 7 8 8 8 [2010]

Fresh Pond Municipal GC, Cambridge. Walter Johnson, 1932.

Right off the bus route from Harvard Square, this nine-hole muni was built by one of Donald Ross's associates at the dawn of the Depression. 1 - - - [1978]

George Wright GC, Boston. Donald Ross, 1935.

This municipal course in Hyde Park south of Boston is an oasis from development, only four miles from city center. Built by the WPA during the Great Depression, as many as 1000 people worked on its construction. The city almost let it go fallow in the mid-1980's, but cooler heads prevailed, and its turnaround since under greenkeeper Len Curtin has been so remarkable that the course will host the 2018 Massachusetts Amateur, its first trip to a municipal course.

With a strict par of 70, George Wright's 6,500 yards pack a punch -- because of its vintage, this is one of the few Ross courses designed with steel shafted clubs in mind. The

tumbling fairways are source of never ending debate. Take the 7th for instance. Do you bomb a drive over a crest of the hill for the sake of a short – albeit blind – approach? Or lay back to the crest of the hill and have a much longer approach, though with a perfect view? There is also an outstanding set of one shot holes. Don't miss this not so hidden gem. - 7 - - [2015]

Kernwood CC, Salem. Donald Ross, 1914.

A 1928 piece in *GOLF ILLUSTRATED* had the par-3 9th at Kernwood as part of "The Ideal Course," but don't ask me why they picked such a mundane hole. The one hole worth seeing was the short par-4 7th, with its tee shot across a finger of Boston Harbor. 3 - 4 - [1986]

Myopia Hunt Club, South Hamilton. Herbert C. Leeds, 1896.

See the "Gourmet's Choice," pp. 28-29. 7 7 8 7 [2007]

Oak Hill CC, Fitchburg. Original nine holes by Wayne Stiles, 1921; extended to 18 holes by Donald Ross, 1927.

Perhaps a good endorsement for Wayne Stiles' work is that most people would have a hard time discerning his work here [the front nine] from Ross's. The difficult greens are the club's main calling card. 5 – 6 - [1996]

Salem CC, Peabody. Donald Ross with Walter Hatch, 1925.

For many years, this was the star of north Boston, thanks to its *GOLF DIGEST* ranking and the fact that no one had tampered with it for generations; but lately the restoration of other courses has stolen some of its limelight. That's silly, because Salem is still a bewitching course. It has less than sixty bunkers, but the topography is so good that it doesn't need more. Holes like the reachable par 5 8th with its 20 foot chocolate drop mound and the short par-4 13th should be much more celebrated. 7 8 7 6 [2007]

The tee shot on the 9th at Whitinsville would still make Donald Ross proud.

Whitinsville GC, Whitinsville. Donald Ross with Walter Hatch, 1925.

A peculiarly quiet spot in the teeming Boston-New York corridor, Whitinsville gets my vote as the best nine-hole course in America. Six of its nine holes are truly outstanding, most of all the finishing par-4, an excellent driving hole skirting a pond to a high plateau fairway, and one of three holes Ross singled out for inclusion in George Thomas's book on golf design. The short holes are both excellent, and the par-5 opener is a beauty. Because it's only nine holes, opportunities for visitors are limited, but if you do get on, they may have to tackle you to stop you from going around it again and again. 8 – 6 - [2013]

Winchester CC, Winchester. Donald Ross, 1903-28.

This fine parkland layout is the hilliest of Ross's Boston-area courses. The first four or five holes climb methodically away from

the clubhouse, but from then on the variety of holes is outstanding, thanks to a superb routing over interesting terrain. There is even a bit of flair from Ross at the par-5 13th, with a split fairway landing area, but it works well as the upper landing area is a natural shelf underlain by rock, surrounded by deep fairway bunkers but offering a much better line for the second. 6 7 7 - [1991]

Worcester CC. Donald Ross, 1914.

Host to the 1925 U.S. Open and 1927 Ryder Cup Matches, Worcester does not have the sort of grandeur you'd expect of a course with such pedigree, but it's still a better course than a lot of today's tournament venues, thanks to the undulating terrain. The difficult par-3 13th is the hole I remember best. 5 – 5 - [1986]

Agawam Hunt C, Rumford, RI. Donald Ross, 1920, with revisions by Geoffrey Cornish.

   Just around the corner from Wannamoisett, this modest club is a bit over-treed, to try and inject some difficulty into a small course. The highlight of the course are the par-3 holes, where you don't have to worry about punching a second shot out from under branches. 4 - - - [1982]

Blue Rock Par-3 GC, South Yarmouth, MA. Geoffrey Cornish, 1962.

   This is a wonderful vacation spot, with eighteen holes ranging from 110 yards to 240 and two or three first-class water holes, so there's enough oomph to keep a good golfer interested while the rest of the family ambles along. It makes me sad that we've never had the chance to build a par-3 course of our own. 4 - - - [1973]

Eastward Ho! CC, Chathamport, MA. Herbert Fowler, 1920.

   Keith Foster's brilliant restoration of Eastward Ho! cements its place as the most exciting course on the Cape, if not New England. Seeing a 6,400-yard course get proper recognition on a few top-100 lists is a welcome sign that character is replacing difficulty as a metric. The set of par threes are wonderfully varied, head in different direction (which is important on such a windy site), and help to ensure that the par of 71 is rarely breached. The roller-coaster fairways are not every golfer's cup of tea – there are several places where your drive either crests a hill and rolls another thirty yards, or falls short and rolls back toward the tee. But there is never a dull moment, and the ridgetop views of Little Pleasant Bay are breathtaking. Its rise in prominence may have come slightly at the expense of Kittansett, which lacks drama by comparison. 7 8 7 8 [2010]

The last hole at Eastward Ho! is representative of the views and topography throughout.

Fishers Island Club, NY. Seth Raynor, 1917.

An old-money enclave in the middle of Long Island Sound, Fishers is one of the world's most beautiful courses. Many of Raynor's routings were constrained by the land planners seeking housing lots; here the course circles the east end of the island, with lots of elevation changes providing tremendous views and the holes utilizing the water's edge in every conceivable manner. It joins Yale as Raynor's boldest design, with audacious holes like the Alps 4th and Biarritz 5th. But the relatively weak four hole finishing stretch makes me wonder if it isn't getting to be a bit overrated: its high ranking by *Golf Digest* seems at odds with their rating criteria. 8 9 8 8 [2007]

Highland Links, North Truro, MA. Willard Small, 1892.

This hilly nine holes on bluffs along the Atlantic coast has gotten more than its share of acclaim by being cited as one of the only "true" links in America, but neither the turf nor the terrain will remind you of Britain's best. 3 - - - [2010]

Kittansett Club, Marion, MA. Fred Hood, 1923, with help from William Flynn.

In one sense, this is a one-hole course, because the famous par-3 3rd, playing across a seaweed-strewn beach to a built-up island of green, is in a class by itself. The supporting cast is less memorable, but its small greens are always hard to find when a breeze is about, and its location at the tip of a peninsula almost guarantees windy conditions. The green complex at the 240-yard 11th with its drop to a lower right tier, and the strategically bunkered sub-400 yard 12th with its perfectly placed fairway bunker left and greenside bunker right, are must-sees for the golf architecture fan. Ongoing tree removal continues to add to the atmosphere. 7 7 7 6 [2009]

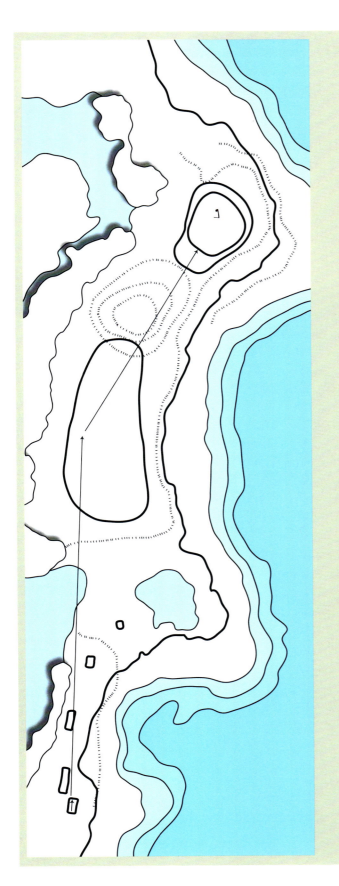

Fishers Island Club
4th hole - 397 yards

    While aficionados of golf architec-
ture love to drone on about the importance
of strategic design, the original spirit of the
game is for the player to surmount great natural obstacles.

    The 4th hole at Fishers Island is as
clear an example of the original type of golf as
one can find in America. Laid out along the
south shoreline of the island, the tee shot requires a carry up an abrupt bank to the start
of the fairway, which sweeps from left to right
high above a natural cove. The high point of
the shoreline comes seventy yards short of
the green, so the second shot must be played
blind over the summit, to a punchbowl green
sticking out onto a point of land, with a rocky
beach around the right side and behind. Two
good shots are essential here; no bunkers are
required to complicate the task at hand.

Metacomet CC, East Providence, RI. Donald Ross, 1921.

Seldom mentioned in the same breath as its neighbor, Wannamoisett, this is a wonderful piece of property for golf, but the club seems to have struggled in restoring the character of Ross' design while its neighbors have all succeeded. The strong par-4 14th might be the best hole in the Ocean State, and it's amazing to reflect that Ross planned the all-carry par-3 10th at today's 230-yard length. I wonder how long he'd want it to be now? 6 5 - - [2002]

Misquamicut Club, Westerly, RI. Willie Anderson, 1895, remodeled by Donald Ross.

For those of you searching Rhode Island for hidden Ross gems, this is not the place: the best part of the course's character derives from the original layout, with its built-up platform greens and yawning grass-faced bunkers. Although the bruising par-fours of yesteryear are middleweights today, the wonderful undulations of the fairways on the front nine give the course its distinctive character. The Ross holes nearer to the shore are relegated to flat ground, although the wild 15th green is worth a look. The long par-3 18th, across a deep grassy chasm and up to the clubhouse, is a memorable and unusual finish. 5 - - - [1989]

Nantucket GC, Siasconset, MA. Rees Jones, 1998.

Initiation fees here set record levels in the boom-boom 1990's, when Wall Street money flocked to Nantucket only to find that the two older courses on the island were impossible to join. Rees' successful project at Atlantic made him the obvious choice for the job, and he responded with one of his best designs – less man-made in appearance than Atlantic, and better programmed to make the most of the windy clime. But, it's still a bit too straightforward to generate real love in my heart. 6 – 7 - [2000]

CC of New Seabury, Mashpee, MA. Ocean course by William Mitchell, 1962.

They compare themselves to Pebble Beach, but 'Spyglass Hill of the East' is more apt as the front nine provides the exhilaration that comes from playing beside a large body of water while the back features standard fare through woods. Alas, the lack of rumples combined with flat topography squelches any aspirations of 'links' golf along the Nantucket Sound while the ponds and sometimes awkward doglegs on the back fail to inspire. None of us have seen it in quite a while so maybe they have done some work to better bridge the two wildly different nines – but we don't know how. The course was built long before the Mike Keisers of the world dedicated the best property for all eighteen holes. - 5 - - [1987]

Newport CC, RI. William F. Davis, 1894, with revisions by A.W. Tillinghast, Donald Ross, and Orrin Smith.

A course with authentic seaside flavor, even though it never gets across the road to the oceanfront, Newport's lack of fairway irrigation can make for some interesting bounces [and interesting shots!] after a long summer. Its classic clubhouse, great history, and unusual bunkering are all charming, though there are not enough great holes to put it in the elite class for me. However, its successful stint as the host for the 1995 U.S. Amateur (won by Tiger Woods) is a great argument against the notion that older courses have to be lengthened to make for a compelling championship; indeed, Buddy Marucci's runner-up performance showed that older courses are more likely to allow shotmakers to compete with the big hitters. 6 7 7 - [2016]

Old Sandwich GC, Plymouth, MA. Bill Coore and Ben Crenshaw, 2005.

I played this course before it had fully matured, and perhaps that's why I'm not as big a fan of it as Ran or Masa. The opening par-5 playing up a long valley is a fine starting hole, but the next three holes were a bit of a lull before the memorable short par-4 5th playing up and over a hog's back ridge. There are a number of other good holes, including the short par-4 7th that seemed to be inspired by the 8th at Pine Valley. 7 8 8 7 [2015]

Oyster Harbors CC, Osterville, MA. Donald Ross, 1926.

As the consultant to Oyster Harbors I get back every couple of years now, thinning out the pines a bit more to let the beautiful fescue roughs out into the sun. It's a wonder they think they need me at all. The star of the show here is one of Donald Ross's finest sets of greens, with their associated chipping areas, which we left untouched. The course only gets a brief peek at the water, since all the views were saved for the surrounding homes -- but it's a beautiful walk. 7 – 6 - [2016]

Pinehills GC, Plymouth, MA. 36 holes by Rees Jones and Jack Nicklaus Jr., 2001.

I only toured Rees' course here, as it was prior to the opening and the Nicklaus course was seeded a bit later.   It's pleasant daily-fee golf, but didn't seem to have any higher aspirations. 4 - 5 - [2001]

Plymouth CC, MA. Donald Ross, 1908.

This hidden gem on the way from Boston to the Cape is laid out over wonderful, undulating property. As a par-69 course it is routinely ignored, but there are outstanding par-4's galore, including a remarkable run from the 408-yard 5th to the 294-yard 6th and 344-yard 7th. Big hitters might be annoyed how often the landing areas drop off into trouble at 260 yards off the back tee, but for everyone else it is a terrific test of shotmaking and a load of fun. 6 – 5 - [2000]

Played from a sloping stance, the approach to the 7th at Old Sandwich is reminiscent of the short par-4's at Pine Valley.

Rhode Island CC, West Barrington, RI. Donald Ross, 1911.

Neither as quirky or as charming as some of the other Ross courses in the area, R.I.C.C. rests its case on a graceful routing across relatively gentle terrain, with occasional abrupt moments at the 3rd, the par-5 8th, and the uphill 14th. There are only three short holes [good ones] and two short par-5's; the variety of two-shot holes is its strength. It must be a good course on which to learn; both Billy Andrade and Brad Faxon grew up here. 6 - - - [2013]

Sakonnet GC, RI. Donald Ross, 1899, with revisions by Gil Hanse.

Donald Ross maintained a summer home just down the road at Little Compton, on the still-unspoiled southeast tip of Rhode Island, and tinkered with Sakonnet over the years as it was expanded from nine holes to eighteen. Ross never made it more than a par-68, but a few years back the club succumbed to convention and added two holes at the far end.

The meat of the course are the first six holes, which play back and forth to the bay, up and over the crest of a low ridge: the 2nd and 4th greens are built on sprawling fill pads right at the water's edge. The 214-yard 6th is in another class: with a sharp swale just in front and a couple of shaggy five-foot mounds just short and left of the plateau green, it's one of the great one-shotters of Ross' career. Once the course heads inland at the 7th, there is less excitement, although the par-4 18th next to the club entrance is a fine finish. 5 - - - [2013]

Sankaty Head GC, Siasconset, MA. H. Emerson Armstrong, 1921.

The established old-money classic on Nantucket, Sankaty is renowned for its breezy conditions and summer caddie camp, but the golf course was a bit less than I expected. It's surprisingly hilly, with several of the long holes taking up 30 or 40 feet of elevation between tee and green, but it all happens in broad, consistent slopes instead of cool wrinkles. The greens have some nasty tilt to them, and the bunkering is deep and decidedly un-flashy, probably to keep the sand from blowing away. So, in the end it might play a bit linksy, but it doesn't look much like a links at all. 5 - - - [2000]

Shelter Harbor GC, Charlestown, RI. Mike Hurdzan and Dana Fry, 2005.

Quite a change of pace from its elderly neighbors throughout the state, Shelter Harbor occupies a 400-acre plateau with remnant rock outcrops and views out to Block Island Sound. The densely forested and rocky site caused its share of headaches for the construction crew and for the developers, and it would have been easy to compromise playability along the way, but their perseverance resulted in a fine course, spacious enough to allow for interesting golf. Hurdzan and Fry collaborated with bunker guru Jeff Bradley to build the course, and the contouring of the greens and bunkers is miles above most of their other work. Among the many highlights are the outrageously contoured 4th green, a clever short par four at the 7th, and the beautifully bunkered par five 9th. - - - 7 [2015]

The candy-striped lighthouse is a perfect aiming point on the 4th at Sankaty Head.

The Vineyard GC, Edgartown, Martha's Vineyard. Donald Steel and Tom Mackenzie, 2002, with recent revisions by Gil Hanse.

Better known originally for its pledge to be an organically maintained golf course, than for the quality of the golf holes, this course has been completely remodeled since I visited in 2011 to interview for the job. Donald Steel's team had never built a course where they'd attempted to move earth on such a large scale, and they moved a bit too much: their small revetted bunkers felt completely out of scale in the face of large, broad hollows. I thought a major revision was required, but I didn't think the club was ready to go there; eventually they hired Gil Hanse to do just that. From all reports, it has been a resounding success. NR [2011]

Wannamoisett GC, Rumford, RI. Donald Ross, 1914-26.

A great study in getting a difficult course out of a small acreage, Wannamoisett's par of 69 is unique among top-ranked American courses -- and seldom challenged! Most designers would have made one of the parallel opening holes a par-5, but even at 449 and 473 yards they are both par-4's here, which can be considered fair warning of the course's intent. The greens feature a tremendous variety of tilt and undulation, and they are maintained at breakneck speed in the cool Rhode Island summers. The routing does suffer a bit from going back and forth so often, but Ron Forse's recent renovation and clearing work have done a marvelous job of making a small property feel big. Perhaps some raters mark it down because the three finishing holes are not as appealing as all that come before. 7 7 7 6 [2013]

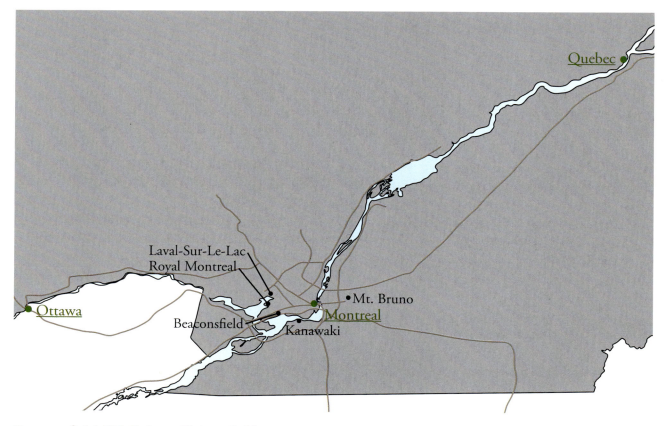

Beaconsfield GC, Pointe-Claire. Golf course from 1904.

Not far from the new airport on the city's west side, Beaconsfield is one of Canada's oldest clubs and has a long history as a venue for tournaments. The routing makes use of the rocky ridge near the clubhouse for many tee and green sites, notably the "Gibraltar" par-3 15th backed up by a granite face. However the holes themselves lack interesting detail. 4 - - - [2016]

Kanawaki GC, Kahnawake. Golf from 1914.

We stopped in here to have a look at the deep punchbowl green of the 230-yard 9th, but kept wandering because we found that all of the holes around the clubhouse were appealing. The strong par-4 2nd and short 3rd with its green hanging out on the end of a ridge make for an appealing start, and the fine par-4 18th with a backboard slope on the green does its best to encourage a bold approach. 5 - - - [2016]

C Laval-Sur-Le-Lac. Blue course by Mike Weir and Ian Andrew, 2013.

The total rebuild of an old course with mismatched nines, this is the first new design for both its architects, and it succeeds in presenting a style of its own. Nearly all the green sites are raised four or five feet above surrounding grade, with short grass down the banks all around -- there is considerably more tilt than one sees on modern courses, and the sweeping breaks on chips and putts are fun to decipher. However the tee shots are less interesting: the fairway bunkers are so far downrange that the mid-handicapper never even tries to carry a hazard. My favorite holes were the par-4 11th and 12th holes which break out into a big clearing, the par-5 4th with its Redan green and 13th with a large bunker obscuring the green, and the strong par-4 finisher with its green falling away and only a small ridge at the right front helping to collect a long approach. 6 - - - [2016]

C Laval-Sur-Le-Lac. Green course by Willie Park, Jr., 1917.

Willie Park's original layout at Laval has remained relatively intact for almost a century now. It gets off to a terrific start with a big, straightaway par-5 descending from the back of the clubhouse in two big steps. Several greens like the strong par-3 2nd are defended by strong ridges, presenting very difficult recoveries if you've gone over the back. The back nine is on fine ground, and the greens offer a challenging combination of tilt and speed. 5 - - - [2016]

Royal Montreal GC, Ile Bizard. Blue course by Dick Wilson, 1959, with modifications by Rees Jones.

The oldest club in North America was founded in Montreal in 1875, though today's facility dates from 1959, so a real sense of history only comes through in the upstairs areas of the clubhouse. The championship Blue course was updated by Rees Jones before the Presidents' Cup in 2007. The routing is only slightly altered, but the curving fairways of Wilson's design have been formalized into doglegs, and the diagonal ridges in some of the revised greens are very difficult to play over. There are lots of raised greens, so that every recovery shot is a deep bunker shot or a flop with the wedge, until you get to the back nine where water is in play next to five greens. 6 - 7 5 [2016]

Royal Montreal GC. Red course by Dick Wilson, 1959.

The Red is mostly a well-preserved example of Dick Wilson's work, but the many fairway bunkers are becoming lost in the trees creeping into play at the margins. Sadly, in the 1980's Joe Lee added a bunch of "bumpers" at the back of greens at the members' request that take the edge off the course. The par-4 5th with its narrow front panhandle and the short 7th with its abrupt fall-offs were my favorite holes. 5 - - - [2016]

Mt. Bruno GC, St. Bruno-de-Montarville. Willie Park, Jr., 1918, with some revisions to the bunkering by Stanley Thompson.

From the driveway up to the clubhouse right through the finishing hole alongside it and the lunch afterward, Mt. Bruno is one of the loveliest places in golf. Its members are also regular visitors to places like Muirfield, Brookline, Hoylake and Myopia, and their taste is most evident in and around the long red-shingled clubhouse, with its screened interiors and grassy sitting areas outside.

The course is set on the side of the mountain, with the holes laid out sidehill, uphill and downhill across a strong grade that makes reading the contours of the greens quite difficult. There are only two par-5 holes, but an excellent set of par-3's: the up-hill 3rd with its small back terrace, the plain-Jane 7th with its green unexpectedly falling away to the back right behind a bunker, the drop-shot 10th to a green in a pocket, and the 230-yard 15th to a huge green divided left and right by a very strong ridge. The longer holes suffer a bit from the clutter of trees, and from narrowed fairways that don't do justice to the scale of the property. Some of the downhill holes are aligned toward gumdrop-shaped mountains in the distance, and it's a shame that those views are now partially obscured. 7 - - - [2016]

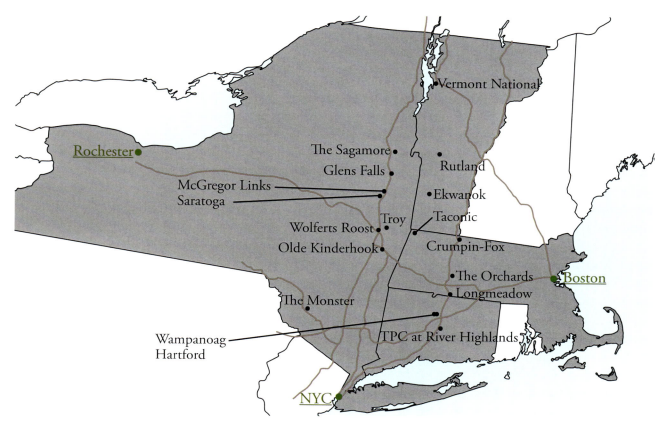

Crumpin-Fox Club, Bernardston, MA. Robert Trent Jones and Roger Rulewich, 1978-90.

This upscale public course was one of the forerunners of the type, drawing most of its play from Springfield and Hartford, each an hour away. It won't be mistaken for an older course, with its modern fairway lines, multi-tiered greens and prominent water hazards, but the golfers who make the two-hour drive from Hartford to play it know what they are doing. The back nine existed well before the front and most of the better holes are found here, including the attractive sub 400 yard 12th whose fairway bends left between a rock outcropping short left and one long right and the daunting uphill approach to the 460 yard 16th green. The highlight on the front comes when playing the par 5 8th where a pond parallels the last 450 yards of the fairway before one pitches over it to a green with several sections. 6 6 - - [1991]

Ekwanok CC, Manchester, VT. John Duncan Dunn and Walter Travis, 1899.

This old club set in a mountain valley is the quintessential summer escape, but the course is also a milestone in the evolution of American golf design. The midsection of the course is an exhilarating stretch of holes over hilly terrain, starting with the 585-yard 7th [at right], with its blind second shot through a gap between two huge knobs. Two design features at the short 340 yard 14th - the diagonal angle of the fairway to the tee and a green full of interesting contours - highlight a turn away from the straight playing corridors and flat greens of earlier American designs. 7 6 - 7 [2007]

Glens Falls CC, Queensbury, NY. Donald Ross, 1912-21.

How has such a fine course escaped attention this long? Far away to the north of New York City, Glens Falls is a summer club that never took itself too seriously, the same formula that kept places like Crystal Downs and Roaring Gap off the radar for many years. There is a big broad hill in the center of the property, perhaps 50 feet high, and the routing works around it and across it and twice up and over, so even though there are many parallel holes, you never have the sense of playing Army golf. The greens have all sorts of variety ... fallaways and punchbowls and severe tilts and tiers, maybe a couple of them in the same green! There are so many standout holes that I would put it comfortably in Ross's top ten courses, and that's a pretty special list. 8 7 - - [2015]

Hartford GC, West Hartford, CT. 27 holes by Devereux Emmet, 1914, with many revisions.

This club has tinkered with its course so many times that there is really no consistent character to latch onto. Its one outstanding moment is at the par-4 7th, with a diagonal tee shot across a creek, followed up by the long par-3 8th to another tiny green. 4 - 5 - [1991]

Longmeadow CC, South Longmeadow, MA. Donald Ross, 1922.

Only a few miles north of Hartford, Longmeadow plays much longer than the first glance at the scorecard might suggest; there are only two par-5's in theory, but with eight other holes over 420 yards, you're bound to put a few 5's on your card. The front nine is wonderfully routed, with many of the fairways interrupted by deep valleys. It's not all big two-shotters, either; the 318-yard 5th presents a bunch of awkward places to land your tee ball, and there is good variety in the short holes. 6 - - - [2014]

The tee of the long par-5 7th at Ekwanok is placed to mirror the backdrop of the Green Mountains.

McGregor Links
3rd hole - 225 yards

Long par threes are the least popular type of hole in the game, for two reasons: most golfers are not good enough to hit them consistently, so designers shy away from including the sort of interesting features that could compound the problem and produce a quick double bogey.

Designer Devereux Emmet was never one to compromise his principles just to be popular, and his 3rd hole at McGregor Links is the rare one-shotter that asks the weaker golfer to consider a two-shot route. There is only one tee, for all golfers [for ladies, it is a par-4], facing a shot across a valley and a line of cross-bunkers set into the face of a diagonal ridge, which partly obscures the green beyond. The golfer is given three options:

(a) a safe lay-up to the left, leaving a blind pitch over the ridge;
(b) a long shot just out to the right, to minimize the carry at 150-160 yards; or
(c) a bold shot straight to the heart of the green, where a carry of 190-200 yards over the bunkers is rewarded by a gathering green.

Today's pampered golfers demand multiple tees for such holes so they are never faced with such tough choices; kudos to the managers of McGregor Links for honoring the spirit of Emmet's design.

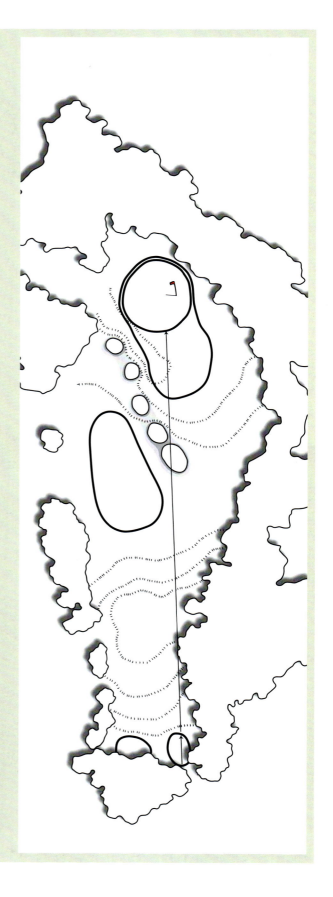

McGregor Links, Saratoga Springs, NY. Devereux Emmet, 1920.

Long past its heyday, the McGregor Links has been squeezed by housing development and overgrown by trees on the periphery, and the conditioning is more what you'd expect of a good municipal course. Yet there is still enough left of it to make an architecture geek giggle with excitement, with a handful of stunning holes like the 230-yard 3rd with its cross-bunkered approach, a rollicking run from the 6th through the 8th, the 13th and 16th with their perched greens, and a glorious version of the Alps for its penultimate hole. I wish I'd gotten to see it before the developers got their hands on it: it's hard to imagine now, but it was once compared to Pine Valley. 5 3 - - [2015]

The Monster GC, Kiamesha Lake, NY. Joe Finger, 1963

For years there have been rumors of rebuilding The Concord Hotel as a big-time casino resort, but nothing has come of them so far; however its famous golf course has remained open all along. "The Monster" was famous in the 1960's and 70's for its prodigious length and prominent use of water hazards. It's not my cup of tea -- many of its fairways are bulldozed flat -- but at least it has a style of its own. 4 – 4 - [1986]

Olde Kinderhook GC, Kinderhook, NY. Rees Jones, 1999.

I was intrigued to see Rees Jones' design for this course, as I had done a routing for the owner in the mid-90's and thought it was a pretty piece of ground. Good players will relish the challenge from 7300 yards over hilly terrain, but double-digit handicappers should stay away, as there are a lot of forced carries into greens on the longer holes, with no good option for playing safe. Favorite hole: the par-5 6th, with its green offset to the right over a series of bunkers. 5 - - - [2014]

Orchards GC, South Hadley, MA. Donald Ross and Walter Hatch, 1922-31.

Friends including Ben Crenshaw and Bradley Klein have raved about this course, but I think it is better kept in the perspective of a hidden gem. Most of the site was woods, not orchard, so the overall feel is much more private than most of Ross's parkland layouts in the region. There is some beautiful wild fescue on the bunker faces, though there are less than 40 bunkers in all; a small stream also makes its presence known on the holes close in to the clubhouse. 6 – 6 - [1986]

TPC at River Highlands, Cromwell, CT. Pete Dye, 1984, with major renovation by Bobby Weed.

None of us have seen Bobby Weed's version of this course, except on television, but I worked on the original TPC of Connecticut with Mr. Dye for long enough to know the property. It's a perfect setting for stadium golf, and Bobby got the adjacent property Pete always wanted, so I'm sure it's turned out well. NR [1984]

Rutland CC, Rutland, VT. George Low, 1902; extended to 18 holes by Wayne Stiles, 1927.

By reputation Rutland is the second-best course in Vermont, after Ekwanok, and I doubt there is much argument except from self-important types who think a 6100-yard course is not testing enough for their skills. Nearly all the holes run north and south, but the terrain is varied as the back nine works its way up a steep ridge at the 14th hole, which provides sweeping views over the course toward Killington and Pico Peak to the east. The stretch of par-4's from the 6th to the 8th is particularly good, as are the short 3rd sited near a rocky ridge and the short par-4 10th close to the Middlebury River which runs through the course. 6 - - - [2015]

The upper reaches of Rutland CC look out to the Green Mountains.

The Sagamore GC, Bolton Landing, NY. Donald Ross, 1928.

One of the few resort courses in upstate New York, The Sagamore sits high on a ridge overlooking Lake George, while the hotel is several miles away, down by the lake. Ross was engaged to find the best property he could, and it's a bit surprising he picked one this rugged. It could really use some aggressive clearing to restore lost vistas. 5 - - - [2014]

Saratoga G & Polo C, Saratoga Springs. R.C.B. Anderson, 1896.

Built pre-automobile, this Victorian nine holes and its stunning clubhouse are a quarter mile from city hall, rivaling Garden City for proximity to the urban core. The 1st hole starts with promise to a viciously canted green defended by wraparound bunkers, and the two one-shotters are equally distinctive. However two of the most dramatic holes, the 2nd and 5th, have had playing features snuffed out over time. Restored, the course would have the charm of Saratoga itself. - 6 - - [2015]

Taconic GC, Williamstown, MA. Wayne Stiles and John Van Kleek, 1927.

After the publication of the first edition of *The Confidential Guide*, I received more letters urging me to get to Taconic than for any other course. Owned and operated by Williams College, the parkland layout makes good use of a hilltop site, with distant church steeples framed against the surrounding mountains. Half the greens are situated above the golfer on his approach shot, and the strategy hinges around keeping your ball below the hole as the sloped putting surfaces can be especially wicked in the ideal New England climate. Four putts can be solicited from top collegiate golfers on such greens as the 6th, 10th and 13th. The uncluttered simplicity of the design helps make it a charmer. 6 7 - - [2008]

CC of Troy, NY. Walter Travis, 1927.

This hidden gem up the Hudson from New York City traverses some steep hills, but Travis' wonderful set of greens make it worth the hike. Their combination of serious internal contours and the general tilt of the land can make deciphering putts quite difficult. Bruce Hepner has done his best to restore the bunkering to the same standard as the greens, and to thin out the trees so the golfer's eye can enjoy the variety of contour he must tackle. 6 - - - [1993]

Vermont National GC, South Burlington, VT. Jack Nicklaus with Jack, Jr., 1997.

This very playable Nicklaus course features some nice golf around a couple of wetland areas. The Cape-style 3rd and par three 4th and 13th holes are its best stuff. The golf is a little formulaic, but it's good enough to add value to your ski condo. - - - 5 [2015]

Wampanoag GC, West Hartford, CT. Donald Ross, 1926.

Though never one of Ross' most prominent layouts, Wampanoag spawned the formation of the Donald Ross Society by a group of club members in the mid-1980's, after a controversial renovation veered away from Ross' original plan, adding tiny pot bunkers in front of a couple of greens. 4 5 5 - [2001]

Wolferts Roost GC, Albany, NY. A. W. Tillinghast, 1921, revised by Leonard Ranier.

Well respected in the capital, the Roost's small, sloping site did not endow it with many great holes. The signature par-3 15th over a pond is memorialized in the USGA's *Decisions on the Rules of Golf*, confirming that the unlucky player whose shot bounces over the small berm behind the green, catches the driveway, and rolls down the hill out the front gate, has no other option but to hit three from the tee. 4 - - - [1993]

The downhill par-3 9th at Taconic finishes underneath the small clubhouse.

NEW YORK CITY METROPOLITAN AREA

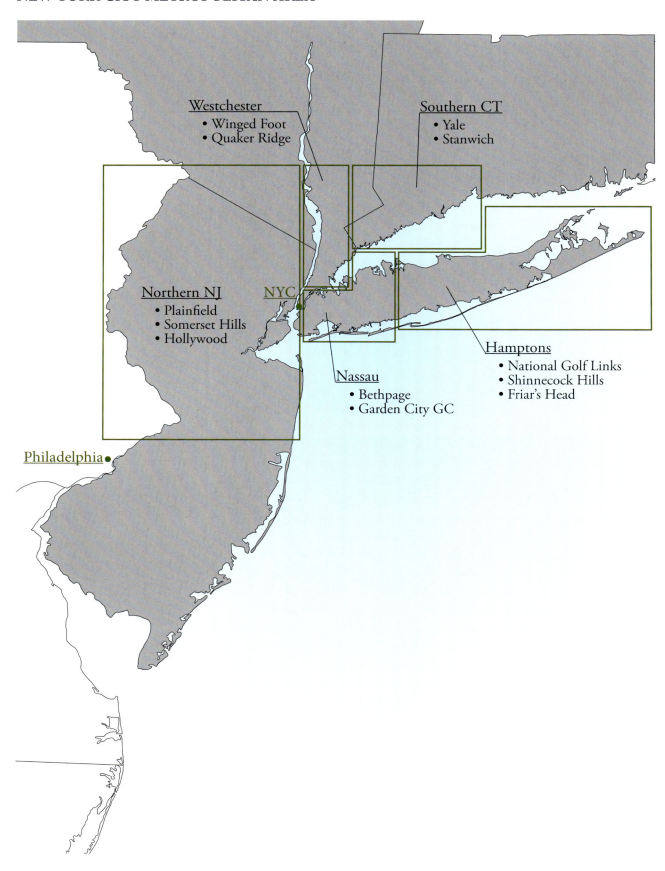

Westchester
- Winged Foot
- Quaker Ridge

Southern CT
- Yale
- Stanwich

Northern NJ
- Plainfield
- Somerset Hills
- Hollywood

NYC

Nassau
- Bethpage
- Garden City GC

Hamptons
- National Golf Links
- Shinnecock Hills
- Friar's Head

Philadelphia

I was born in New York City, and grew up in the Connecticut suburbs. Since my family weren't serious golfers, we were not members of a private golf and country club, but once I got my driver's license I discovered that great golf architecture was all around me.

A big part of my education as a golf course architect came from trespassing around the courses of the Metropolitan Golf Association, which stretches from Fairfield County, Connecticut, into Westchester and northern New Jersey, and all the way out to the Hamptons near the tip of Long Island. With the greatest concentration of wealth in the country, there has always been the money not just to develop new courses but for people to buy memberships in them, even at prices unimaginable to Midwesterners. [That's what it took to develop Bayonne and Sebonack and Friar's Head, but also Lido and Timber Point and The National Golf Links, pictured below.]

Thirteen of *Golf Digest's* 100 Greatest Courses in America reside the in the Met Section; the second tier of courses is even more amazing. Seth Raynor and Charles Blair Macdonald built nearly two dozen courses here, in settings as diverse as Westhampton [on the beach] and The Creek [sweeping down to Long Island Sound] and Sleepy Hollow [looking over the Hudson River]; all are well worth your time. It was also home for A.W. Tillinghast, who built so many outstanding courses in Westchester and north Jersey that a few were bound to go unsung.

If you like difficult greens, there's Winged Foot and Deepdale and Sebonack; in fact, Tillinghast's Somerset Hills [only a few miles from the USGA headquarters at Far Hills] was used as the standard for a "10" on the Slope System scale for greens difficulty.

If you like bunkers, you have everything from the open sands of Maidstone and Friars Head to the staggering depths built by Charles "Steam Shovel" Banks at Forsgate and Whippoorwill.

And if you like Donald Trump, he owns three projects around here, including the new Ferry Point public course at the foot of the Whitestone Bridge, complete with a "Trump" sign aimed at passengers on their final approach to LaGuardia airport. Who'd-a-thunk he would write it off as part of a presidential campaign?

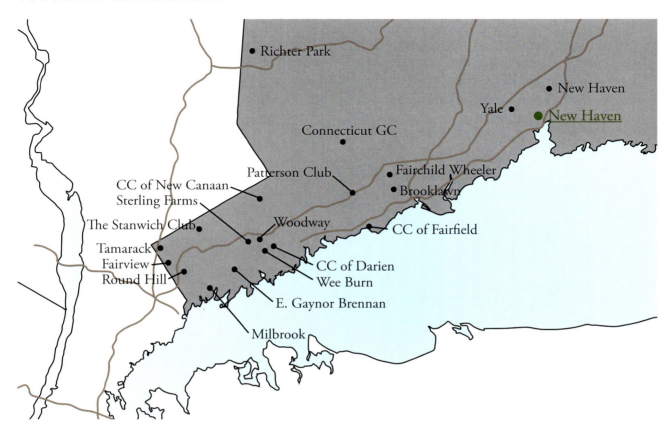

E. Gaynor Brennan GC, Stamford. Maurice McCarthy, 1925.

The former Hubbard Heights, this was the other public course of Tom's youth, and one he dreaded playing because of several opportunities to put a ball through someone's windshield. Crammed into just 70 acres, the fairways are so scrunched together that it is possible at times to see four golfers in the eighth fairway, who are actually playing four different holes! 2 - - - [1978]

Brooklawn CC, Fairfield. Golf from 1896; present course by A. W. Tillinghast, 1929.

Tillinghast inherited a routing from a previous course that featured several parallel fairways playing up and down a steep grade, so the course relies heavily on his fine greens contouring for its interest. The par-5 7th with its green guarded by a creek used to be the best hole, but lengthened now to 580 yards, I doubt many members can go for it. 5 - - - [1980]

The Connecticut GC, Easton. Geoffrey Cornish, 1966.

Developed in the mid sixties by the fellow who owned the Empire State Building, this course is unabashedly modeled after Augusta National, thanks to the scale of the property and the hilly terrain. However, Mr. Cornish never tried to test golfers with greens contouring the way Dr. MacKenzie did. 5 - - - [1980]

CC of Darien. Alfred Tull, 1958.

The only memorable hole here is the 620-yard 13th, so flat that it ought to be used as an emergency landing strip for airplanes. 3 - - - [1981]

CC of Fairfield. Seth Raynor, 1921, with revisions by A. W. Tillinghast.

This Raynor gem flew under the radar for years; that has changed as a result of methodical restoration work by Bruce Hepner over the past fifteen years. Virtually all the subtleties that Raynor imbued in this property are now fully realized. Standouts include the short 310 yard 7th played to an angled green that runs away and the Redan 9th, both of which might make a list of Raynor's eclectic best eighteen. Tillinghast's contributions include the short 4th and par-4 Cape 6th. Though the best holes are found on the front, the lovely coastal setting, rich texture from the fescues and fresh winds ensure the golfer is never bored. 5 7 6 5 [2008]

Fairview CC, Greenwich. Robert Trent Jones, 1968.

Fairview is the usual Trent Jones fare, but the steeply sloping site makes it one of his less compelling layouts. Tee and green sites required massive cuts and fills, detracting from the natural feeling of being out in the woods, without easing the walk. 4 - - - [1989]

The Millbrook Club, Greenwich. Geoffrey Cornish, 1963.

An affluent housing community surrounds these nine holes, woven tightly through the rocky and wooded terrain. It's a nice place to live, but you needn't bother visiting. 4 - 4 - [1988]

CC of New Canaan. Willie Park, Jr., 1909, extended to 18 holes by Alfred Tull.

This rolling, wooded course is built across difficult terrain, so I was surprised to find three outstanding long holes: the par-4 6th, and the par-5 13th and 16th. 4 - - - [1983]

New Haven CC, Hamden. Willie Park, Jr., 1920.

Little changed since 1920, the front nine ascends a ridge overlooking the clubhouse, with the back nine below. There are a couple of wonderful greens, but the preponderance of 390-yard holes fails to challenge today's golfers. 5 - - - [1994]

The Patterson Club, Fairfield. Robert Trent Jones, 1947.

Typical of Trent Jones' work in his early years, this parkland layout features elevated greens with some really savage contours, and the club has always been known for keeping the greens fast. But there are a lot of straightaway holes: the only one I remember as something different was the 284-yard 7th, with a lot of bunkers scattered around to punish a wild swing off the tee. I honestly can't think of another hole of that length in any of Mr. Jones's work. 4 - - - [1986]

Richter Park GC, Danbury. Edward Ryder, 1970.

For years Richter Park featured prominently on lists of the best public courses in America, but that is more an indication of how modest our expectations were for public golf, before the great boom of daily-fee courses in the 1990's. The holes that have the most potential or visual interest are the worst holes architecturally. 4 - - - [1988]

Round Hill Club, Greenwich. Walter Travis, 1922.

A short course with character, Round Hill suffered more than most from the Dutch Elm blight, as several holes played under and around massive American elms. The 2nd and 16th holes are both fine short par-5 holes, even if they are easily reachable in two for today's best golfers. 5 - - - [1980]

The Stanwich Club, Greenwich. William and David Gordon, 1960, with recent renovation by Tom Marzolf.

A lot of people consider Stanwich to be the best course in Connecticut, which is mostly a testament to how spotty the conditioning of the Yale course has been at times. Stanwich is a difficult course, an ideal test for U.S. Open qualifying with its length and fast, back-to-front greens; but it feels like it was pasted on top of the ground instead of built into it. The most memorable holes are a pair of Z-shaped par-5 holes, the 12th and 17th. 6 - - 5 [2001]

Sterling Farms GC, Stamford. Geoffrey Cornish, 1971.

Built on an old farm in a residential suburb of New York City, this is the quintessential Geoff Cornish design, with all the bunkers built above grade to avoid digging in rock. The routing is cramped, but there are a few interesting holes, such as the short par-4 16th which doglegs around the old family cemetery. It wouldn't have made this book, except that this book probably wouldn't exist if not for Sterling Farms – it's the course that gave me the opportunity to learn the game, for just a dollar a round, just a mile from the house where I grew up. If only more towns had a junior program that good. 3 - - - [1986]

Tamarack CC, Greenwich. Charles Banks, 1929.

I'd heard that Tamarack was one of the steepest and deepest examples of the Macdonald/Raynor/Banks lineage, so perhaps my expectations here were too high. The greens have been expanded back out to their original 15,000 square foot dimensions, and a couple of them exhibit impressive contouring, and there are indeed some very deep bunkers, such as left of the Biarritz 12th where the sand is 15 feet down a bank from the putting surface. But the extensive use of sod for renovations gives the impression that the course is a modern knockoff of Banks' style rather than a classic, and there are a lot of new fairway bunkers that add little strategy. 5 - - - [2015]

Wee Burn CC, Darien. Devereux Emmet, 1923, with revisions by Tom Fazio.

This was the club we couldn't justify joining when I was a kid; I was really the only one in the family who played golf, and I would have been in college before we'd climbed the waiting list, anyway. I haven't seen it since the Fazio revision, so won't try to give it a grade here. NR [1980]

D. Fairchild Wheeler GC, Fairfield. Red course by Robert White, 1934.

I only played the lesser of the two courses at this 36-hole facility with my brother, and I remarked in the previous edition of this book that it should not be allowed to display the same numeral as Pinehurst No. 2. Glad to see they've changed the course names to Red and Black! 1 - - - [1980]

Woodway CC, Darien. Willie Park, Jr., 1916.

Woodway was the closest country club to the home where I grew up, but I didn't know any members, so I never played there. The course makes good use of its two natural features: a rock-studded hill in the center of the property, and a rushing stream that's been dammed up in two places to make par-3 holes across ponds. But, like many American clubs it's been heavily overplanted with trees, and they are behind the curve in opening things back up. 4 - - - [1990]

The Course at Yale, New Haven. Charles Blair Macdonald and Seth Raynor, 1926.

See the "Gourmet's Choice," pp. 42-43. 8 8 - 6 [2015]

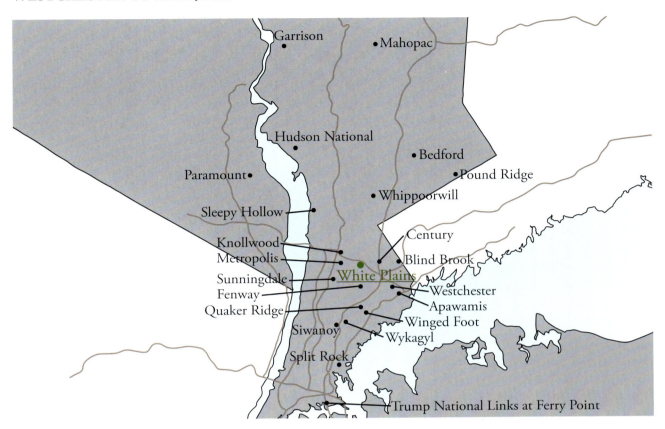

Garrison
Mahopac
Hudson National
Bedford
Paramount
Pound Ridge
Sleepy Hollow
Whippoorwill
Knollwood
Century
Metropolis
Blind Brook
Sunningdale
White Plains
Fenway
Westchester
Quaker Ridge
Apawamis
Winged Foot
Siwanoy
Wykagyl
Split Rock
Trump National Links at Ferry Point

Apawamis Club, Rye. Maturin Ballou and Willie Dunn, 1901.

     A very conservative club, epitomized by the name given to the double row of cross-bunkers guarding the 4th green, known as "Eleanor Roosevelt's teeth." Despite several attempts at revisions, the small greens and semi-blind shots between rock outcroppings still feel like it's 1911, when Harold Hilton won the U.S. Amateur here after a fortuitous bounce out of the woods at the 37th hole.   4 - - - [1983]

Bedford G & Tennis Club. Devereux Emmet, 1891.

     The sleepy town of Bedford has gotten even more tony over the past 30 years – Martha Stewart and Richard Gere are among the residents now – but this pleasant parkland course is nothing that will attract the paparazzi. 3 - - - [1983]

Blind Brook Club, Purchase. Seth Raynor and George Low, 1917.

     I dismissed this course in previous editions of *The Confidential Guide* as being home to an all-male club with an elderly membership. That much is true, but the course is perfectly tailored to that audience, reaching deeper into the bag than the usual Raynor templates. I need to get back here. 4 - - - [1985]

Century CC, Purchase. C.H. Alison, 1926

     This parkland layout is set across rolling land with very attractive brawny bunkers. I haven't been back since a restoration ten years ago, and they are about to embark on another. For history buffs, the fact that Ben Hogan spent a couple of years as an assistant professional here is another lure. 5 – 7 - [1985]

Fenway GC, Scarsdale. A.W. Tillinghast, 1924.

Fenway is an underrated parkland course over very good property, though we wouldn't mind seeing 100 more trees disappear. There is a great set of greens, and just the right number of bruising two-shot holes so that good players can't dismiss it. Even with Quaker Ridge and Winged Foot as neighbors, it shouldn't be lost in the shuffle. The start of the back nine is the best stretch of holes, but the super-narrow green at the short par-4 15th has probably had the most influence on consultant architect Gil Hanse's subsequent designs. 7 7 6 6 [2011]

Garrison GC, Garrison-on-Hudson. Dick Wilson, 1961.

I would never have guessed the provenance of this course; the narrow clearings through the woods and steep inclines of fairway are hardly what comes to mind when one thinks of Dick Wilson's work. The name derives from the town's previous tour of duty as a Revolutionary War stronghold, and the course does offer a couple of fine views of the Hudson River. It might be a pleasant change of pace after one too many gussied-up parkland layouts. 4 - - - [1984]

Hudson National GC, Scarborough-on-Hudson. Tom Fazio, 1996.

This course was supposed to be a blockbuster – Tom Fazio in New York City! – but it was just a bust for me. High up above Sleepy Hollow, the course commands huge views of the Hudson River, particularly from the back tee of the par-3 16th. But the rocky terrain interspersed with wetlands didn't suit golf so well, and the course had to be constructed on three distinct levels, making for a disjointed experience. There are a couple of very memorable holes, but also a couple of real stinkers, which might be chalked up to the environmental restrictions. 5 – 6 6 [2007]

Knollwood CC, Elmsford. Golf from 1897; present course by A. W. Tillinghast and Seth Raynor, 1927.

The two most memorable holes here are Raynor's work – the superb 18th, playing back and forth over a deep hollow that contains a long narrow pond to an elevated fortress green, and the 90-yard 19th, one of the earliest surviving examples of a "bye hole" in U.S. golf. 5 – 5 - [1984]

Mahopac G & Beach Club. Devereux Emmet, 1913.

As proof that it's still possible to find a hidden gem, Darius found one just 25 miles from where I grew up! An utterly charming old club north of Westchester County, Mahopac members play on a very attractive and undulating property overlooking Lake Mahopac. The closing holes on the front nine and vast majority of the back occupy boldly rolling ground and boast a bunch of really fun, strong challenges for all manner of player. The side-hill, then uphill 9th is particularly memorable, along with long par threes at the 6th, 12th and 14th, which are well bunkered and demanding of different shapes and different shots. Although short, the course is no pushover thanks to a number of nervy approach shots into aggressively leaning greens. The bunkering is also a feature, the traps deep and fringed by fescue grasses in the faces and around the edges. The club has done a lot of good work in recent years, clearing trees and restoring fairway and green dimensions. - - - 6 [2015]

Metropolis CC, White Plains. Herbert Strong, 1922, with revisions by A. W. Tillinghast and Joe Finger.

This is yet another fine parkland course, a bit more wooded and hilly than most of its neighbors. There is one renowned hole, the strong par-4 6th, a narrow downhill dogleg. 4 - - - [1984]

The par-3 16th at Sleepy Hollow, at right, alongside the 2nd green.

Paramount CC, New City. A. W. Tillinghast, 1920.

Built for the founder of Paramount Studios, on an estate 45 minutes from Manhattan, this course has been revived by my former colleague Jim Urbina, after years in disrepair. The strength of the design lies in its greens which follow the broad slopes of the property, but we doubt Tillinghast ever envisaged green speeds this fast: many approach shots land on these tilted putting surfaces only to be summarily shunted off. Always Tillinghast's pride and joy, the par-3 holes here are exceptional, including the 18th hole which is one of the few examples of his "Reef" concept in existence. - 6 - - [2015]

Pound Ridge GC. Pete and Perry Dye, 2008.

A dramatic course weaving its way around granite ledges, Pound Ridge has several holes which are too narrow for their own good, including the last two. It's not a course we'd want to play every day, but the topography does provide some compelling shots. - 5 - 5 [2011]

Quaker Ridge GC, Scarsdale. A.W. Tillinghast, 1926.

Perhaps a more honest layout than its illustrious neighbors, the Quaker Ridge course relies more on natural undulations and less on wicked greens for its challenge; but the club has shunned tournaments as steadily as Winged Foot has embraced them. It's an excellent layout, especially from the 4th hole around to the Sahara 14th, but there is a bit of a letdown with three parallel holes at the finish. It's one of Tillie's best, but not as original as San Francisco Golf Club or as diverse as Somerset Hills. 8 8 8 7 [2011]

Siwanoy CC, Bronxville. Donald Ross, 1913.

The only Ross design in Westchester, Siwanoy hosted the first PGA Championship in 1916, but has rarely attracted attention since, perhaps in part because it had gotten very overgrown. Recent work has helped expand the playing corridors and surfaces so the members can enjoy it, but the lack of space and lack of doglegged holes limits its potential. - - - 5 [2007]

Sleepy Hollow GC, Scarborough on Hudson. Charles Blair Macdonald and Seth Raynor, 1911, with revisions by A.W. Tillinghast, 1928.

This sprawling course climbs up a ridge, with knockout views of the Hudson River as the backdrop for the short 16th. Seven of Macdonald's original holes were co-opted for a third nine, with Tillinghast enlisted to extend the main course at the top end, which produced some more good holes but a strange dichotomy between two styles of design. In 2006-07 Gil Hanse and George Bahto were hired to marry the two styles into a more cohesive course. Not many parkland courses deliver this much drama. 7 7 8 7 [2015]

Split Rock GC, Bronx. John Van Kleek, 1934, from an earlier layout.

The pride of the New York City municipal course system, prior to the opening of its brand new neighbor at Ferry Point Park, Split Rock occupies a woodsy setting between the Hutchinson River Parkway and the MetroNorth train line. The opening holes are difficult but quite plain; its character changes for the better at the short par-4 7th, and from there on the course features a number of exciting greens of the kind rarely found on public tracks. Favorites included the 439-yard 11th with a sweeping bunker across the approach and two small raised hole locations, the 347-yard 15th with a large mound right in the middle of the green, and the difficult finishing hole with two ridges running across its long green. 4 - - - [2015]

Sunningdale CC, Scarsdale. Seth Raynor, 1918, with revisions by Walter Travis, A.W. Tillinghast and Mike DeVries.

Of the lesser-known clubs in this golf-rich neighborhood, Sunningdale seems to have the most potential for major improvement, with its generous fairways and constantly moving terrain. They have recently found new direction under Mike DeVries, who has re-designed the mid-length 5th while recovering lost hole locations on other greens. The strong one-shotters on the front side and Raynor's gently rising par-5 7th to a Road Hole green are a solid base to work from. - - - 5 [2011]

Trump National Links at Ferry Point Park, Bronx. Jack Nicklaus with John Sanford, 2015.

As ambitious as the guy with his name on it, the new public course at the foot of the Bronx-Whitestone Bridge was funded by the New York City Parks Department through years of delays and cost overruns. The result is challenging and well manicured and undeniably a big course, and the short game options around the greens are some of the best of any Nicklaus course I've seen. However it doesn't play like a links, because the many angled greens and bunkers on the approaches make it hard for lower-trajectory golfers to bounce the ball in. Too much of the shaping is wasted in between the holes, and not enough spills over into the fairways themselves. 6 - - 5 [2015]

Westchester CC, Rye. West course by Walter Travis, 1922.

I've only seen the West course as it used to be set up for the PGA Tour's Westchester Classic, when the two nines were reversed. It's the hilliest course in the area, but the contours are well employed in the routing, so that abrupt features come into play without it being a difficult walk. The clubhouse is enormous, a hotel-sized building that makes Riviera's look like a mud hut. 5 – 5 - [1986]

Whippoorwill Club, Armonk. Donald Ross, 1925, revised by Charles Banks, 1930.

Ran likens the spirit of Whippoorwill to The Addington outside of London, where golf and adventure are served up in equal parts. It is clearly Banks' masterpiece, because his steam-shovel bunkers fit easily into the abrupt contours of the site. Unusually for a course in the Macdonald/Raynor family, the par-4 holes steal the show from the par-3's: the roller-coaster 455-yard 5th, the 425-yard 7th with its steeply uphill second shot to an enormous punchbowl green, the 440-yard split-fairway 14th and the underrated Home hole pull off the rare combination of being daunting and inspiring. 6 8 6 - [2013]

Winged Foot GC, Mamaroneck. West course by A.W. Tillinghast, 1923.

Winged Foot West is still one of America's most demanding tests of golf, perfectly fulfilling the club's request for "a man-sized course." The greens are small and steep, and every green but the last is flanked by bunkers to both sides, though the approaches are less frightening now than when Hale Irwin was hitting 4-woods and 2-irons to get home. There is nothing unique about the contour or scenery; it seems like you ought to be able to build a course just like it on any good parkland site, yet no one has. It's a clay-soil counterpart to Pinehurst #2: the architecture from fifty yards in and including the greens is amazing, though the topography isn't. Ran declares the 1st hole as the single finest green complex in America; Mr. Nicklaus might disagree, having putted off it in the 1974 U.S. Open. With greens such as this, it's a pity that the club is so fixated on keeping narrow fairways and thick rough. No one aims for a particular side of a 26-yard-wide fairway, so the strategy of Tillinghast's design is negated. The West could be a lot more fun, if the members would let it be. 9 8 8 8 [2011]

Winged Foot GC. East course by A.W. Tillinghast, 1923.

Some believe the East course to be the equal of the West, lacking only the championship tees; others insist that without its big brother to protect its reputation, it would never be rated so highly. Our numbers seem to put us in the latter camp, even though we believe the East's set of short holes, the short par-4's, and its set of greens are superior to those on the West course. [When I look at it that way, I start to question whether I'm overrating the West course for its championship history.] The 440-yard uphill 16th and the downhill 220-yard 17th stand with the best holes on the property, but I do miss the great elm that used to overhang the green of the East 10th. 7 7 7 6 [2014]

Wykagyl GC, New Rochelle. Lawrence Van Etten, 1905, with revisions by Donald Ross in the 1920's, A.W. Tillinghast in 1930, and Coore & Crenshaw.

When people think golf in Westchester County, they think of either Winged Foot over mundane ground with great greens or Sleepy Hollow where tumbling land takes precedence over interior green contours. Wykagyl falls in the later camp, set over rollicking terrain with some sort of a surprise always just around the corner. A member laid out the original eighteen and over half his playing corridors are still in use. Ross's bunker work ramped up the design's sophistication and then Tillinghast took it higher still when he created today's holes 4, 5 and 6 that play around and in a valley with a brook through it. Ran considers the stretch from the 3rd through the 8th to be as good as any in Westchester. Only in New York State could a course of this quality fly still under the radar. As one dimensional macho layouts continue to wane in favor, look to hear a lot more about this unusual 6,700 yard gem that features 5 par threes and 5 par fives. - 7 - - [2016]

Bethpage State Park GC, Farmingdale. Black course by A.W. Tillinghast, 1936.

Since I first played it as an 18-year-old with my mom, the Black course has gone from a neglected municipal course to a storied U.S. Open site. It's a muscular course, but [dare I say it] the greens are pretty boring. The bunkers are cavernous and captivating, but the fairways have been narrowed to the point where you no longer try to play near the hazards. Instead, the contours of the ground are the real making of the best holes -- the par-5 fourth which is best approached in three distinct steps, and the par-4 fifth with its slanting fairway and summit of green. Though it is probably the single best site on which he ever worked, we would not put it in Tillinghast's top tier of work because of the dearth of shots that require finesse. Kudos to the state for keeping the Black course cart-free, a tradition that separates it from the other four courses in the park, and keeps pretenders away. 8 8 7 7 [2007]

Bethpage State Park GC. Red course by A. W. Tillinghast, 1936.

Had the Black course never been built, the Red, with its many strong doglegged holes, might have received similar acclaim. It hasn't got the big, bold bunkering of the Black, but the opening and closing holes are far superior, the 5th is a fine long hole, and the short par-4 6th gives aggressive tee shots the cold shoulder. 6 - - - [2015]

Clearview Park GC, Queens. William Tucker, 1927.

I was hoping this might have some remnants of the Alister MacKenzie-designed Bayside Links, built just after 1930, but apparently that course was further down the hill, and entirely consumed by the construction of the approach to the Throgs Neck Bridge. Clearview is a slightly older municipal course with not much to recommend it. 2 - - - [1995]

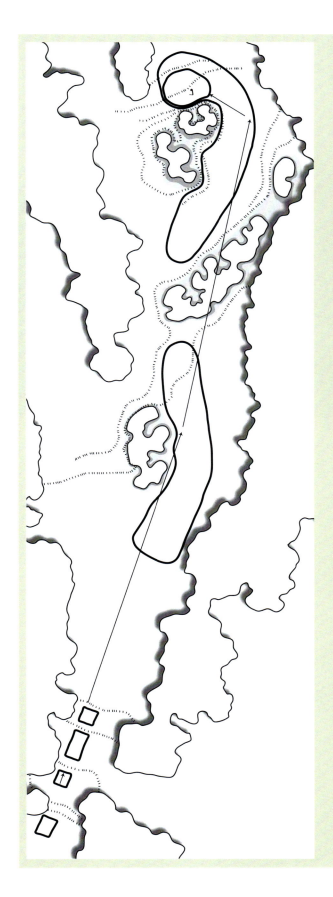

Bethpage State Park (Black Course)
4th hole - 521 yards

Few par-5's present themselves more boldly from the tee than the 4th at Bethpage Black, A.W. Tillinghast's championship-level public facility. From the elevated tee, you can see most everything about the hole, as the fairway wraps around a gigantic fairway bunker inside left of the driving area, stops, and then resumes behind an even bigger Sahara of sand running away diagonally from left to right. It's immediately obvious that a tee shot close to the bunker on the left will make the line for the second much less daunting, yet just as clear that the second bit of fairway will be hard to reach if one pulls the tee shot into the sand.

The less obvious challenge of the hole is that the green, hiding behind two smaller bunkers across its front, tilts away from the line of play and is none too deep, so that a long second shot [or a third shot out of the rough] will have difficulty holding onto the putting suface. Indeed, the safest play for the longer hitter is hole-high just to the right of the fronting bunker and the green, for an easy up-and-down chip ... but few who can reach the green in two will be patient enough to settle for the best way to make four, when a three for the ages seems within their grasp.

The 6th (left) and 16th (coming back) at The Creek are two of Long Island's finest par-4's.

The Creek Club, Locust Valley. Charles Blair Macdonald and Seth Raynor, 1923.

It's hard to believe a course in this magnificent setting was dismissed as no more than an old man's course, but that's what years of neglect and tree growth can do to a classic design. The first five holes, on the inland side of the clubhouse, will have you wondering if we are crazy to recommend this place, but the par-4 sixth is a wild ride down the hill toward Long Island Sound, and from then on the course is outstanding – touching the beach at the short par-4 10th, playing back across the creek to a low island green at the Biarritz 11th, fending off wetlands at the strong par-4 13th and 14th, and playing up a beautiful valley toward the clubhouse at the long par-4 16th. 7 7 7 7 [2012]

Deepdale Club, Manhasset. Dick Wilson, 1956.

Deepdale is one of the most reclusive clubs in America, due not only to its elite membership, but also to the memories of a scandal in the early 1960's, when the club's Calcutta tournament was busted for gambling excess. You never see it in the rankings of great courses, because if you're on one of those panels, they'll ask the members not to bring you out. Too bad – it's one of Dick Wilson's best courses, although there are too many sharp doglegs to put it among America's best. Conditioning is routinely compared to Augusta National, because there are a few greens with such a steep back-to-front slope that you can easily putt off them. Legend has it that when one guest questioned whether the greens were really that fast, his host called up a jet and flew the guest down to Augusta the same afternoon, just to prove him wrong! 6 6 - - [2004]

Engineers GC, Roslyn. Herbert Strong, 1918, with lots of revisions.

Nothing at all like you'd expect from a course with a name like Engineers, this course has a bit of a cult following – you'll either love it or hate it. The hilly property gives plenty of opportunity for creative shotmaking, but it's the large and severely terraced greens that will leave the most lasting impression … you won't find greens like them anywhere else. There are several strong candidates for list of the best, worst, and most unusual golf holes, but the signature hole is a part-timer – the 94-yard 14th, with a narrow fallaway green and death to both sides, christened the "Two or Twenty" hole back in the club's heyday. This tiny hole had been abandoned for many years, but was reintroduced as part of an alternate configuration for the course. 6 6 - - [2001]

Fresh Meadow GC, Lake Success. C.H. Alison, 1923.

The original Fresh Meadow course was a Tillinghast design that hosted the 1932 U.S. Open, but that course was plowed under for housing and the club moved further out onto Long Island, taking over Alison's Lakeville CC course. It's not a bad course, but this is a tough neighborhood. 4 – 4 - [1986]

Garden City GC. Devereux Emmet, 1898, with revisions by Walter Travis.

See the "Gourmet's Choice," pp. 20-21. 8 9 8 7 [2015]

Glen Head CC. Devereux Emmet and Marion Hollins, 1924.

Glen Head began its life as the Women's National Golf & Tennis Club, founded by Marion Hollins and funded by the wives of Wall Street's elite, with the landing areas tailored to the needs of women golfers. Sadly, the club was not able to survive the Depression, and after a few years under the wing of The Creek Club [where many of the husbands were members], it was spun off into a new club. There are a few cool greens, but for some reason the routing was changed a bit, and the par-3 7th is a shadow of what was. 4 - - - [1999]

Inwood CC. Herbert Strong, 1911.

Basically the same course as it was when Bobby Jones won his first major championship there – the 1923 U.S. Open – the aura of this low-lying course was forever changed by the construction of Kennedy Airport just across the marsh. Due to a change in the sequencing, it has the unusual feature of three consecutive par-5 holes from the 3rd to 5th, followed by back-to-back short holes no less. Look for the plaque in the right rough on the 18th hole -- it marks the spot from which Jones hit a 2-iron across the water to six feet in the Open playoff, and finally broke through to become a champion. There is a lot of good, subtle golf here for such a flat property. 5 5 - - [2004]

Village of Lake Success GC. Orrin Smith, 1956.

Built over the site of C.B. Macdonald's original Deepdale course, after construction of the Long Island Expressway caused the club to build anew, the current course is almost completely re-routed from the original design and has little to recommend it. 3 - - - [1994]

Town of Hempstead GC at Lido, Lido Beach. Robert Trent Jones and Frank Duane, 1965.

For some reason, years after C. B. Macdonald's original Lido course went bankrupt and was sold off for housing and town offices, a half-assed public course version of it was built on a new landfill just next door. The design imitates some of the original holes, but it's pancake-flat and poorly maintained. 2 - - - [1981]

The opening hole at Meadow Brook is a sharp dogleg, a staple of Dick Wilson's work.

Meadow Brook Club, Jericho. Dick Wilson, 1955.

This is an unusual course compared to other Dick Wilson designs; it is typically long and difficult, but the greens are twice the size of his other famous courses, or anything else on Long Island. Approach shots are given more latitude, but playing long and safe may result in many three-putt greens. The scale of it is eye-opening even by today's big-course standards. 6 7 6 - [2005]

Nassau CC, Glen Cove. Devereux Emmet, 1896, with revisions by Seth Raynor and Herbert Strong.

A sister club of sorts to The Creek and Piping Rock, this club has always had a more diverse membership, but a lesser golf course. The course has been changed around several times and they are still trying to get it right. Hopefully Raynor's short 5th hole is safe from tinkering. 4 – 3 - [1992]

North Hempstead CC. A. W. Tillinghast, 1916.

One of the lesser-known moments in Tillinghast's career, this course is laid out over a small property on the north shore, on the way to Sands Point. The bunkering looks more like Raynor than Tillie, but I guess that was more his style in his early years. 4 - - - [1999]

North Shore GC, Roslyn. Seth Raynor, 1916, with revisions by Tom Doak and Brian Schneider, 2010.

One of Raynor's first solo designs, its early vintage was a drawback because the most interesting driving features were located only 180-200 yards off the tee, and tees backed up against property lines left little room to address the issue. The club almost disappeared a few years ago under extreme financial pressure – they lost 30 members to the Bernard Madoff scandal – before it was rescued by Donald Zucker, whom had learned to play golf here years earlier. He asked us how to give the course a bit more character and variety, and to do so we reversed the two starting and two finishing holes, creating a drivable short par-4 2nd, a wild version of Macdonald's "Short" hole at the 17th [missing from the original design, which had only three par-3 holes], and a very long par-5 18th coming home from the old 2nd green to the old 1st tee. But the par-5 16th, which crosses a deep gully twice, is still the most arresting hole. 6 - - - [2011]

Piping Rock Club, Locust Valley. Charles Blair Macdonald and Seth Raynor, 1917.

In the middle of Long Island's north shore, Piping Rock is an amazing club – more than 200 acres of golf and skeet and indoor tennis and all sorts of other diversions for the moneyed set. The golf is pretty strong, too, particularly after Pete Dye's renovation in the mid-1980's, which added several hundred yards to the course with room to spare. As with the 15th at St. Louis Country Club, the top tier hole location on the par-5 6th hole will move the scoring average by half a shot. You'll find many of the standard Macdonald/Raynor features here, but a novel addition is the snaky ridge that runs across the 15th green. 6 7 7 6 [2012]

Rockaway Hunting Club, Lawrence. Devereux Emmet, 1900, with revisions by A. W. Tillinghast.

The seaside setting along the south shore of Long Island is promising, with golf holes overlooking Broswere Bay at the start, in the middle, and at the end of the round. But the terrain is pretty flat and low-lying, making it impossible to build deep bunkers to give it any muscle. The par-4 9th hole along the water was well known in the 1920's, but it was much more unusual before Pete Dye came along. 5 - - - [1986]

Sands Point GC. A. W. Tillinghast, 1927.

Almost amazingly secluded for being just twelve miles from Manhattan, Sands Point resides in anonymity on the north shore of Long Island, as do most of its members. Several holes on the front nine play into and over a depression at the corner of the property while the open, windy back nine feels akin to ambling across an open heath. The land is gentler than elsewhere on this long island but that doesn't make it any less appealing as a place to enjoy one's everyday golf.
5 6 - - [2014]

Tam O'Shanter CC, Glen Head. Steve Kristoss, 1963.

This course was a mess when I saw it ... there was a spring leaking right out of the middle of the 9th green! I'm told it's been totally redone since, but there are too many really good courses in the vicinity to bother with going back. 2 - - - [1985]

The Village Club of Sands Point. Tom Doak with Bruce Hepner, 2000, from a nine-hole layout by Robert Trent Jones.

The old Guggenheim estate had been scooped up by IBM as a corporate retreat, and then was sold to the town; it is an impressive property, with some massive trees and a bit of land overlooking Long Island Sound. The golf course operates out of the former stables, with the mansion serving as a restaurant and overnight accommodation for guests of town residents and members. But as this was also a public project, town politics handicapped the design process, as three neighbors wrecked the routing for the front nine by threatening to sue and hold up progress, forcing the 4th hole to be played as a dogleg around the tennis courts, with a giant net protecting them. 4 - - - [2008]

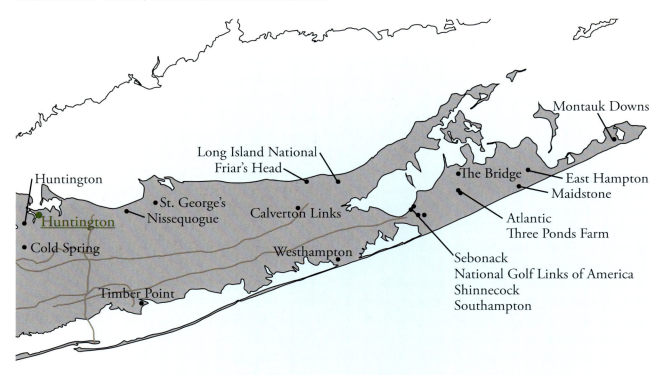

Atlantic GC, Bridgehampton. Rees Jones, 1991-2007.

The original layout of Atlantic epitomized the "tough but fair" mantra of Rees's designs, but the golf never seemed to connect with anything on the ground. In recent years, a makeover of the bunkering, plus the removal of some earthworks that reinforced its artificial feel, have improved the atmosphere and injected more strategy. Whatever it lacked in visual interest, it has always compensated for with perfect conditioning, thanks to the efforts of greenkeeper Bob Ranum, who's been here from day one. 6 6 6 5 [2009]

The Bridge GC, Bridgehampton. Rees Jones, 2002.

Built on the site of the former Bridgehampton (auto) racetrack, The Bridge is an unusual new club, in that developer Bob Rubin was a fairly novice golfer when he started the project: his interest was geared more toward

the ultramodern clubhouse and art installations around the course. The original routing had lots of elevated tees offering great views, but it was a difficult hike; ever since, they have been tinkering with the holes to make the course more walkable and playable. It's come a long way. - - 6 6 [2015]

Calverton Links, Riverhead. Kelly Blake Moran, 1994.

A modest daily fee course for the mid-priced market, there are rumors it may go away soon as it sits on leased land. It's quite narrow in one stretch. 3 - - - [1993]

Cold Spring CC, Cold Spring Harbor. Seth Raynor, 1923.

Originally designed as a private course on the estate of Otto Kahn, the great railroad financier, the remains of Raynor's course is no match for the splendor of Kahn's home, the adjacent Oheka Castle, a veritable Versailles.

Some are up in arms about a Jack Nicklaus proposal to redevelop the site, but this was always a milquetoast example of Raynor's work, so it won't be missed much. 4 - - - [1995]

East Hampton GC. Bill Coore and Ben Crenshaw, 2000.

Though it's been overshadowed by Friars Head which came along just a couple of years afterward, this is a fine course. Crammed onto a small property which had been permitted and cleared many years earlier, the back nine is a short and tight jaunt through scrub oak and sand, with the smallest and most severe greens anyone has built in two generations, and a great mix of 450-yard and 300-yard holes. It's quite a contrast from the open field of the front nine [which was originally the back]. It's got great variety, but to be honest, I wished it had all been like the back nine, just because it's so different than other modern courses. 6 – 7 7 [2015]

Friar's Head GC, Baiting Hollow. Bill Coore and Ben Crenshaw, 2002.

After Sand Hills, this very private club on the north shore is generally accepted as Coore & Crenshaw's second-best design. A dune ridge splits the property in two, and all of the most dramatic holes either start or finish on the ridge or sit in the dunes to the north; my personal favorite is the par-4 9th, with its wild green, but the great set of par-5's also get their share of acclaim.

In contrast, the middle of each nine occupies what were open, rolling fields, and instead of trying to marry the two diverse properties by moving large quantities of earth, it continues to be transformed through added bunkering and landscaping at the direction of Bill Coore and developer Ken Bakst. Friar's Head has gotten better every time I've gone back to see it, and that's the way great courses become iconic ones. 9 9 8 9 [2015]

The 15th at Friar's Head, in brilliant fall colors.

The short par-4 7th at Maidstone is the last hole before one enters the coastal dunes.

Huntington CC, Cold Spring Harbor. Devereux Emmet, 1911-28.

    Huntington was a quite unexpected discovery, as it has little reputation in the New York area, but it is a wild ride. The old aerial photo we were shown looks like an early Desmond Muirhead design – or a message to another world! – with unusual fairway bunkering galore. Nearly every hole features a rugged combination of uphill or downhill or sidehill stances, and the deep fairway bunkers are right in your face in many of the landing areas. Emmet's take on the Road green at St. Andrews is the most severe version since the original, but the par-4's on the back nine are a great combination of topography and whimsy. 6 - - - [1999]

Long Island National GC, Riverhead. Robert Trent Jones, Jr., 2002.

    This faux links makes a big first impression, with the driving range featuring large dunes around a 30-foot deep cut, and the course spreading out through some impressive earthworks in the distance. But the biggest ups and downs of the man-made terrain rarely come into play, while the greens and bunkers are fairly dull. The one really noteworthy hole is the short par-4 13th, with an elevated green that falls away quite sharply to the back, rewarding the player who drives well out to the left over anyone who plays the beeline to the green and comes up short. 4 - - - [2013]

Maidstone Club, East Hampton. Willie Park, Jr., 1922, from an original 1891 layout.

    One of the oldest clubs in America, Maidstone is a social institution, even in the elite precinct of the Hamptons. It is a schizophrenic course, with the starting and finishing holes on very flat ground traversing inland lagoons, and the middle of the course on true links ground protected by a narrow strip of dunes from the Atlantic itself. The par-4

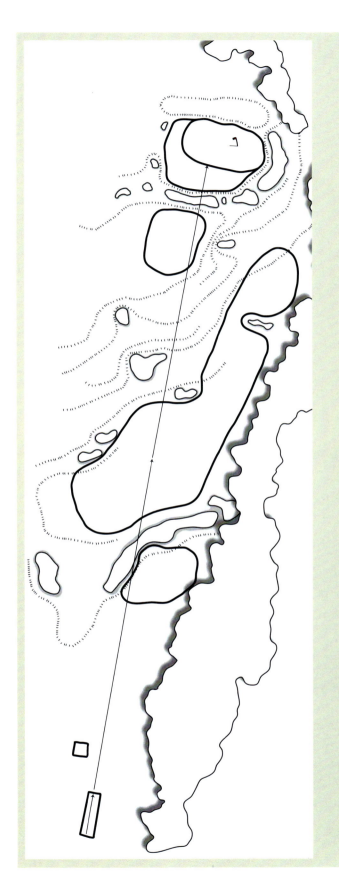

National Golf Links of America
3rd hole - 426 yards

Though Charles Blair Macdonald was
never a fan of blind holes, he acknowledged
the grandeur of the Alps hole at Prestwick
in Scotland, and was determined to have a
hole of similar demanding nature on his U.S.
masterpiece, The National Golf Links. But
Macdonald's version of the Alps is bigger,
bolder, and better.

After a diagonal tee shot over a cross
bunker, the green is hidden from the fairway
not by a dune ridge, as at Prestwick, but over
the top of a large, round hill. This gives every
golfer who comes to the tee a sense of where
the hole is going, and an alternate route of
play. The golfer who has not [or cannot] hit
a sufficient tee shot may continue down the
fairway to the right of the hill, and then play
a pitch up to the green over its steeply banked
right shoulder to try for a one-putt par.
But those who have the strength to get home
in two will almost always take the heroic
approach toward the green, which requires
great confidence after the two opening par-4's
have asked nothing nearly as demanding. A
second shot that isn't perfectly struck will
find a deep cross-bunker short of the green
which may cost them the hole, but to hit this
green in two is still one of the great thrills in
the game, even 100 years after the hole was
built.

9th is a classic British links hole to a raised green, while the short 14th with the ocean for a backdrop is postcard material. It isn't long at just 6655 yards, but there is usually enough wind around to make golfers execute shots, instead of overpowering the course. None of us have seen it since the recent restoration work in the dunes. 7 8 8 7 [2007]

Montauk Downs GC, Montauk. Capt. H.C. Tippett, 1927, redesigned by Robert Trent Jones, 1968.

I'm told Tippett's original course was quite interesting, but the state-park version retained few of the quirky or small-scale undulations that would give it some character. Yes, it's a windy site and that will always provide opportunities for interesting golf; but it's a long way from Southampton out to Montauk, and not worth the drive if you have access to some of the courses in between. 4 - - - [2004]

National Golf Links of America, Southampton. Charles Blair Macdonald, 1909

Thirty-five years ago when I first visited The National, conventional wisdom was that its huge fairways and blind shots were a thing of the past; the course wasn't rated in *Golf Digest's* 100 Greatest Courses at all! Today it's back in the top ten where it belongs, and a generation of young designers pays homage to Macdonald's templates on almost every course they build. Holes like the Alps 3rd and Redan 4th that are improvements on the originals that inspired them, while the par-3 6th, the alternate-fairway 8th and the beautiful finishing holes are originals that haven't been surpassed. There should be no argument that Macdonald's own homage to the greatest holes in Scotland and England remains one of the crowning achievements of American golf course design. 10 10 10 9 [2012]

The par-5 18th at Sebonack plays toward the giant flag pole of The National Golf Links of America.

Nissequogue GC, St. James. Edgar Senne, 1968.

The early holes lead out to Long Island Sound, with a great view along the beach from the tee at the par-3 2nd, but the rest of the course is inland and as uneven in quality as the terrain itself. 4 - - - [1995]

St. George's G & CC, East Setauket. Devereux Emmet, 1917.

Built on a part of Emmet's own estate, a tree-clearing program at St. George's has restored the beautiful sweep of the terrain. The run home from the 11th requires an amazing number of stout shots for a course that measures just under 6,400 yards. Thrown into the mix is the tiny short iron 17th, a hugely appealing penultimate hole that tests nerves more than brawn. England is littered with quality courses of this length; America needs more like it. 6 7 4 - [2013]

Sebonack GC, Southampton. Jack Nicklaus and Tom Doak, 2006.

Sebonack is certainly the hardest course that bears my name -- that's what our client wanted, and that's what happens when you combine all my tricks for making a course challenging [undulating greens, uneven fairway stances, and difficult recovery shots] with Jack Nicklaus' normal repertoire [length, smallish greens, and lots of bunkers]. Two of my clients' wives are big fans, so I guess most men just play it from too far back.

Though my collaboration with Mr. Nicklaus was newsworthy, I never expected that it would continue to divert attention from the course we built. It was always going to be hard for either of us to judge, but there are a bunch of very good holes here, from the wicked par-4 2nd to the drive-and-pitch 5th, the par-4 11th and Postage Stamp-inspired 12th with Peconic Bay to the right, and the par-5 finisher with the bay along the left. 8 6 8 7 [2015]

Shinnecock Hills GC, Southampton. William Flynn, 1931, from an earlier layout by Willie Dunn and C.B. Macdonald.

See the "Gourmet's Choice," pp. 38-39. 10 10 10 10 [2008]

Southampton GC. Seth Raynor, 1925.

The club that Hamptons locals play, it is a good Raynor course recently restored by Brian Silva that would shine in other neighborhoods, but goes largely unappreciated as the smallest house on the block here. 5 - - - [2012]

Three Ponds Farm GC, Bridgehampton. Rees Jones, 1996.

Built as a private course for the late real estate mogul Edward Gordon, the farm has only five fairways and four oversized greens [plus three ponds], but you can play back and forth in different combinations that result in a 6,300-yard par-70 course with several big carries. It's a great backyard course. 4 - - - [1997]

Suffolk County GC at Timber Point, Great River. C. H. Alison, 1925, expanded to 27 holes by Bill Mitchell, 1972.

This could be an awesome reclamation project, if only the county could see the light and give up 27 holes of revenue in order to restore the original 18 holes, which was one of Colt and Alison's most impressive U.S. designs. The only remnant of its grandeur on the present-day course is the par-3 5th on the Blue nine, with its Gibraltar-like profile against the bay. 4 - 5 - [1982]

Westhampton CC. Seth Raynor, 1915.

Westhampton was Raynor's first solo design, so you will find a couple of holes here that you don't typically see on his courses, such as the short 3rd with its unusual punchbowl green. Ran enjoyed the 6th and 15th holes with their elaborate fairway bunkering, but it's a tough neighborhood for a course this flat to shine. 5 6 6 - [2000]

Alpine CC, Demarest. A.W. Tillinghast, 1928, with revisions by Ron Forse and Jim Nagle.

Reportedly this was the most difficult construction job of Tillinghast's illustrious career -- he lived close by in Harrington Park and was on site regularly, which was a good thing as Alpine lies atop the granite cliffs of the Palisades. Carved out of a dense forest, little fairway bunkering was required: a menagerie of canted, contoured greens are the primary defense, though I cringe when I hear of sloping greens being softened for more hole locations. Standout holes like the mountainous, uphill short 10th (339 yards) with its pitched green containing snake-like contours, and the reachable downhill par 5's that conclude each nine are the center piece of the course. Sadly, Tillie's favorite hole, which played to a green pinned by water was sacrificed in favor of a swimming pool in the 1950's. Unfortunately, the club still allows trees to dictate the golf as opposed to the other way around. - 6 - - [2013]

Baltusrol GC, Springfield. Lower course by A. W. Tillinghast, 1922, with modifications by Robert Trent Jones.

I suspect that the Upper was the better course at Baltusrol when Tillinghast finished it in the 1920's … but the Lower course had more space for expansion and for tournament facilities, so it was the course that Robert Trent Jones lengthened in the 1950's, to become the championship course we know today. The Lower does have several memorable holes, including the short 4th and the back-to-back par-5 holes at the finish, but the far end of the course is as plain as the ground itself. Acres of bluegrass sod laid down after a recent renovation have snuffed out the rough-hewn texture in the roughs and bunker faces it had in the 1980's, when I ran around to see every shot of the last two rounds of Jack Nicklaus' last U.S. Open victory here, head to head against Isao Aoki in 1980. With those memories intact, I'd rather play the Upper. 7 6 8 7 [2013]

Baltusrol GC. Upper course by A.W. Tillinghast, 1922.

The Upper course has no dull holes; the starting run and the finishing holes represent some of the best steep sidehill architecture I've seen, although the huge fill pads Rees Jones built for new back tees are very distracting. Its greens are notoriously difficult to read, because of the influence of the ridge above the course. The par-3 3rd and uphill 14th are the two most distinctive holes on this course, and perhaps the whole property, but a well struck approach into the long 18th green nestled below the imposing clubhouse is the single most satisfying shot of the day. 7 7 7 6 [2013]

Bayonne GC. Eric Bergstol, 2006.

Just across the harbor from lower Manhattan (and serviced by a club ferry from Wall Street), Bayonne is one of the most ambitious golf projects ever built. The heavily contoured site was once dead flat, but designer/developer Bergstol cut a deal to take contaminated dredge material from the Hudson River as fill, and entomb it underneath the golf course, providing a platform for his artificial dunescape as well as the funding to get the course built. The site is quite cramped for a golf course that aspired to be 7000 yards long, and feels so in places, with lots of strange walk-backs to tees and steep mounding to hide surrounding warehouses. But the setting is one of a kind, and considering what he started with, Mr. Bergstol should be congratulated for his creativity. 6 – 5 5 [2007]

Canoe Brook CC, Summit. South course by C. H. Alison, 1924.

I only saw the course as set up for the 1983 U.S. Women's Amateur, which for some reason borrowed a bit from the North course, too. There are no bad Alison courses, but the widening of Route 24 caused substantial changes here. 4 - - - [1983]

The tee shot on the 18th at Bayonne plays uphill toward the clubhouse and flagpole.

Essex County CC, West Orange. Seth Raynor and Charles Banks, 1925, from an original layout by A.W. Tillinghast.

Darius reports the revised back nine here should be considered among the best in the state – you can never say more in a state that includes Pine Valley! Amazingly, he cites all the holes I don't remember, including sharply angled greens like the 12th, 17th and 18th, the obscured punchbowl green on the 14th, the really cool double plateau target at the 16th and the long, downhill par three 15th with its rectangular green set at an angle to the tee. The hole that impressed me was the par-3 11th, with a small diagonal brook running across the approach and down into a larger ravine at the foot of the tee, which is the best of a wonderful set of short holes. I saw it several years before the restoration, but notice that no one is saying much about the front nine. 5 6 6 7 [2011]

Forsgate CC, Jamesburg. East course by Charles Banks, 1931.

Located just off the New Jersey Turnpike in the middle of the state – exit 8A, for you Joe Piscopo fans – Forsgate has been lost right in between the spheres of influence of New York and Philadelphia. Banks' steamshovel bunkers and enormous greens are a marvel. Steep and deep aside, there are some wonderful holes including the Punchbowl 5th and the long 8th. Ran thinks the set of one-shot holes are the best from the Macdonald/Raynor/Banks camp. Ownership was dangerously close to replacing three of the better holes on the course for housing twenty years ago before their director of golf at the time, Peter Ooosterhuis, intervened. 6 7 6 - [2016]

Hollywood GC, Deal. Walter Travis, 1915, from an original layout by Isaac Mackie.

The great depth of golf in the Met Section is illustrated here: Hollywood received

Bunkers galore on Walter Travis' long par-4 12th at Hollywood.

scant attention before a recent restoration by Brian Schneider, an avowed fan of Travis's greens. These are some of the old man's best: the four-tiered 7th is not as excessive as it sounds, and the lower back-left hole location at the 9th a thing of beauty. There are also a few really quirky features [such as the mounding around the par-3 4th green] which may date from the course's origins. The club stopped short of restoring every last bunker at the par-4 12th, nicknamed "Heinz 57," but there are enough to make the thoughtful golfer smile. 7 7 5 5 [2013]

The Knoll CC, Parsippany. West course by Charles Banks, 1929

This late-model Banks design features his typical deep greenside bunkering, along with some very strong tiers and internal contours to the greens, but the fairway bunkers are 20-30 yards too close to the tee to influence the line of play. Our friend George Bahto's curiosity about the design of his home course led him to become the foremost researcher into the work of Banks and his mentors, Seth Raynor and C.B. Macdonald. 5 - - - [2014]

Metedeconk National GC, Jackson. 27 holes by Robert Trent Jones and Roger Rulewich, 1987.

This 27-hole complex is one of Robert Trent Jones's last designs, a nice woodsy escape from the hustle and bustle of the NY-Philadelphia corridor. The main 18 holes are plenty strong – in fact, stronger than they look, the opposite approach of Dr. MacKenzie's ideal that players enjoy a hole which looks impossible, but is not really so severe. It's never busy, so you can fly around all 27 holes in not much more than four hours, and still have time left over to go look at Hollywood, or down the parkway to Atlantic City. 5 - - - [1989]

Montclair GC. First, Second and Third Nines by Donald Ross, 1920; Fourth Nine by Charles Banks, 1928.

The only way to run four separate nines interchangeably is if the quality of golf is consistent across the board, and Montclair has never had a problem making it work. Robert Trent Jones was a member here for 65 years (!) but he didn't find much to mess around with. - 4 - - [1986]

Morris County GC, Morristown. Seth Raynor, 1923.

Morris County is one of Raynor's less renowned works, due to the steepness of the hills and a relatively tight rectangular property. There are some memorably deep bunkers guarding greens perched on the edge of steep slopes, and the 415-yard 7th is the sportiest of par-4 holes, with the drive to the crest of a high hill followed by a paratrooper's delight of an approach shot to a partially hidden green. 5 - - - [1996]

Mountain Ridge GC, West Caldwell. Donald Ross, 1929.

Now that Plainfield is receiving its just props, the restored Mountain Ridge may be the most underrated course in golf-rich New Jersey. The hilly nature of this property led logically to a set of steeply sloped greens, which serve as the course's primary defense, though the steep-faced bunkers restored by Ron Prichard in 2007 also take their toll. At top speed, greens like the par-3 7th, with nearly six feet of back-to-front slope, are some of the toughest greens in the tri-state region to putt. Studying a green pad like the 8th is a good way to appreciate how Ross's work evolved with time. 6 7 6 6 [2011]

North Jersey CC, Wayne. Walter Travis, 1928.

The membership here seems stuck in a dilemma of their own making. The course they have is full of blind shots, and Travis's wild

Somerset Hills CC
7th hole - 484 yards

The putting surfaces at Somerset Hills are one of the great wonders of the golf world, especially on its many fine two-shotters. The toughest of these is the long 7th, playing over a bit of a rise and down into a wooded corner.

In recent years, longer hitters were driving past the gentle hilltop in the landing area to a dip where the fairway narrows dangerously. The recent addition of a back tee puts them back in their place, facing a long second shot down the hill. An extra-wide apron of fairway leads into and wraps around the green, which tilts away to the left so that an approach that will bounce home must be carefully judged. There are bunkers left and long, and they're placed just far enough away from the green to present awkwardly difficult recoveries for even a good sand player trying to make par the hard way.

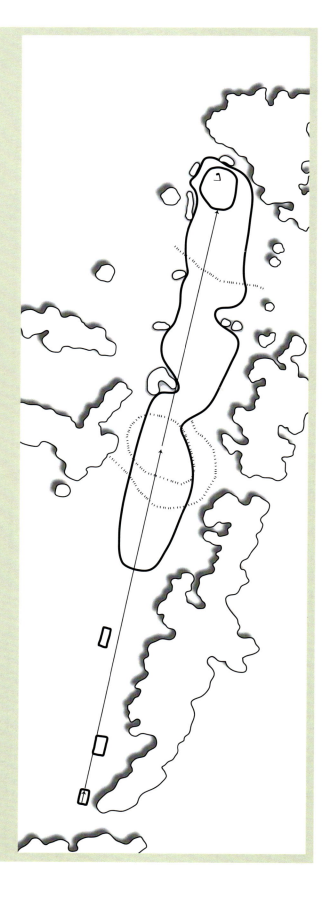

greens are a good fit for the hilly property, but not with the sensibilities of younger members. So they've been slowly chipping away at the course's most distinguishing features, one hole at a time. About a dozen of Travis's greens are left; go see it before they tear up any more of them. 5 - - - [2016]

Plainfield CC. Donald Ross, 1921-28.

Often overlooked in the pantheon of Ross courses, this one is just different enough to stand apart. It's a great piece of property that yielded a great variety of green sites. The start is outstanding, with two long par-4's followed by a difficult par-3. After a couple of good shorter par-4's, the long two-shot 7th is a thing of beauty; and after the turn, the exacting par-3 11th and the long par-5 12th with a brook running down the middle of it are the best holes. However, of the run home only the 16th hole is a standout; I didn't realize until recently that the 13th through 15th were changed from the original design to make room for a practice range up by the clubhouse. We doubt Ross would enjoy seeing the Tour players attempt to drive his uphill, dogleg finishing hole. 8 7 7 7 [2007]

Ridgewood CC, Paramus. 27 holes by A. W. Tillinghast, 1929.

Aptly named even though the club originated elsewhere, Ridgewood's property is bisected by a wide dominant ridge which is a feature of many of the best holes, including the 7th East, 2nd Center, and 5th on the West nine. Though having 27 good holes is an undeniable boon for the members, the penchant of visitors to want to play the "main" course can be the only explanation for how a course this good could be consistently overlooked in the magazine rankings.

The West and East nines are generally considered the main course, but the recent Barclays events featured an even more alluring sampling from all three nines, including the sub 300 yard "Nickel and Dime" 6th on the Center course, so called because Byron Nelson always played it with a 5-iron and a wedge, to a plateau green a scant nine paces wide. It must not have been easy to get six good holes coming and going from the stately Tudor-style clubhouse, but Tillinghast did it so well that you never even think about such logistical difficulties. 7 8 7 7 [2015]

Somerset Hills CC, Bernardsville. A. W. Tillinghast, 1917.

See the "Gourmet's Choice," pp. 40-41. 8 8 8 8 [2015]

Trump National GC, Bedminster. Old course by Jim Fazio, 2004.

Developed on the John DeLorean estate and purchased by Donald Trump mid-construction, this is a well built and attractively finished course that was certain to appeal to a subset of New York area golfers. It's a stout test of golf slated to host the 2022 PGA Championship, but the golf is all about execution, not strategy. That's probably why the par-3 holes are the only ones we remember. - - 5 6 [2007]

Upper Montclair CC, Clifton. 27 holes by Robert Trent Jones, 1956.

Here is another 27-hole course, but with none of the majesty of Ridgewood. The 415-yard par-4 3rd was often cited as one of Trent Jones' best holes, but I'm not fond of holes where a shot through the green can wind up in the water. 4 - - - [1981]

White Beeches G&CC, Haworth. Walter Travis, 1920.

Though the course was one of the more celebrated in the Met area back in the 1920's, little remains that really grabs your attention, other than the large oaks which you must squeeze between at the short par-4 4th. 3 - - - [1984]

MID ATLANTIC STATES

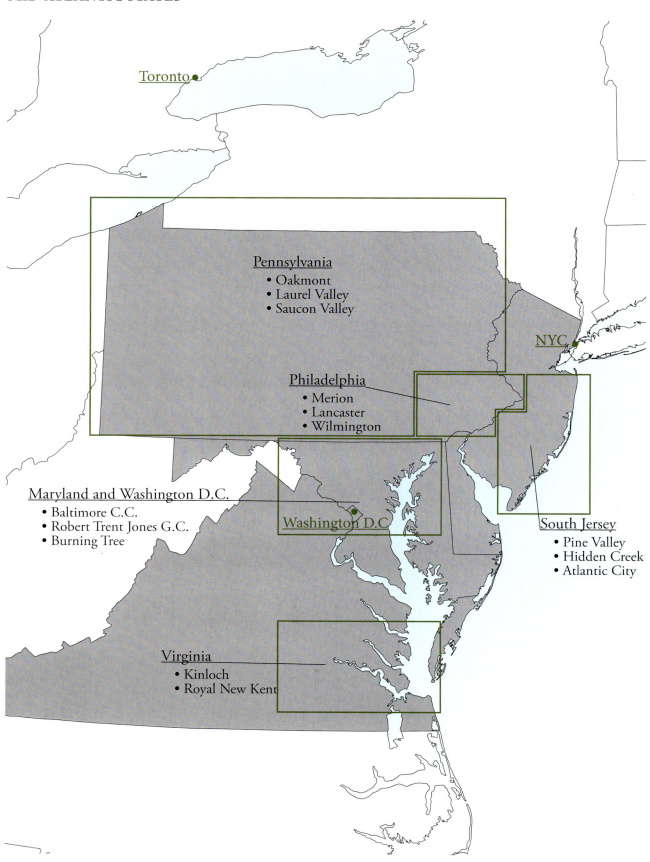

Toronto •

Pennsylvania
• Oakmont
• Laurel Valley
• Saucon Valley

NYC •

Philadelphia
• Merion
• Lancaster
• Wilmington

Maryland and Washington D.C.
• Baltimore C.C.
• Robert Trent Jones G.C.
• Burning Tree

Washington D.C.

South Jersey
• Pine Valley
• Hidden Creek
• Atlantic City

Virginia
• Kinloch
• Royal New Kent

The Mid Atlantic states are home to some of the best golf in America, and to some of the worst. This acute divide owes in large part to the climate. As one moves south from temperate New Jersey and the humid summers of Philadelphia, to the sweltering beltway around our nation's capital, great golf falls lower and lower on people's priority list for their free time. If you've wondered why President Obama plays so much at the Andrews Air Force Base course, which no one has ever recommended to us, just consider his options, and you'll see the choice isn't only about security issues.

I lived in Philadelphia for a summer while I was building the Old course at Stonewall, and for most of the project, my associate Gil Hanse and I would take a day off on Tuesday and go to play another area course, courtesy of Stonewall members who were also members at those other clubs. What a great summer that was! At the time, Gil had been living in Colorado, and was very partial to Cherry Hills in Denver; and nearly every week, when we were done playing another Flynn hidden gem, or perhaps a course by A.W. Tillinghast or Donald Ross, I would conclude, "Well, that was better than Cherry Hills!" Courses like Rolling Green and Manufacturers would be standouts in almost any other city in America; but being in the same vicinity as Merion and Pine Valley gives them little opportunity to attract attention.

To a lesser extent, the same is true of western Pennsylvania: Oakmont is the 600-pound gorilla, and everything else is ignored. I'm guilty of this myself, never getting to Sunnehanna or New Castle or Bedford Springs to see how they stack up.

Galloway National, across the marsh from Atlantic City, is one of Tom Fazio's finest designs.

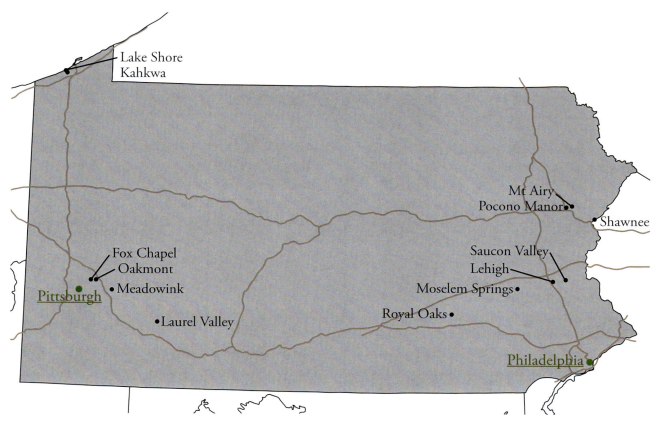

Fox Chapel GC. Seth Raynor, 1925.

This lesser-known Raynor design took a turn in the spotlight as host to the Senior Players Championship. Several holes make use of a small brook which meanders down the middle of the valley, most notably the short par-5 8th with its approach to a high platform green hanging out over a severe drop to the right. 6 – 7 - [1993]

Kahkwa C, Erie. Donald Ross, 1915.

A relatively unheralded Ross course, due to its location, I found Kahkwa to have a great variety of holes and a great variety of greens – built-up plateau, half-punchbowls, and others just laying at grade. I'd love to get back here to play it. 6 - - - [1995]

Lake Shore CC, Erie. Tom Bendelow, 1929.

Though cut in two by a busy road and confined to rather flat ground, the Lake Shore course is a challenging test of golf with some interesting design features. One is the short par three 5th, a decent hole from today's tee but very cool from the original pad (current 15th tee) from where the green was blind. Steeper greens like the 9th and 14th are also noteworthy, as is the par three 3rd near the road and the par three finishing hole, played back toward the clubhouse and the vicinity of the otherwise unseen lakefront. - - - 4 [2015]

Laurel Valley GC, Ligonier. Dick Wilson, 1960.

A championship course somewhat lacking in character, Laurel Valley occupies some gently rolling bottom land in the valley below Ligonier. The elite membership of CEO types generally fall well short of the course's demands: it weighs in at over 7000 yards, with medium-sized greens vigorously defended by bunkers and mounding, and a variety of water features emanating from a small stream. Fifty years of tree growth have transformed what was a fairly open site, but it's still more parkland than woods. 6 – 6 5 [2007]

Lehigh CC, Allentown. William Flynn, 1928.

This outstanding layout is the equal of Flynn's Philadelphia treasures, without the exposure of tournament play that might have put it on the map. The hilly property encompasses both sides of a deep valley, with the Little Lehigh River flowing through the bottom, and the character of the course is a combination of parkland and woodland. There are only two par fives but both are distinctive: the dogleg 6th has a narrow entrance and fallaway green, while at the go-for-broke 11th the river crosses just in front of the green, baiting second shots from the fairway high above. It's a tough walk, but a fine course. 7 7 6 6 [2007]

Meadowink GC, Murrysville. Ferdinand Garbin, 1970.

Included in memory of my late uncle, who took me out to play it as a kid. I don't miss the course, but I do miss uncle Ken and his quirky sense of humor. 2 - - - [1974]

Moselem Springs GC, Fleetwood. George Fazio, 1964.

As Tom Fazio's brand has skyrocketed to prominence, his uncle George's work has been relegated to obscurity, which is too bad. The senior Fazio was a fine player -- runner-up to Hogan at Merion in 1950 -- and he was the perfect fit for a project like Moselem Springs, a difficult course out in the country where good players joined to test themselves. 6 - - - [1995]

Mt. Airy Casino Resort & GC, Mt. Pocono. Hal Purdy, 1972; redesigned by Dan Schlegel, 2009.

This course has been completely redesigned from the day of my one visit, thank goodness. I still can't believe the first hole I

saw, a double-dogleg par-5 climbing up a steep hill, with a small pond hiding up top, right smack in front of the green! NR [1991]

Oakmont CC. Henry and William Fownes, 1903.

See the "Gourmet's Choice," pp. 30-31. 9 10 9 9 [2007]

Pocono Manor Resort. East course by Donald Ross, 1912.

The sharply downhill, 77-yard 7th is locally famous: you're advised to "take it back about hip high with a sand wedge, and if it feels like you're going to chip it in the water, you'll probably be on the green." [Rumor has it they've built an extra hole to take this one out of play.] The 200-yard 3rd, with a tiny green at the bottom of a V-shaped cut, is almost as strange. Hard to believe they could charge resort-course prices for the conditions I saw there in the early 90's. 2 - - - [1991]

Royal Oaks GC, Lebanon. Ron Forse, 1992.

Ron Forse has gone on to a successful career as a restorer of classic courses; this is one of his only original designs, and like many young architects' early opportunities, it wasn't the best property or client to let him show his stuff. Still, he wasn't able on his own to mimic the great greens and bunker shaping of all the courses he admires. 3 - - - [1992]

Rolling Rock C, Ligonier. Donald Ross, 1917, expanded to 18 holes by Brian Silva.

Built within the 1300-acre preserve of the Mellon family, this was one of the very best nine-hole courses I've seen, and surely the only one with an international membership of 2,500. [At that, they host only 9,000 rounds a year.] The Ross nine occupies sloping parkland that makes for an occasional blind tee shot, but it is the greens that make the course. Some of them look more like Pine Valley's greens than anything else I can think of, with high shoulders at the edges and fairly steep levels running from side to side. The par-3 3rd green should be protected for the ages, but really all the greens from the 2nd through 8th are pretty wild. At a shade under 3000 yards it was never going to be considered championship stuff, but it amazes me that they decided to build another nine holes, when Donald Ross didn't think it would help. 6 - - - [2007]

Saucon Valley GC, Bethlehem. Old course by Herbert Strong, 1922, with modifications by Tom Marzolf.

It was the Old course that the USGA turned to for two U.S. Senior Opens and more recently the U.S. Women's Open. The new platform tees and swollen bunkers from the renovation seem like a miss on what was a low profile Golden Age design. 6 6 6 5 [2007]

Saucon Valley GC. Grace couse by William and David Gordon, 1953-58.

For years I had seen the Grace course listed in *Golf Digest's* rankings of the best in the country, but I found it to be quite dull – a distant second and perhaps even third among its siblings. Therein lies the danger of a lofty ranking: Ran found it a pleasant walk, with his expectations in check. 5 6 4 4 [2007]

Saucon Valley GC. Weyhill course by William and David Gordon, 1968.

The less trafficked Weyhill course, with its own separate clubhouse in the woods a couple of miles away, has some of the most dramatic golf on the grounds, with a couple of par-4's playing along the edge of sharp drops. In earlier years it was the most exclusive of the three courses – you pretty much had to be playing with somebody from U.S. Steel to see it – but with that aura lost, the more awkward holes are too easily remembered. 5 – 4 4 [2007]

CC of Scranton, Clarks Summit. Old course by Walter Travis, 1927.

You'll be hard pressed to find a more undulating set of 18 greens than Travis' greens here, set on a hilltop outside of Scranton: I have never seen interior contours like those on the 7th, 9th and 18th greens. However new bunkering, prompted by calls from the membership to make the bunkers deeper and tougher, resulted in weird slopes at the edges of the greens that sometimes spoil the show. The juxtaposition of modern features with old, lumpy, pitched greens is awkward, but these greens are definitely worth seeing. Miss them short and straight on; recovery from a wide approach can be almost impossible! 6 7 - - [2016]

Shawnee Resort and CC, Shawnee-on-Delaware. Original 18 holes by A. W. Tillinghast, 1906, remodeled to 27 holes by Bill Diddel.

Tillinghast's first design was a remarkable debut. The resort hotel lies on the mainland, but all but the first hole and the last three are set on a island in the Delaware River, as it carves its way through the Delaware Water Gap beneath 300-foot wooded slopes on both shorelines. The crossing was originally made by horse-drawn barge over the shallows of the Binniekill tributary, following one's tee shots on the par-5 2nd and par-3 16th holes. Sadly, the expansion to 27 holes changed the routing of almost all the holes on the island, so that while twelve of Tillinghast's original greens are still in play, only four of his 18 holes survive intact. We discussed a complete restoration of the course a few years ago, but they never pulled the trigger on it; I suspect they'd rather do it after a big flood, than just before one. It could be terrific if they ever put it all back, but it's nothing close to that at present. 4 - - - [2008]

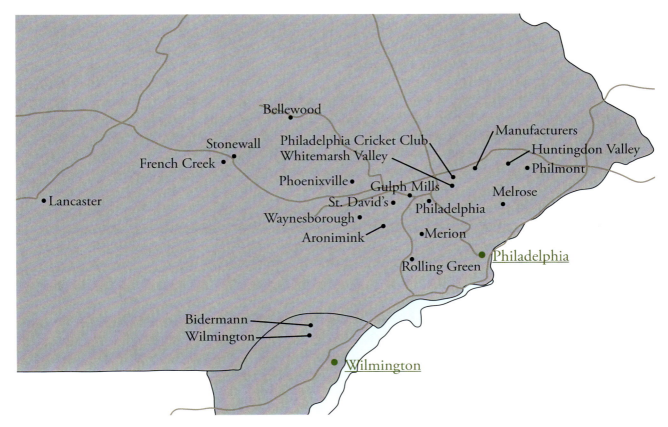

Aronimink GC, Newtown Square. Donald Ross, 1928-30.

Mr. Ross spent a considerable amount of effort on his one prominent Philadelphia course, and succeeded in building a difficult test that holds up well for today's professionals. The club had tinkered with the course incessantly to try and maintain its championship credentials over the years, but a restoration by Ron Prichard has made it feel like Ross' design again, cemented by the fact that the great set of greens was never touched. 7 7 7 7 [2009]

Bellewood GC, Pottstown. Tom Drauschak, 1999.

Our contractor for the original course at Stonewall fancied himself a golf course architect, and subsequently built this private club on a site that the Stonewall founders had passed over. The mansion clubhouse is everything Stonewall is not – posh, haughty, and un-golfy – and much the same can be said about the golf course. Surprisingly, the large and slightly crowned greens are the best feature of the design. 4 - - - [2000]

Bidermann GC, Wilmington, DE. Dick Wilson with Joe Lee, 1965.

Dick Wilson was in poor health when this course was constructed (and indeed died shortly after it opened), so Joe Lee is largely responsible for this lovely "country" course on a farm formerly owned by the DuPont estate, with the barn converted into a beautiful rustic clubhouse. Their big bunkers and greens are well suited to the open, rolling countryside, while the native grasses and bushes give it the texture many of Wilson's sites lacked. The course has a fine quartet of sub-400 yard par-4's, highlighted by the 321-yard 7th, which help make the course fun for the members. As with most Wilson courses, the good player is given the opportunity to shape the ball to gain an advantage. 6 6 - - [2012]

French Creek GC, Elverson. Gil Hanse, 2003.

Just across the street from Stonewall, where we worked together, French Creek is one of Gil Hanse's earliest designs. It's combined with a residential estate over some very difficult ground, with restricted wetlands set between steep hills, which inevitably led to an awkward routing with some serious gaps between holes. Nevertheless, there are a few stunning holes in the mix, perhaps in part because necessity is the mother of invention. The 117-yard 5th over a deep hollow is a hole not many designers would find; the same could be said for the blind 231-yard 17th, or for that matter the short 3rd with its long forced carry over wetlands. The long par-4 12th, with its three islands of fairway set and large green set next to a small brook, is another beautiful hole; the 456-yard 13th, grinding back uphill, not so much. But my favorite hole is the 404-yard 9th, with the upper half of its split-level fairway guarded by an intimidating bunker, but a much tougher approach to its punchbowl green for those who bail safely away to the right off the tee. 5 - - - [2003]

Gulph Mills GC, King of Prussia. Donald Ross, 1916, with revisions by Perry Maxwell and Gil Hanse.

I've simplified the credits for this course – everyone from Flynn to Bill Gordon to Robert Trent Jones tinkered with it at some point, but Gil Hanse has thankfully sorted through the hodgepodge of styles and restored the best of Ross' and Maxwell's work. There are a few holes that would rate with Philly's finest, including the short 4th across a deep valley, and the 6th and 11th with their distinctive and severe Maxwell greens – but there are also some clunkers, and the cramped and hilly site does not allow it to surpass the second tier of Flynn's many fine courses in the area. The most amusing feature was the steeply uphill finisher, a par-5 on the card even though it's only 421 yards from tee to green. 5 5 - - [2004]

Huntingdon Valley G & CC. 27 holes by William Flynn, 1927.

In the Golf Association of Philadelphia, many consider this the third best course in town, on the basis of its difficult back nine and its unusually strong playing membership. Set in a wooded bowl that bottoms out just a bit too abruptly, the front nine goes around the exterior of the property like it was routed by Richard Petty – every hole is banked up right to left. The back nine, crisscrossing the bottom of the valley and the stream that runs through it, is better stuff. Ran reports that the restored third nine [which was still overgrown by woods when I visited] has the strongest holes of the 27, with several carries over wetlands. 7 7 6 6 [2007]

Lancaster CC. William Flynn, 1920.

It could just be that I'm partial to Lancaster because it is set a little bit apart from Flynn's great Philadelphia cluster of courses geographically. Its strengths are similar to those of Huntingdon Valley and Manny's and Rolling Green – a varied parkland setting and a great set of par-3 holes – but it also has the most interesting set of greens among its peer group, and that always gets my attention. The front nine has several interesting shorter par-4's, with an especially memorable green next to the creek at the 5th, but the back nine stretches out considerably. There are several greens where it's frightening to be above the hole, not least at the 430-yard uphill finishing hole with its 10,000 square-foot green. 8 7 7 6 [2009]

Manufacturers G & CC, Oreland. William Flynn, 1925.

It's scary to think a course this good doesn't always make lists of Philadelphia's top 10. (It would be there with room to spare on my own list.) Like most of its neighbors, it lies in a valley with some steep holes along the top edges and a creek in play on several holes along the bottom. The five par-3 holes offer great variety, from the strong uphill 199-yard 6th to the 117-yard 8th guarded by its own small quarry. Hopefully they've taken steps to remove some of the more recently planted trees, which were starting to detract from the giant sycamores that are the nucleus of the landscape plan. 7 - - - [1992]

JC Melrose CC, Cheltenham. Perry Maxwell and Alister MacKenzie, 1928.

In digging through Alister MacKenzie's correspondence, we came across a note to Perry Maxwell singing the praises of his beautiful work at Melrose, which was a shock since no one I knew in Philadelphia had ever mentioned the course. Sadly, the course did not survive the Depression intact, as some of the land was confiscated for a road expansion. What's left is a 5,800 yard affair with a few roller-coaster features. I still hope I get back one day, if only to play the par-5 2nd hole. 4 – 4 - [1994]

Merion GC, Ardmore. East course by Hugh Wilson, 1912, with revisions by William Flynn, 1924.

See the "Gourmet's Choice," pp. 26-27. 10 10 10 9 [2009]

Merion GC. West course by Hugh Wilson, 1911.

Some think of the West course as where Merion's older members go to ride in golf carts, but more of Hugh Wilson exists on this 5800 yard course than on the East, and everyone could use a break from the relentless rough next door. The greens are invariably well located: Wilson's use of the creek at the drop-shot 6th and the short par-4 7th are prime examples, but we are equally impressed by the small puff contour in the 9th green, located out in the open. Trying to carve an approach into the 14th to use the left-to-right slope to your advantage is another highlight. 5 5 6 - [2010]

The quarry hole at Manufacturers is half the length of Merion's, but just as fearsome.

Merion Golf Club (East course)
5th hole - 504 yards

The new, U.S. Open yardage for this hole suggests a par-5 to most readers, but the 5th at Merion is in fact a long par-4, stretched to the breaking point for modern tournament play.

The design is simplicity itself. The entire length of the fairway slopes sharply from right to left toward a stream along the low side; the hope is to play as close to the creek as possible, to gain a flatter lie for the second shot. The green is just an extension of the fairway, tilting to such a degree it appears impossible that a shot will stay on it, especially since the approach is almost always played with the ball well above one's feet. All of this tempts the golfer to play out to the right with the second shot, even though he or she knows that winding up above the hole in two will almost surely cost a shot, as the third shot careens past the hole to the bottom of the green.

Such simple tilted targets are slowly going out of favor as modern green speeds make them impossible to hold, but this great par-4 illustrates perfectly what we will have lost if the green speed arms race continues unabated.

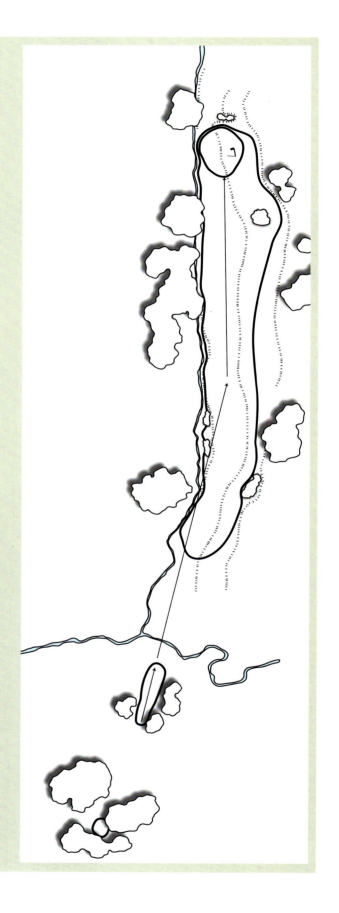

Philadelphia CC, Gladwyne. William Flynn, 1927.

Known locally as Spring Mill, this is yet another fine parkland course with a great set of par-3 holes. It seems a bit less taxing than Huntingdon Valley or Lancaster, so it's surprising to remember that it was host to the almost-forgotten 1939 U.S. Open. In those days the clubhouse was on the other side of the property, so that Sam Snead's heartbreaking 8 at the 72nd hole was actually recorded on today's 3rd hole – but it's still hard to imagine when you look at it! 7 – 7 6 [2007]

Philadelphia Cricket C, Flourtown. Wissahickon course by A. W. Tillinghast, 1922.

"The Tillie in Philly" was sometimes elevated in local rankings because the Flynn courses tend to split the vote, but a recent restoration by Keith Foster has the locals drooling. Perhaps I was too embarrassed to notice its finer qualities after playing my approach to the par-4 2nd off the roof of the locker room. The dueling par-3 3rd and 10th holes are much too close for comfort, and the par-4 18th with its approach over a stream might well be the best finishing hole in town [and country!]. There is a newer 18 holes here by Hurdzan and Fry which we have not reviewed, while the club's original nine holes, host to the U.S. Opens of 1907 and 1910, are still open for play at the club's original St. Martins facility, three miles to the south. 6 – 5 6 [2015]

Philmont CC, Huntingdon Valley. South course by Willie Park Jr., 1907.

The older, more open South course is not the main attraction at Philmont, but it's less like the many fine parkland courses in town than its sister, so if you are seeking something different you might give it a try. The opening hole, crossing a rushing brook below the clubhouse on the second shot, is about as good as it gets. 4 - - - [1992]

The par-3 6th highlights the steeper terrain found at Merion's West course.

The 12th at Rolling Green.

Philmont CC. North course by William Flynn, 1924.

The tree-lined North course is the better of the two courses here, but not in the top tier of Flynn's Philadelphia gems. Its 600-yard, boomerang-shaped 9th hole plays around the 10th, 11th, 17th and 18th holes, so they'd better hope those trees stay healthy! 5 - - - [1992]

Phoenixville GC. Hugh Wilson, 1915.

My old friend Bill Kittleman who has done work to these nine holes swears that they were originally laid out by Hugh Wilson of Merion fame, though there is still some dispute about whether this has been proven. A deep ravine behind the clubhouse has to be crossed with the tee shots at the 1st, 4th and 8th holes, and the 9th green sits down in the hollow, a bit reminiscent of the 9th at Wannamoisett. Most golfers would be inclined to overlook a course which tops out at 2800 yards, but the greens are small and sharply tilted, and Bill has done some

remarkable fairway bunkering that adds some flair to it. 4 - - - [1992]

Rolling Green GC, Springfield. William Flynn, 1926.

Last alphabetically of the great Flynn courses, but certainly not last in terms of the property it inhabits, Rolling Green's terrain culminates in a dramatic ravine that must be crossed with the approach to the par-4 13th, and then back again at the long par-3 hole immediately following. For those who like to analyze by scorecard, the 600+ yard 9th hole is a rarity in town, but for me the par-4 8th with its landing area in the arc of a small brook was more of a highlight. Shot for shot, some consider it Flynn's most difficult test in Philly. 7 7 – 6 [2007]

St. David's CC, Wayne. Donald Ross, 1927.

I played most of the Philly courses the summer we built Stonewall, and St. David's was not a standout. The first few holes are length-restricted by the shape of the property, and it ends on a sour note with the walk back to the 18th tee. But the restored cross-bunkering at the 8th and the five difficult par-3's would be enough for most courses to brag about. 4 - - - [1992]

Stonewall, Elverson. Old course by Tom Doak with Gil Hanse, 1993.

An important milestone in my career, Stonewall was my first private club, and I will always be indebted to the late Jack May for teaching me the nuances of developing and operating a private club. The Old course has a deserved reputation as a difficult test of golf, thanks to its small greens and thick native roughs, and the par-4 18th is a personal favorite because it cozies up so intimately to the stone buildings that comprise the clubhouse. Most of all, I love going back because the staff are like family, and because you learn much more about your work from members who have played the course 500 times than you can from golf course raters. 7 – 7 7 [2012]

Stonewall. North course by Tom Doak with Don Placek, 2003.

The newer North course, developed ten years later on land that had been acquired to protect the Old course from neighboring development, has gotten mixed reviews. Built to allow the membership an option for cart play without relaxing the walking-only ambiance of the Old course, the routing of the newer course flows more naturally, so it's actually easier to walk. Our goal was to build a set of greens that required more changes of strategy due to hole locations than the original 18 holes had, and we may have succeeded too well. You are bound to love them or hate them, if not both on the same day. 6 6 7 6 [2012]

Waynesborough CC, Paoli. George Fazio, 1965.

Substantially remodeled since my one and only visit. It was originally a classic early Fazio parkland course, with sweeping greens, sprawling bunkers, length and lots of doglegs. Not my type, but pretty good if you like the style. 5 - - - [1992]

Whitemarsh Valley CC, Lafayette Hill. George Thomas, 1908.

Shoehorned into a hilly and tight property bordered by public roads, Whitemarsh has no real aura to it, but it is the course that gave native son George Thomas a chance to try out some of his early architectural ideas before he moved west. It's hard to imagine they managed to find enough space here to host a Tour event, the long-defunct IVB-Philadelphia Classic. The short holes are the most interesting feature of the course, but not always in a good way: the par-3 12th green is frighteningly close to a busy public road. 4 - - - [1992]

Wilmington CC, DE. North course by Dick Wilson, 1962.

This is the only place I know of where the two great architectural rivals of the 50's and 60's built courses side by side, and it's surprising that Wilson let his rival get the better of him so easily – the North course is a yawner. 4 - - - [1996]

Wilmington CC. South course by Robert Trent Jones, 1962.

The South is a classic Trent Jones layout over a nice parkland site, with large slicked-up greens and some do-or-die par-5 holes on the back nine. It's probably one of Trent's personal top ten. 6 - - - [1996]

Atlantic City CC, Northfield. Tom Doak with Tom Mead, 2001, from an original layout by Willie Park, Jr., modified by William Flynn.

This was the kind of project I don't usually take on – a substantial modification of an historic old course with architectural pedigree. Yet the layout as it existed was a mish-mosh of three previous architects' work, cut up by a few houses where land had been sold off to finance improvements to the course, and there were several flat holes on the upper end and several which went underwater down along the marsh. We tried to preserve the best of the older holes [the par-4 3rd and the par-3 12th, among others] while fixing the problems. The short par-4 14th, and the par-3 that follows it, are built around a newly-created salt marsh bay that not only broke up a monotonous long line of downwind par-4's, but added environmental benefits as well. 6 – 6 - [2002]

Bedens Brook Club, Skillman. Dick Wilson, 1965.

For a golfer accustomed to a steady diet of Golden Age courses, Wilson's greens will seem like huge targets in comparison. Scoring isn't easy – and a winding brook adds to the challenge – but the fairways were hit pretty hard by bulldozers so the course lacks the subtle appeal of courses built forty years prior. - 5 - - [1987]

Galloway National GC, Galloway. Tom Fazio, 1994.

Set on the marshy banks of Reeds Bay, Galloway is an eye-catching Tom Fazio design built across a series of small wooded sand hills. Although its most memorable holes are the par threes that play directly across the marshland and look out toward Atlantic City, the heart of this course are the longer holes within the scrubby dunes. Here Fazio set a number of small greens atop dangerous plateaus and strategically used sloping terrain and a number of large sandy waste areas to complicate matters for the approaching golfer. The front nine scores higher for variety and quality holes, though the back does feature one of the best holes on the property, the uphill 15th played spectacularly across an enormous central bunker complex. Were it not for some non-descript water holes on the back nine, Galloway might rank as Fazio's finest work in America. - - 6 7 [2007]

Hidden Creek GC, Egg Harbor Township. Bill Coore and Ben Crenshaw, 2002.

Sometimes compared to the heathland gems around London, Hidden Creek is located a short drive from Pine Valley and similarly set within a scrubby forest of mature pines. There are no great undulations or bold ground contours here, but instead subtle humps and soft rises, exploited beautifully in an intelligent routing that seems to capture each and every interesting change of topography. The bearded-lip bunkering is first rate and the par threes are exceptional, particularly the picturesque 230-yard 4th and the short, uphill 11th with its away-angled green set atop of a small knoll. – 7 7 7 [2012]

Lawrenceville School GC. John Reid, 1925.

The tattered condition private school layout belies the wealth of the school's many benefactors. 2 - - - [1995]

Medford Village GC, Medford Lakes. William and David Gordon, 1964.

Originally named after its owner, "Sunny Jim" Himmelein, this course was built to be as tough as Pine Valley, and in its first few years no one could take a prize offered for beating par. Narrow fairways and thick trees were (and still are) the major part of its defenses, but there are some fine holes here, especially the set of three-shotters. 6 - - - [1989]

Pine Valley GC, Clementon. George Crump, with some help from his friends and from H.S. Colt, 1918-22.

Most golfers concede Pine Valley's place as the greatest golf course in the world, and as one of a handful of courses to receive perfect scores across the board on the Doak scale, we're not out to dispute that assessment. If you believe that a golf course is the sum of its holes, then there is no course that dares challenge Pine Valley: any one of its 18 holes would be a welcome addition to almost any other course. You never hear people come away talking about the par-4 4th, for example, but its blind drive up over the top of a big hill, and downhill second to an undulating green set right on the ground, would be the signature hole at 90% of golf courses in America. Yet there aren't many others on the course where approaching on the ground is an option.

Since the golf magazines started rating courses in order in 1985, Pine Valley's consensus #1 position seems to have had an outsized influence on what today's designers and developers want to build, right down to the "destination golf" model that is struggling to prove itself in many markets. Unfortunately, it also spawned some people's ideal that players should never see a hole except the one they're playing, and others' belief that resistance to scoring is the most important ingredient of a great course, which are false conclusions. And the pressure to build 18 postcard-ready holes? That derives from the set of 18 postcards they used to sell as a souvenir in the Pine Valley pro shop.

Meanwhile, the most overlooked aspect of Pine Valley is its terrific set of short par-4 holes [the 2nd, 8th, 12th, and 17th]. Their inclusion has actually helped the club not overreact to changes in technology, and make it the complete design. 10 10 10 10 [2009]

Pine Valley GC. Short course by Tom Fazio and Ernie Ransome, 1991.

Created to take some of the traffic pressure away from a course crowded with members and guests, eight of these ten holes are close reproductions of approach shots on the big course, and the "tees" are fairways so you can play them from anywhere you like. It's an excellent solution for the club, because no original design was going to be good enough to get regular use; but it's hard to know how to grade something so derivative. 5 6 - - [2007]

Sand Barrens GC, Swainton. 27 holes by Dr. Michael Hurdzan and Dana Fry, 1997.

On a formerly flat and sandy site, every fairway was excavated between two and eight feet below natural grade, and all the dirt was collected to build up elevated tee complexes in central locations, producing a course with lots of visual relief. At the double green for the 2nd and 6th holes, a careless approach might leave you a 200+ foot putt. 4 - - - [1999]

Stone Harbor GC, Cape May Court House. Desmond Muirhead, 1989.

Without a doubt, Stone Harbor was the most ridiculous course I've ever played. The late Desmond Muirhead was an erudite fellow, but I have no idea whether the overt symbolism he built into his courses of this period was a serious attempt at art, or just a mockery of golf.

Whichever the case, the course was full of extreme holes. The most famous was the par-3 7th with a football-shaped island green flanked by two zigzagging island bunkers. My tee shot landed on the bulkheaded edge of the green, bounced into the air and didn't make a splash – instead, it had landed in the bunker on the left, leaving me a 20-yard sand shot out of a fried-egg lie over water, to about 40 feet of green, with more water beyond. It was the single dumbest golf shot I have ever faced.

Alas, the gaps between the island green and its flanking bunkers have been filled in, and some other features like the tree growing in the 3rd green or the ax-handle bunker at the 12th have been removed; yet there are still more bizarre features on this course than on all the other courses you've ever played, put together. Even the earthworks for the tees will make you laugh out loud. It's interesting to look at, but hell to play. 0 - - - [1989]

Trump National Philadelphia, Pine Hill. Tom Fazio, 2000.

The former Pine Hill Golf Club, this project was begun as a high-end daily fee course on property quite near the back gate to Pine Valley. With Tom Fazio at the helm, it sounded like a dream. But it turned out that a good part of the wooded site was classified as wetlands, so the routing of the front nine is marred by several ridiculous 200-yard cart-ride transitions from one hole to the next. No amount of re-branding could overcome this mess: my advice to Mr. Trump would be to lose the front nine entirely, and promote the unblemished back nine as Tom Fazio's finest nine-hole design. 4 - - - [2000]

Twisted Dune GC, Egg Harbor Township. Archie Struthers, 2001.

This faux links near Atlantic City was completed by a friend of mine after a disagreement with the architect who did the original layout. It's a pretty difficult tee-to-green test, as you'd expect from an amateur designer who's a good player, but there are too many straight holes between the artificial mounds. They would have been wiser to spend more of their earthmoving money in the fairways, and less in between them. 4 - - - [2001]

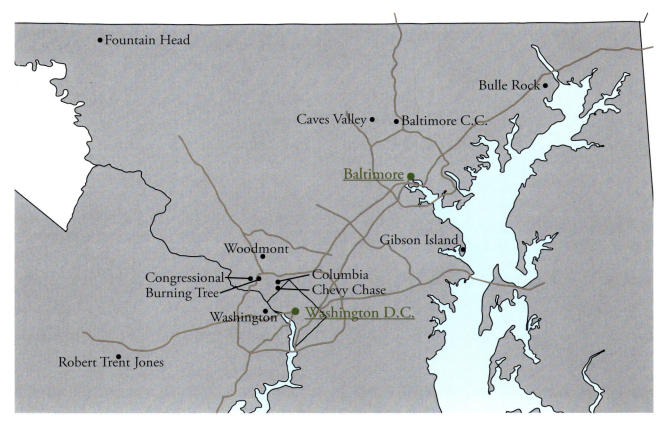

Baltimore CC. Five Farms East course by A.W. Tillinghast, 1926.

A.W. Tillinghast laid out 36 holes at the new Five Farms location for Baltimore Country Club, but only his East course was built at the time. It's still a wonder; Keith Foster's work ten years ago softened the tilt in a handful of greens, but they are still treacherous even after the changes. The most memorable holes are the dogleg par-5 6th, with the maintenance barns in play on the tee shot something like the railway sheds at St. Andrews, and the very long 14th, with its Sahara cross-hazard that has to be cleared on the second shot. 7 7 7 7 [2015]

Baltimore CC. West course by Bob Cupp and Tom Kite, 1990.

When the West course was eventually added the club ignored Tillie's original plan, and has never overcome this stumble. 3 – 4 - [2007]

Bulle Rock GC, Aberdeen. Pete Dye, 1998.

This brawny Pete Dye design has received a lot of acclaim, but I think much of it can be attributed to the lack of other Dye courses in the northeast corridor; it's really not his best work. The course is big enough and strong enough for anyone who will pay the freight to pay its daily fee – the par-5 11th is 599 yards from the third set of markers! – but some holes feel contrived, most of all the long par-4 finisher with a skinny lake dug into the side of the hill along the left of the hole. 5 - - - [1999]

Burning Tree Club, Bethesda. C. H. Alison, 1922, with revisions by Robert Trent Jones.

A D.C. institution, Burning Tree was Eisenhower's favorite golfing haunt during his years as President, though most of today's politicians are wary of the potential hassle of frequenting an all-male club. It's a graceful layout, with outstanding holes like the 4th

This fairway bunker on the 8th at Chevy Chase must be avoided to reach the green in regulation.

and 16th draped over the rolling terrain, and plenty of greens you can putt right off of, to the amusement of the deer in the woodsy triangular spaces between the holes. I expected it to be stuffy and Secret Service secure; instead, it's one of the most low-key clubs I've ever visited. 6 - - - [2014]

Caves Valley GC, Owings Mills. Tom Fazio, 1991.

The brainchild of former USGA president Reg Murphy, Caves Valley set a new standard for private-club service and class, inadvertently becoming the forerunner of a generation of courses where the ambiance and the maintenance overshadow the golf. It all falls to pieces because the golf course is too hilly, and because none of the holes are standouts. 5 – 5 5 [2007]

Chevy Chase Club. Donald Ross, 1910, with revisions by Colt & Alison and by Arthur Hills.

An historic old country club close to downtown Washington, D.C., Chevy Chase is known locally for its charming clubhouse, unhurried atmosphere and pleasant golf course set on gently rolling topography. The reachable par-5 10th, its fairway leaning toward a hazard that runs along the left side of the hole and then cuts in front of the green, is one of those rare holes that technology has improved, as more people can reach in two and the second shot from a slightly hanging lie over the water is exhilarating. With lots of good bending holes and some effective plateau green sites, the club affords its members some of the best golf inside the Beltway. - - 5 6 [2007]

When Ernie Els clinched his second U.S. Open, the last green was located by today's 10th tee.

Columbia CC, Chevy Chase. Herbert Barker, 1911, with modifications by Walter Travis and others.

The Mall and our national monuments were built on flat ground – landfilled into a swamp, actually – but I had forgotten just how hilly the rest of the District is. Columbia is a prime example, laid out within tight boundaries on a roller-coaster property of hills and deep valleys. It's an uneven test, with the back nine presenting most of the good golf, and the turf is always a struggle here in the transition zone. There are several very interesting shots to be played, and a couple of the greens were memorable, especially the "Split Level" 10th, with the left third of the green a punchbowl dipping three feet below the right-hand plateau. Most observers would identify the par-4 11th as the class of the course, though. 5 – 5 5 [2007]

Congressional CC, Bethesda. Blue course by Devereux Emmet, 1924, with modifications by Rees Jones.

Were it not in our nation's capital you might never have heard of Congressional, so inflated is its reputation by Beltway hype. It is the most straightforward of golf courses imaginable, and the land has too much character to yield nothing more than an examination of hitting fairways and greens in regulation. There are some good par-4's on the back nine, but the only really memorable hole is the last, with its green set on a peninsula jutting out into a large lake. 6 7 7 5 [2007]

Congressional CC. Gold course by Robert Trent Jones, 1960, and George Fazio, 1975.

The Gold course is more difficult than most clubs prefer for a second 18, but mostly it's a well landscaped bit of overflow parking when they have tournaments on the Blue course. 4 – 4 4 [2007]

Fountain Head CC, Hagerstown. Donald Ross, 1929.

Hemmed in by housing and tree growth, the appeal of this vintage Ross course is that little has been done to its bare bones. The ground is wildly undulating in places, and the greens, although much smaller than Ross intended, retain their venom thanks to some nasty tilts and slopes. With some sensible clearing and restoration, this place could be terrific: they just have to stop worrying about the long hitters so the other 90% can enjoy it. - - - 5 [2015]

Gibson Island GC. Charles Blair Macdonald, 1922.

Only nine holes are left of this, the least-known of Macdonald's twelve original designs, and what is left is so decayed that it's not worth seeing. Located at the tip of a peninsula jutting into Chesapeake Bay, it might have had a hint of Fishers Island about it in its heyday, but that heyday was short-lived and it's hard to imagine it now. 1 - - - [1982]

Robert Trent Jones GC, Lake Manassas, VA. Robert Trent Jones, 1991.

Mr. Jones purchased this land himself back in the 1960's, and waited decades to find the right developer to fund the project. It is one of his most dramatic designs, with most of the inward holes playing alongside Lake Manassas, and two greens [the par-3 9th and 11th] sticking right out into the lake ... they must have had friends in high places to secure the permits for these. The land near the lake is pretty sloping, so the fairways do feel grafted onto the terrain, but the beautiful backdrops soften it. 6 - - - [2014]

Washington G & CC, Arlington, VA. Donald Ross, 1907, modified by William Flynn.

Just five miles from the Washington Monument, this is a short but difficult test [and walk], with never a flat lie for your second shots. It doesn't really feel much like a Ross routing; I'd guess he kept some pieces of the original 1898 layout due to space constraints. 5 - - - [2014]

Woodmont CC, Rockville, MD. North course by Alfred Tull, 1950, with renovations by Arthur Hills.

A sprawling 450-acre oasis in suburban Rockville, Woodmont is home to contrasting parkland courses. The meaty, tournament-ready North Course was redesigned by Arthur Hills a decade ago, and is both hillier and harder. It also has bentgrass fairways and bentgrass greens, many of which are placed uphill with steep false fronts and often lightning fast speeds. With no tournament headed this way, all the effort feels wasted. - - - 4 [2015]

Woodmont CC. South course by Alfred Tull, 1951-61.

Woodmont's more user-friendly South course was Darius' preference of the two. Its longer holes tend to play left-to-right a little too frequently, but otherwise this is the more enjoyable test over decent undulating ground. The zoysia fairways are superb. In all, it seems a better fit for a suburban country club with the full range of non-golf amenities including tennis, swimming and dining. - - - 5 [2015]

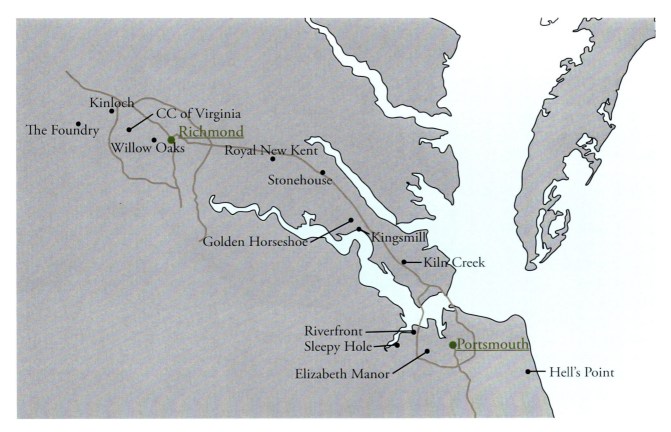

Elizabeth Manor GC, Portsmouth. Dick Wilson, 1956.

Site of the annual Eastern Amateur, won by golfers including Deane Beman, Ben Crenshaw and Lanny Wadkins, Elizabeth Manor is an unassuming, flat layout built fairly early in Dick Wilson's career. It is reminiscent of Wilson's Florida work, like Pine Tree, but with smaller greens and low-profile bunkering. 4 - - - [1991]

The Foundry GC, Powhatan.   J. K. Timmons, 1991.

Designed and developed by a local engineer and property developer, the Foundry is a beautiful high-end development on a rolling piece of ground cut by the appropriately named Fine Creek. Design inexperience shows in some of the shaping and greens contouring, but overall this is pleasant golf with a peaceful setting the principal attraction. The fact you can play beside the place where Robert E. Lee spent his final evening as a Confederate General is also pretty cool. - 5 - 5 [2015]

Golden Horseshoe GC, Williamsburg. Gold course by Robert Trent Jones, 1964.

Adjacent to the old-money Williamsburg Inn, Golden Horseshoe was considered a top-of-the-line resort course in the 1960's, which just goes to show how high our standards have grown in the fifty years since it opened; the property seems small and cramped today. The focus of the course has always been the four short holes, all of which revolve around ponds in a deep ravine that runs through the center of the property; each has its own identity, but I've played dozens of classic courses with better sets of par-3's. The 10th and the two finishing holes are among the more difficult two-shotters you'll find on any resort course, but as usual with Mr. Jones's work, the shorter par-4's don't measure up to the same standard. 5 6 5 - [2006]

Hell's Point GC, Virginia Beach. Rees Jones, 1982.

A creek divides this property into two sections, but they weren't allowed to use it as a feature of the golf. Instead, a couple of holes built around man-made ponds are the main feature of the course. It's a good but basic public layout. 4 - - - [1991]

Kiln Creek GC and Resort, Newport News. Tom Clark, 1989.

Many of the dozen courses which received the dreaded "0" rating in the original Confidential Guide have since been modified or closed, but Kiln Creek survives, because the homeowners around it don't want to see it close. The oddball design came about when the architects received last-minute instructions from the developer to "lose" 2.5 million cubic yards of fill excavated from a drainage canal around the housing, so they didn't have to pay to haul off the dirt. Instead of changing their design in light of the new circumstances, and using the fill to create some drama, they just built up the golf corridors between the homes with 8-10 feet of fill, creating shallow bunkers one story up! The golf tends to look down on the homes [and slice into them], rather than the homes looking down on the fairways. 0 - - - [1991]

Kingsmill GC, Williamsburg. River course by Pete Dye, 1975.

The handsome dogleg right 16th that heads toward the broad Potomac and the par-3 17th playing from high point to high point along its shore aren't enough to save this course from being a clunker, according to Ran. Mr. Dye might agree: he told me he should have walked away from this project after his original client, Anheuser-Busch, forced him to re-route five holes to make room for a housing development. With Busch Gardens nearby, there are better things to do on a family vacation. - 3 - - [1990]

Kinloch GC, Richmond. Lester George with Vinny Giles, 2001.

Kinloch is often lauded for its over-the-top service and pristine conditioning, but those things are down the list of important factors for us. A lot of neat and refreshingly original design features were attempted here, like the split fairway landing areas at the 2nd and 9th holes, the latter of which would be mistaken for two parallel holes by any casual observer. But whether the options presented are all good choices for some subset of the members is debatable. For sure, the number of forced carries into greens makes Kinloch more appealing to low-handicappers than to the rest of us. - 6 6 6 [2007]

Riverfront GC, Suffolk. Tom Doak with Bruce Hepner, 1999.

Laid out along tidal marshes which feed into the Nansemond River, Riverfront is quite dramatic, considering its highest point is just twenty feet above sea level. My assignment to Eric Iverson [who was doing his first shaping work for us] was to look at every green from 20 yards left of the landing stake and 20 yards right, and try to make each green look as different as possible from those two vantages … which turned out to be a great prescription for a strategic golf course. However, we stretched out the golf course along as much tidal marsh as possible, which also increased development frontage, so many of the holes now feel crowded by the homes The par-5 14th was once one of my best holes; today, if you don't take on the second-shot bunkers, your ball might wind up in someone's swimming pool. 5 5 - - [2004]

Royal New Kent GC, Providence Forge. Mike Strantz, 1997.

An epic design with some wonderfully creative holes, Royal New Kent was the forerunner of a new golf market – the course that everyone should play once – but it is severe enough that few players are good enough to enjoy regular engagements. There is a market for such a course in certain resort areas, but I always wondered if Williamsburg was big enough to support it. The bold features of the course don't scale down well for short game play; everything around the greens is either straight up or straight down, and the putting contours are either dead flat or seven-foot tiers that no one can judge. I would have been a bigger fan if the water laden finishing holes didn't abandon the rugged links theme of the rest. Now that homes are starting to be built around the perimeter – the par-3 12th, always a weak point in the routing, has been laid siege – the appeal of the course is really starting to erode. 5 5 - - [1999]

Sleepy Hole GC, Suffolk. Russell Breeden, 1972.

Host to an LPGA event in the early 1980's, Sleepy Hole is a heavily-played municipal course with one of the most difficult 18th holes I've ever seen. The long second shot off a downhill lie has to carry a patch of cat-tails in front of the green, with water left and the clubhouse too close for comfort on the right. 4 - - - [1991]

The Tradition GC at Stonehouse, Toano. Mike Strantz, 1996.

A sensation when it opened, Mike Strantz's Stonehouse is now struggling to survive, and in both cases it's been all about the design. The grand scale of the course attracted attention, but also caused problems … if you're going to make the holes severe anyway, why space them so far apart? [When you checked in to play, they proudly announced they had 8 miles of continuous concrete cart paths.] A couple of the greens set in deep valleys struggle to maintain any sort of turf cover. Ran thinks the four dramatic finishing holes over and around ravines make it worth a visit, but clearly I disagree. 0 4 - - [1997]

CC of Virginia, Richmond. James River course by Fred Findlay, 1928.

The late Bob Jones watched a teenaged Jack Nicklaus compete here during the 1955 U.S. Amateur championship; not much good has occurred since. A 1990's renovation saw bunkers reduced in depth, water added and natural features destroyed. Most egregious was how the landing area of the dogleg right 12th was expanded to make the once-unique hole more 'fair.' Originally, the golfer had to place his tee ball near the bunker on the inside of the dogleg in order to earn a level stance for the long approach; once the landing area was leveled, there was no need to think about where to hit it. - 5 5 - [2014]

Willow Oaks CC, Richmond. William F. Gordon, 1957, with revisions by Lester George.

Founded on the grounds of an old Virginian farm by the banks of the James River, Willow Oaks was extensively modified by Lester George in 2007, who retained the old Gordon routing but added plenty of length and modern difficulty. Drainage was improved by digging waterways through the lower riverside areas, though utilizing the dirt generated for mounding makes these holes seem very confined. The 16th and 17th holes, for example, require forced carries on each shot, the par-5 16th particularly cruel on shorter hitters and the less accurate. The short 15th, which drops down into this area, is better, as are the closing holes on each nine, which rise back toward the clubhouse. It feels like they were a little too preoccupied here with making this course hard, rather than fun for the membership. - - - 4 [2015]

THE APPALACHIANS

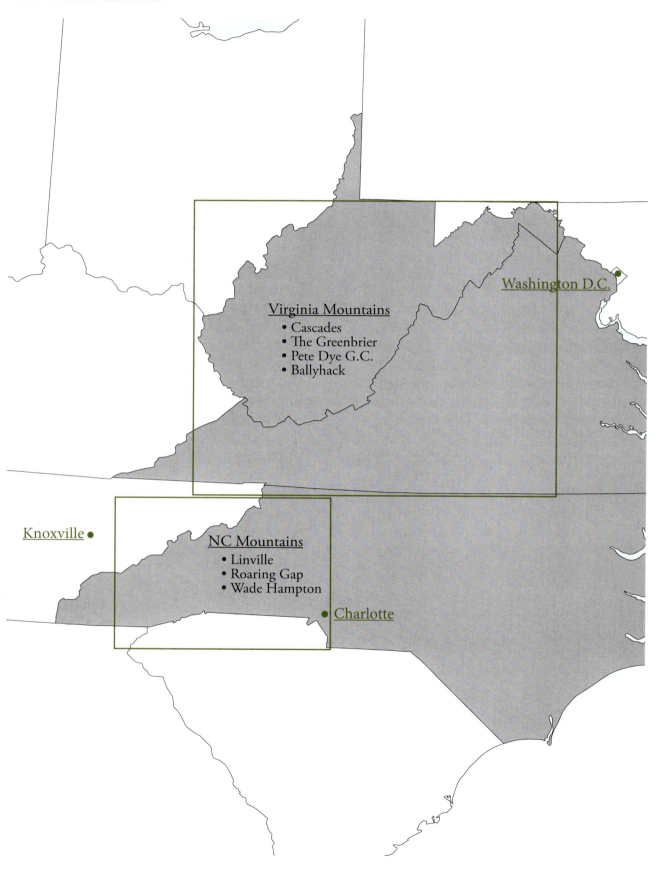

Virginia Mountains
- Cascades
- The Greenbrier
- Pete Dye G.C.
- Ballyhack

Washington D.C.

Knoxville

NC Mountains
- Linville
- Roaring Gap
- Wade Hampton

Charlotte

My friend Fred Muller, the professional at Crystal Downs, and I would sometimes make a small golf trip in April, before our summer club opened for play on May 1. One year, when we were headed to Tennessee, I suggested jumping over the mountains into North Carolina to play at Highlands Country Club, which P.B. Dye had fallen in love with when he and his dad were building The Honors Course. We tried to call the club, but got no answer; we only later realized that Highlands, like many other clubs in the Appalachians, doesn't open until May, either. They shut down early, too: on my one visit to Linville, the trees were at the peak of fall color, but the clubhouse was already boarded up for winter!

The short golf season up here means that the mountain courses of West Virginia, Virginia and North Carolina were rarely noted in the mainstream golf press, at least until twenty years ago when newer developments started seeking to advertise their courses. There is just so much attention devoted to the famous courses of the Northeast and the Great Lakes that there hasn't been much space left over to talk about golf in the mountains.

Almost all of these courses are aimed at residents of the southern states seeking to find relief from the heat and humidity of summer: it was residents of Pinehurst who started Roaring Gap Club, while Bobby Jones himself went to Highlands to escape the worst of the heat in Atlanta, years before air conditioning. [A/C is still not a thing in Appalachia.]

It's a small section of our book but do not overlook it -- there is a lot of fine golf here. The more I read about these courses, the more I wish I'd had a chance to build one up there.

Pikewood National's Redan-like 12th green overlooks layers and layers of mountains.

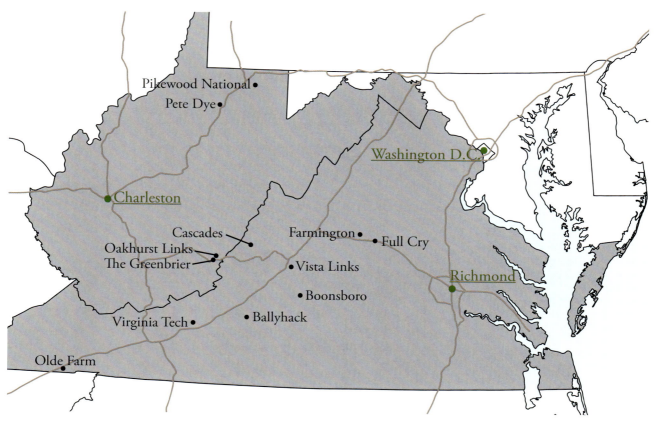

Ballyhack GC, Roanoke, VA. Lester George, 2010.

    This is a love it or hate it design. Ran chooses the former, believing that the many exciting golf shots more than justify having to take a cart to traverse the property, set in the chop hills outside of Roanoke. The hazards are the deepest in the state and work in concert with the broad slopes to provide a different brand of golf. The par-5 2nd is a fine example: tee balls gravitate toward the central fairway bunkers and the golfer must calculate how to avoid them. Just seeing the ball run along the ground for long distances is rare in this part of the country, and a welcome change.

    Like Tobacco Road, some will think the design overdone and it will never feature in any course rankings because of those naysayers. But for those who yearn for something bold and different, Ballyhack has it in spades. - 7 - 6 [2015]

Boonsboro CC, Lynchburg, VA. Fred Findlay, 1929.

    According to club records, Willie Park, Jr. actually laid out this course, but Findlay built it after Park passed away. That fine duo of Scots explains why there is so much to like across this rolling property. The great amateur Vinny Giles developed his game here and has always spoken glowingly of home: being able to shape the ball both ways and hit from a sloping stance are imperative to one's success here. Take the 6th: a power fade will find a speed slot and drastically shorten one's approach to the small, tilted green 460 yards on. - 6 - - [1993]

Cascades GC at The Homestead Resort, Hot Springs, VA. William Flynn, 1923.

    A mighty design accomplishment, Flynn found a way to build a world class course after A.W. Tillinghast passed on the site. Its construction was anything but easy, and Flynn's use of dynamite was judicious. It should still be the best course in the state, but years of neglect have seen the bunkers flattened, and streams that were integral to Flynn's design have been piped underground in the name of playability. It's a shame -- the back nine flies in the face of convention with its superb two-shot holes and unusual 3-5-5-3 finish. 7 6 7 6 [2007]

Farmington CC, Charlottesville, VA. Fred Findlay, 1928.

Fanning out around the impressive clubhouse that Thomas Jefferson had a hand in building, Farmington offers something for every golfer. You and I will enjoy the rare chance to try for the par-5 7th in two, thanks to 80 feet of elevation change in our favor. The scratch man will struggle to conquer the monster 240-yard 10th, and all classes will be inspired by the long 14th, played across rolling ground toward the Blue Ridge Mountains. Ran grew up in Virginia, and considers this the state's best course. - 7 5 - [2015]

Full Cry at Keswick Hall, Charlottesville. Pete Dye, 2014.

Here is the most user-friendly Dye course we've seen in ages: a lower profile design set in a pleasant valley. The most striking hole is the home hole with views of the Blue Ridge mountains beyond, but the graceful sweep of the 3rd fairway as it jogs left, then right before feeding onto the green from the high right side represents uncluttered architecture at a high level. Both club members and guests of the five star, 48-room Keswick Hall much prefer it to the Palmer design that it replaced. - 6 - - [2015]

The Greenbrier Resort, White Sulphur Springs, WV. Old White TPC course by C.B. Macdonald and Seth Raynor, 1913.

The only course in America named after its patrons, Old White was a watered-down Macdonald design until Lester George's renovation in 2008. The course is quite short

Ballyhack's 13th and 15th holes [played from across the ravine] finish on an enormous double green.

for its role as host to a Tour event, but it is fun to watch the professionals attempt to handle some of Raynor's angles and features. The Short hole, played as the 18th with a big hump in the middle of the green, has provided the most excitement. Regardless, we find the less emulated Narrows hole [here the 14th] to be the best on the course. 6 6 6 - [2009]

The Greenbrier Resort. Greenbrier course by Jack Nicklaus, 1977.

The Greenbrier course was originally a second 18 holes by Macdonald – the old photos indicate that he must have included several adaptations of British holes he never used anywhere else. But the course was quite short overall, and to lengthen it for the 1979 Ryder Cup, Jack Nicklaus obliterated all trace of its origins. The holes where ponds were added seem particularly out of place. 5 - - - [2006]

Oakhurst Links, White Sulphur Springs, WV. Russell Montague, 1884, restored by Bob Cupp.

Formed by a small group of Scots immigrants, Oakhurst would be the oldest golf club in America, but when the founders died the course simply grew over, and the course remained in pasture until its nine holes were rebuilt (by hand) in 1994. Maintained by gang mowers and sheep, it probably plays much the same as it did 120 years ago, if you use the replica gutty balls and vintage hickory-shafted clubs provided for guest play. As an exercise in understanding that the thrill of golf is not a function of how far you hit the ball but how well, it cannot be surpassed. The view of this mountain valley from the clubhouse porch is lovely, as is the short par-4 9th hole playing back up the hill. 5 - - - [2006]

Olde Farm GC, Bristol, VA. Bobby Weed, 2000.

As construction manager at Long Cove, Bobby Weed was my first boss, and this is his best solo design. His client was a wealthy coal man and there were no limits on how to use the expansive property. Two short par-4's on the front side are offset by the 240-yard 4th, while the back nine offers some exhilirating tee shots before the back-to-back ballbusters at the 16th and 17th. The pastoral setting is dotted by farm structures, and you might even play your approach shot off a barn roof onto the 6th green. - 7 - 7 [2015]

You can play off the barn on the 6th at Olde Farm, but don't go through the barn door!

Pete Dye GC, Clarksburg, WV. Pete Dye, 1994.

Begun in 1978, this might have been one of Mr. Dye's most attention-getting designs, had it opened on time; but there were so many battles between Pete and his client, Jim LaRosa, that the course took forever to build, and it opened with a bit of a yawn.

The 1000-acre property is gorgeous – bisected by a winding river and surrounded by wooded hills that are a riot of fall color, all for just 18 holes. There are some strange gimmicks, including relics of the coal mining history of the property, and the waterfall that comes out of the 10th green [right underneath it], but the sheer number of outstanding holes trumps these oddities. The par-4 2nd and 18th and the par-5 5th all play dramatically along the river, while the par-5 8th with its long quarry bunker emphasizes the monumental scale of the course. 7 7 6 7 [2007]

Pete Dye River Course of Virginia Tech, Radford, VA. Pete Dye, 2005.

Set hard along the rushing New River, Dye's routing is a loose figure eight familiar to those who know Kiawah and Whistling Straits. The excitement of playing along the river at teh par-5 3rd or the bruising finisher is never equaled by the artificial mounding and small bunkers on the interior holes. The Tech golf team gets more out of it than we did. - 5 - - [2008]

Pikewood National GC, Morgantown, WV. John Raese and Bob Gwynne, 2009.

Designed by two Oakmont members along the top of a steep mountain ridge, one's first thought at Pikewood are the marching orders given to A. W. Tillinghast at Winged Foot, to produce a "man-sized course." This is purist golf at its purest -- a relentless "but fair" test of golf that has been enthusiastically received by low-handicap visitors for its insistence on solid ball-striking. You don't want to have a bad day with the driver here!

Pikewood is a different take on minimalist design, with just two sets of tees at 7,500 and 6,800 yards [with a few extras to accommodate higher-handicap visitors], and only 23 bunkers in all. With only three fairway bunkers, few would label it a strategic course, yet there are several holes where hugging to one side leaves an easier or shorter approach -- notably at the par-5 8th which swings boldly around a deep hollow. And there is a lot of short-game interest, with tricky chipping areas surrounding many greens. From the 2nd hole onward, there are many spectacular moments with thirty-mile views over layers and layers of mountains.

Another point for the founders was to build the course for walkers only, despite the steep elevation changes on the front nine, as their vision of golf is that it's an athletic endeavour. To my great surprise, the walk was the greatest attraction, focusing the player's attention on narrow paths and small views in between all the big vistas. The walk from the waterfall-backed 5th green up to the 6th tee, alongside a stream lined with rhododendrons, is the prettiest thing I've seen on a golf course in ages, and can only be the product of a designer who takes the time to get to know and love the property he's working with. Ultimately, that's what makes the whole course special. 7 - - - [2016]

Vista Links, Buena Vista, VA. Rick Jacobson, 2004.

This muni has been in the news since city of Buena Vista defaulted on the loans to build it, against which they had pledged as collateral certain municipal buildings. Yikes! Lost in the ensuing handwringing is the golf course, which is still open. Set on a hilltop within a lovely valley, standout holes include the drivable 4th where staggered bunkers make even a lay-up tricky, and the bunkerless 5th, downhill to a Volcano green. - 5 - - [2016]

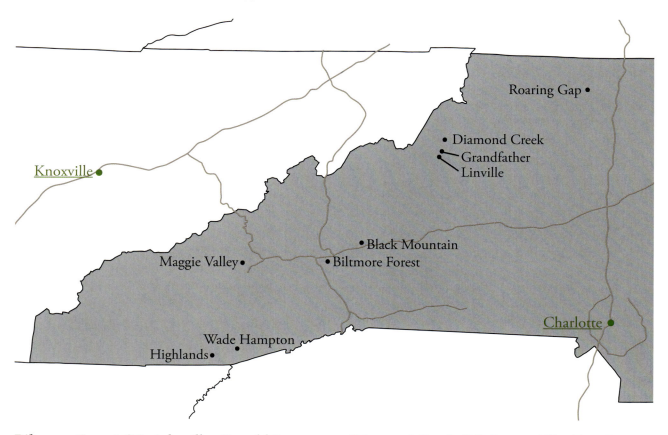

Biltmore Forest CC, Asheville. Donald Ross, 1922.

Developed by the Vanderbilts as the centerpiece of a new community south of Asheville, Biltmore Forest is a spacious "core" course that could pass for an opulent Tom Fazio design, apart from the classic architecture of the surrounding homes. During World War II, Ben Hogan won a Tour event here three years in succession, and it is not hard to imagine him pulling away from the field on the bruising quartet of finishing holes. Brian Silva has been working here for years slowly restoring Ross's design. - 6 - - [2003]

Black Mountain GC. Nine holes by Donald Ross, 1929; expanded to 18 holes in 1962.

Black Mountain is the site of the longest golf hole I've personally seen, a 747-yard par-6 that somehow fails to stand out from a crowd of ordinary golf holes. 2 - - - [1989]

Diamond Creek GC, Banner Elk. Tom Fazio, 2006.

Tom Fazio has plenty of high-end, private golf courses in his design portfolio, and Diamond Creek, in the mountains of Banner Elk, is among his most attractive. The front nine tends to wander higher into the upland areas, with the back set mostly down into the wooded glades. On both, the use of tall fescue roughs contrast beautifully with the immaculate bentgrass surfaces.

This course was a major engineering achievement, with large hillsides blasted and rocks cleared to create the playing corridors. Things get a little steep early in the round, but the holes are mostly fun and the conditioning, scenery and superb amenities are sure to satisfy most who visit. The most photogenic hole is the par three 17th, played across a meandering creek and toward a green backed by a large natural waterfall. - 6 - 6 [2009]

Grandfather G & CC, Linville. Ellis Maples, 1967.

Grandfather Mountain is one of the tallest in North Carolina's Blue Ridge Mountain Range, and the golf course is set in the valley between two large ridges. Maples once worked for Donald Ross, and it shows in an effortless routing which is eminently walkable despite the mountain environs. These are some of the most confounding greens in golf: between the speed and the difficult-to-discern slopes, putts can break four feet more than you see. There are also several creeks that cut across fairways, most memorably on the 15th where both shots are challenged. The 18th is another notable hole, for the manner in which the final green juts into the club's 35-acre lake. - 7 6 5 [2010]

Highlands CC. Donald Ross, 1928.

A mountain retreat for well-to-do Southerners [including the late Bobby Jones], Highlands is a billy-goat layout in immaculate condition that zealously guards its privacy. In places it becomes a bit too narrow, especially on the front nine where the combination of sideslope and trees rivals the difficulty of The Olympic Club, but the back nine widens out a bit to better holes. There are some excellent long two-shotters, like the sidehill 5th and the dogleg 10th which is pinched by a mountain stream in the landing area, such that you have to flirt with the water off the tee if you want to reach the elevated green in regulation. The greens are not as complex as Ross's best work, and the short overall length of the course will cause some good players to dismiss it. Don't believe them. 6 6 6 - [2000]

Linville GC. Donald Ross, 1928.

This well-known mountain resort sits in a tranquil mountain valley just outside of Linville. A winding brook comes into play on no less than twelve holes, but in many instances it intersects the holes in relatively meaningless

The 16th at Diamond Creek plays sharply back down grade.

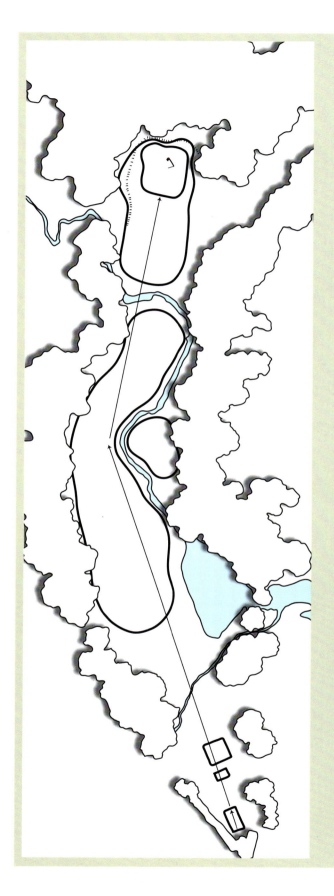

Highlands CC
10th hole - 434 yards

A small creek makes a much better hazard than a large pond, because the line of the hazard has more twists and turns to add strategy to the hole. [Plus, the average golfer can get away with a miss sometimes, by recovering from the opposite bank.]

The S-bend of the creek on the 10th at Highlands was perfectly employed by Donald Ross on this long two-shot hole. Short hitters must flirt with the creek on the right in order to have a chance to reach the elevated green with their second shots, or just get across the creek in two. The long hitter is tempted to carry the elbow of the creek off the tee to make the approach easier, but he will often cost himself a shot attempting to gain a fraction of one. The small bit of fairway to the right of the creek is a restored feature; it wasn't an option back when I fell in love with this hole, 25 years ago.

locations, or restricts the long hitter from using his driver. Exceptions are the distinctive one-shot 14th to a green high on a ledge above the creek, and the par-4 3rd hole whose long approach plays over a big loop of water, unless one chooses to lay up on an island of fairway in between. However the greens and the bunkers lack in sculptural interest, which might suit the older members but prevents the course from being in the class of Roaring Gap.
6 5 5 - [2015]

Maggie Valley Club and Resort. William Prevost, 1972.

This small family-owned resort used to advertise a lot in *GOLF DIGEST*, so my family stopped through when I was young. It made no great impression. 3 - - - [1975]

Roaring Gap C. Donald Ross, 1926.
See the "Gourmet's Choice," pp. 32-33.
7 7 - 6 [2015]

Wade Hampton GC, Cashiers. Tom Fazio, 1988.

Wade Hampton is rightly thought of as one of the best of a generation of new courses, and a talented on-site team that included Dana Fry, Tom Marzolf and Mike Strantz is reflected in the finished product. It is a development course, but most of the lots overlook from high above, leaving the golf experience uninterrupted by road crossings, and the green-to-tee walks are manageable apart from the long hike to the 6th tee. The layout makes use of a couple of winding streams and its views toward Chimney Top Mountain, though the looming granite dome is in no way reflective of the relatively gentle terrain. Three of the four short holes are postcard material, but the best holes are in the stretch of two-shotters from the 13th to the 16th, capped off by the long downhill par-3 17th [at left] across the brook. 7 8 7 7 [2012]

THE GREAT LAKES

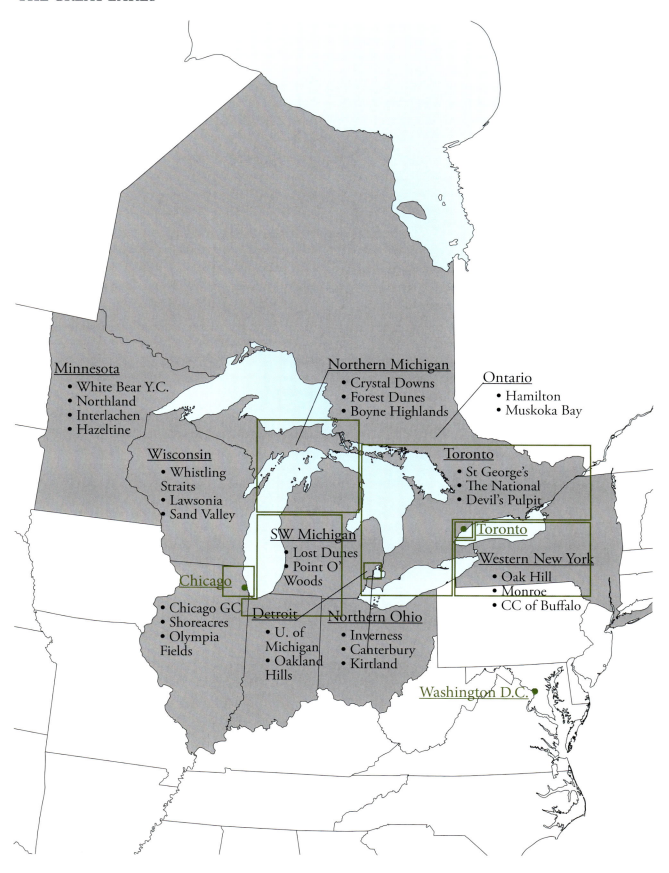

Minnesota
- White Bear Y.C.
- Northland
- Interlachen
- Hazeltine

Northern Michigan
- Crystal Downs
- Forest Dunes
- Boyne Highlands

Ontario
- Hamilton
- Muskoka Bay

Wisconsin
- Whistling Straits
- Lawsonia
- Sand Valley

Toronto
- St George's
- The National
- Devil's Pulpit

Toronto

SW Michigan
- Lost Dunes
- Point O' Woods

Western New York
- Oak Hill
- Monroe
- CC of Buffalo

Chicago
- Chicago GC
- Shoreacres
- Olympia Fields

Detroit
- U. of Michigan
- Oakland Hills

Northern Ohio
- Inverness
- Canterbury
- Kirtland

Washington D.C.

Though I was born and raised on the east coast, the Great Lakes have been my home for the second half of my life, ever since I was hired to design High Pointe Golf Club in Traverse City, Michigan -- my first solo design -- at the ripe old age of 26.

That opportunity came about because the Great Lakes region is blessed with attributes that make it relatively cheap and easy to build a golf course. The soils, in many places, are excellent for construction; irrigation systems can be under-designed because natural rainfall is enough to maintain the roughs in all but the worst of droughts. It's easy to put the numbers together and think you can make a go of it, especially if you already own the ground.

In fact, it was so easy to build golf courses that too many were built. The present oversupply of courses means that most have to cut prices to the point that they're financially unsustainable. It's a burden on the member of an undersubscribed club, but it's a win for the golfer paying retail -- right up until his favorite course goes under, as High Pointe did.

The Great Lakes include some of the most highly-developed golf markets in the world. Golf in Toronto has boomed along with the city itself over the past twenty years, while the disadvantaged old industrial cities from Utica to Buffalo to Cleveland and Detroit can still boast of classic courses from their heyday. Michigan advertises itself as "America's Summer Golf Capital," but just across the lake, Wisconsin's star is ascending with recent developments like Erin Hills, Whistling Straits and the new Sand Valley [its par-3 8th hole is pictured below]. And though I'm not as big a fan of golf in Chicago as they are of themselves, there are a ton of clubs with distinct personalities and old-school charm.

What's more, where other regions of the world and even the U.S.A. are struggling to justify the use of water resources on golf, the Great Lakes have both a temperate climate and the world's largest natural reservoir. One of my professors in college told my class that by the end of our lives, people would be moving back to the Great Lakes from the Southwest because of water, and his sense of timing is starting to look prophetic.

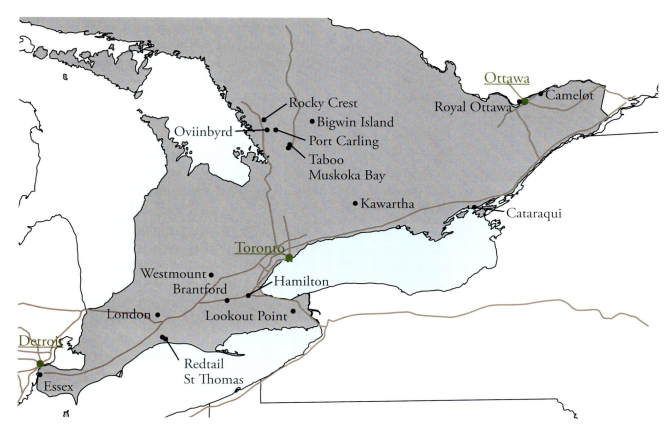

Bigwin Island GC, Baysville. Doug Carrick, 2002.

Set on a 520-acre island in the Lake of Bays, a ten-minute boat ride from civilization, the Bigwin Island course is the centerpiece of an ambitious second-home development. Home sites are strewn around the shoreline, with most of the golf draped over the hilly center. It's not really meant to be walkable, but sweeping holes like the par-5 18th back down to the harbor might be worth taking a cart. - - 6 5 [2004]

Brantford G & CC. Stanley and Nichol Thompson, 1919.

Thompson's old-fashioned parkland course in Brantford has a fine set of five short holes, highlighted by the 10th with its green set at the edge of a steep fallaway to the left, and five par-5's that dare you to attack the second shot, as none of them longer than 530 yards. - - 4 5 [2004]

Camelot G&CC, Cumberland. Thomas Mc-Broom, 1992.

Created from farm fields and woods on the south bank of the Ottawa River, Camelot is very modern in its presentation. The homeward stretch starting with the alternate-fairway short par-4 14th is promising, but the parallel finishing par-4's to a double green are by now a well-worn cliche. - - 5 - [2004]

Cataraqui GC, Kingston. Stanley Thompson, 1933, from an earlier layout.

Halfway from Montreal to Toronto, Cataraqui's fine parkland course makes for a pleasant stopover. Some of the best holes are early in the round, including the par-3 2nd and par-5 4th with their demanding greens, and I was also quite fond of the long par-4 7th with its tilted green laying on the ground. The back nine also starts strong, but the two finishing holes are each out of place in their own way. 6 - - 6 [2013]

Essex G&CC, Windsor. Donald Ross, 1929.

Just a few miles across the bridge from Detroit, Windsor - Essex is one of the few Ross courses in Canada. The greens were much admired by pros like Ben Crenshaw and Jerry Pate when it hosted the Canadian Open in 1976 -- Pate won that year -- but there are scores of Ross courses built on property with more interest than this flattish site, including four or five on the Detroit side of the river. 6 5 5 - [2003]

Hamilton G&CC, Ancaster. Harry S. Colt and C.H. Alison, 1914.

Known throughout Canada by the suburban name of Ancaster, Harry Colt's layout over wooded, rolling terrain has always placed high on the lists of best courses in Canada, but on my last visit I could not help think it has been a little bit overrated. None of the bunker work or plantings in recent times have done the original design any justice. The little switch-backing streams which cut through the lows of the property make for pretty pictures, but the new math of how far good players can drive the ball make for some awkward tee shots to the steep fairway landing areas on either side of the valley. 7 6 8 7 [2013]

Kawartha G&CC, Peterborough. Stanley Thompson, 1932-38.

A mix of parkland and woodland terrain, Kawartha is a low-key place packed with smiling golfers. There are several greens tilting madly along with the natural grade, but they are maintained at just the right speed to make position play paramount without the game becoming silly. My favorite holes were the par-4 2nd with its better-than-a-Redan tiered green, the short par-4 3rd with a tree in an awkward spot right atop a big diagonal bunker, and the sharply downhill par-5 11th with its green across a small brook. 6 - - - [2013]

Stanley Thompson's bunkers at Kawartha are features of the landscape.

London Hunt & CC. Robert Trent Jones, 1959.

London Hunt is a boilerplate Robert Trent Jones design, refurbished by Rees Jones in 2000 so that it now has six sets of tees. The most memorable stretch are the 8th through 11th holes, playing on the low ground alongside Canada's own version of the River Thames. 5 – 5 - [1991]

Lookout Point GC, Pelham. Walter Travis, 1922.

From a clubhouse at the edge of the Niagara escarpment, providing a grand view to the east, the 1st and 10th holes plummet down to the valley below. After that, many of the holes play across the side of the hill, including some wild holes like the par-4 6th and 13th and a fine set of Travis' small, undulating greens. There are a couple of awkward holes, in particular the par-3 8th and par-4 18th which attempt to scramble back up toward the clubhouse, but there is too much good stuff here to miss. 6 - - - [2013]

Muskoka Bay C, Gravenhurst. Doug Carrick, 2007.

Hip-hopping around granite outcrops, Muskoka Bay is one of the best courses in the spectacular Muskoka Lakes region, though visitors are well advised to play one tee up from where they usually do, unless they've brought plenty of ammo. The quartet of par-3's are all postcard material, and the short par-4 4th outstanding, but squeezing through the gauntlet of rocks with one's second shot at the 9th is downright frightening. - - 6 - [2007]

Royal Ottawa GC, Gatineau, QC. Tom Bendelow, 1904, with revisions by Willie Park, Jr.

A deep valley close to the clubhouse interrupts the fairway at the par-4 9th and each of the four finishing holes, often requiring lay-up tee shots followed by 200-yard approaches. - - 4 - [2004]

Oviinbyrd GC, Foots Bay. Thomas McBroom, 2005.

With the smallest membership of any of the Muskoka area clubs, Oviinbyrd is a rare sighting. Eschewing returning nines, the routing wanders over a vast property, though many of the best holes gravitate toward water: the par-3 8th, played across a natural wetland into a skinny green at the base of a rocky cliff, is distinctive, as are the two following holes, which dogleg around large lakes. The dimensions and dogleg on the 9th are very similar to the famous 14th hole at The Lakes in Australia, apart from the new green site at the latter.

Though most of the course was built for the enjoyment of the membership rather than to impress visitors, the long, plunging par three 14th and the all-carry tee shot on the 15th ramp up the difficulty considerably. The par-5 18th along a lake is a sadly unremarkable end for such a high-quality modern course. - - - 6 [2004]

Port Carling G & CC. Thomas McBroom, 1990.

One of the first of the modern wave of golf courses developed in Muskoka, Port Carling has always been held back by a difficult ridge-and-valley site and a routing that tackles it almost head-on. The par-4 4th, known as the Wall, plays straight up and over a hill that had been terraced to prevent short balls rolling all the way back to the tee. We understand the Wall has been modified since our visit, but anyone who dares to walk the course is likely still as exhausted standing on the 5th tee as they always were. Thankfully the rest of the course is less extreme, save for a nasty cross canyon par three at the 6th and the violently falling and then rising par five at the 8th. - - - 5 [2004]

Redtail GC, St. Thomas. Donald Steel with Tom Mackenzie, 1992.

One of the more perfect golf operations we've seen, Redtail is the brainchild of two partners from London who built it for themselves and share it with a select group of friends. Everything is done with taste and class, from the beautiful clubhouse with guest rooms above, to a difficult but understated course.

The course takes its character from several deep ravines, though the architects had to route their holes carefully to limit the number of bridges, which would have blown their construction budget. The greens contouring is also excellent, with a variety of difficult hole locations created by the interior slopes. There are less than thirty bunkers, though I'm not a big fan of the low mounds used in place of bunkers in a few of the green complexes -- they're the only piece of the course that looks man-made. The finishing hole, a par-5 played past the clubhouse à la the 18th at The National Golf Links of America, is a real beauty. 7 6 6 5 [2004]

Rocky Crest G Resort, MacTier. Thomas McBroom, 2000.

ClubLink's premier course in the Muskoka region, nearly all of the 18 holes at Rocky Crest have some of the Canadian Shield granite in play, as well as dense trees to both sides. The par-5 6th, with a big carry over exposed rock to reach the fairway, is probably the most distinctive hole. - - 6 5 [2004]

St. Thomas G&CC. Stanley Thompson, 1922, with expansion by Robbie Robinson, 1970.

St. Thomas is a wild ride of a routing, with both nines dropping down to play alongside Beaver Creek on the holes added by Robbie Robinson, and then fighting their way back up to the clubhouse. The entrance drive crosses a shooting gallery of fairways at the 14th, 11th and 12th, but these are some of the most interesting holes on the course, along with the undulating 5th and Robinson's sidehill par-4 16th. 6 - - 5 [2013]

Taboo GC, Gravenhurst. Ron Garl, 2002.

While most of the Muskoka courses seem like a missed opportunity, considering the natural drama of the terrain, Taboo is actually among the most pleasant to play because the ground is a bit less severe. Garl's bunkering is eye-catching but not over the top, and there is plenty of rock, too: depending how you play the par five 18th, you might hit all three shots over areas of exposed granite. Aside from the slightly cramped side-hill 10th hole, the longer par fours and early par threes are the pick of the holes. - - - 6 [2005]

Westmount G&CC, Kitchener. Stanley Thompson, 1931.

Set in a residential area, Westmount's fine routing invites members to skip around and play a few holes late in the day. However, there is only a little drama in the undulations, and neither the greens nor the bunkering really have the feel of a Golden Age course. 5 - 6 5 [2013]

Beacon Hall GC, Aurora. Bob Cupp, 1988.

This difficult club course is Bob Cupp's most highly-regarded design, though we don't agree with the Canadian magazines who have it in the country's top ten. The front nine is laid out through woods and features some dramatic elevation changes, while much of the back side is in an open meadow, hemmed in by pretty fine fescue roughs. The par-5 15th offers an optional carry to the left that cuts 50 yards off the hole, though I don't understand the merit in rewarding length with length. - - 6 5 [2004]

Devil's Paintbrush GC, Caledon. Mike Hurdzan and Dana Fry, 1991.

The Paintbrush was considered a bit of a novelty when it opened, but the course has proved to have great staying power as the business has come around to fescue fairways and the like; the run out on these fairways trumps anything in a 200-mile radius. The creativity that is afforded the golfer has earned this

course many a staunch supporter. Sleepered bunkers and stone ruins are also incorporated into the design. - 7 6 6 [2004]

Devil's Pulpit GC, Caledon. Mike Hurdzan and Dana Fry, 1989.

Developed by the guys who invented the game *Trivial Pursuit*, this course was meant to be a big deal but it turned out to be something of a grab bag of design features. The opening hole, with its elevated tee and two alternate fairways, is a glitzy start, but by the time you have to choose which of the alternate 11th holes you want to play, your head will be spinning from all of the mismatched parts. The "routing" of holes is so disjointed it gives the impression they threw all their toys out of the box and left them on the floor for the golfer to pick up. Oddly, after all that comes before, the last four holes are fairly conventional and sedate. 5 6 5 5 [2004]

Don Valley GC, North York. Howard Watson, 1956.

Don Valley appeared to be a decent layout that was suffering from neglect when I saw it: the par-3 7th had willows overhanging the right side of the tee, forcing it to be played as a dogleg par-3. 2 - - - [1991]

Eagle's Nest GC, Maple. Doug Carrick, 2004.

Eagle's Nest is a strong, intimidating faux-links wedged between a couple of regional roads and what appears a future housing estate. Naturally or otherwise, the site is dominated by a series of peaky dunes and ridges that frame many of the holes and screen the course from suburbia. Carrick insisted upon the links theme with his design, but curiously used both smooth, grass-faced pot bunkers and more rugged, sprawling sand wastes – often in very close proximity to each other. He also routed holes around two large irrigation dams and built a lot of pushed-up greens that are particularly cruel to those who catch an edge and feed away.

In some ways Eagle's Nest is like playing a slightly toned down Arcadia Bluffs or Whistling Straits, but away from the water. Some won't enjoy it, but it seems perfect for the muscular public course golfer in Toronto looking for a stern test of their game. - - - 5 [2004]

Emerald Hills G&CC, Stouffville. Rene Muylaert, 1982.

Set on the Oak Ridges Moraine, Emerald Hills now has 27 holes but Masa only saw the original 18, cut out of hardwoods. Pine trees planted to separate holes in the open areas have grown to isolate them from one another and crowd the golf. It features sprawling white bunkers and sharp elevation changes. - - 5 - [2004]

Glen Abbey GC, Oakville. Jack Nicklaus, 1974.

One of Nicklaus' first design efforts, the inclusion of elementary spectator mounds was the first time I'd ever seen the feature, a few years prior to the TPC network making them famous. The old abbey overlooking the course is the home of the Royal Canadian Golf Association, and they hosted the Canadian Open here for so many years that the course became too familiar. I've heard a lot of people in Canada bash the design, but I disagree, apart from the 430-yard 17th where it's too easy for amateurs to get on the wrong side of the horseshoe green and have no way to putt at the hole. 6 – 6 5 [2004]

King Valley GC, Toronto. Doug Carrick, 1991.

I just happened to be in Toronto during the grand opening of this course, when the "design consultant" Curtis Strange was given credit for the course and the actual architect's name was never mentioned. It's a modest parkland course over gentle terrain that tries to sell itself as "classical" in style, but it doesn't have the artistry of featuring to pull off the comparison. 4 – 5 - [1991]

Ladies' GC of Toronto, Thornhill. Stanley Thompson, 1924.

This is the only golf club in the world where memberships are restricted exclusively to women, and men may only play the course in their company. [It seems like an idea that could go big in South Korea, or at some resort destination with multiple courses.]

The only real standout hole was the par-3 7th, but the course did present an interesting study in how fairness and quality depend on one's perspective. Its 200-yard dogleg points make perfect sense for many of the golfers who play it, yet were it not for the club's membership, most people would dismiss these holes as ridiculous. 4 - - - [1991]

Maple Downs G & CC, Toronto. Bill Mitchell, 1954.

I had an interesting experience here; a friend and I just stopped in and wound up playing with a member he knew, so I arrived with no knowledge of the course, but on the first tee I asked who had built the bunker through the fairway, because it was obviously a modern positioning on an older course. [It was part of a Ron Garl redesign.] The course is built across a good piece of property, but I don't think they've gotten the most out of the ground. 4 - - - [1991]

The National G&CC, Woodbridge. George and Tom Fazio, 1976.

For three decades, The National was rated the #1 course in Canada by a magazine poll, a result clearly at odds with our own ratings. It's tough and it's in great condition, but the same is true of hundreds of other courses. The land is too handsome and diverse for there not to be more memorable holes here.

The first five holes are a bracing start; they're so difficult that they'd be a good finishing run on most courses, and that sets the tone for the day. In the end, it just amazes me that a couple of promotional events at the club's beginning could keep it in the limelight for so long. 6 6 6 6 [2004]

St. Andrew's East G&CC, Whitchurch/ Stouffville. Doug Carrick, 1989.

This private, equity club was the first of the new wave of Toronto courses, and still enjoys a fair degree of prestige. However the design has a very modern look to it: there are lots of extraneous bunkers, and several holes play through thick evergreens where you'd be lucky to find a wayward tee shot. - - 5 - [2004]

St. George's G&CC, Islington. Stanley Thompson, 1929, with revisions by Robbie Robinson, 1966.

The heavily rolling terrain of St. George's front nine is some of the most exciting land I've seen for a parkland golf course, and Stanley Thompson's routing made the most of it, though a couple of the approach shots [especially at the 4th and 15th holes modified by Robbie Robinson] are steeply uphill. St. George's strength is a terrific collection of two-shot holes, and I was pleased that when we rebuilt the greens they let us restore the par-3 3rd green to its original position, where we rediscovered the visual trickery of Thompson's original bunkering. 8 8 8 8 [2014]

Scarboro G&CC. A. W. Tillinghast, 1924, from a routing by George Cummings.

On a steep site to the east of the city, this course features three outstanding short par-4 holes at the 7th, 16th and 17th, but the par-4 18th hitting over fences and across the road is a letdown of a finish. 5 - - - [2013]

Summit GC, Richmond Hill. Stanley Thompson, 1919, from an original layout by George Cumming and George Lyon.

Compared to other cities of its size, there are fewer genuine old school hidden gems around Toronto. One pleasant exception is The Summit, designed originally by a couple of local Toronto golfers and later upgraded by a young Stanley Thompson.

Cut from thick woods, this is an out and back design with a twist, as the 10th through 15th holes loop back inside the far end of the first nine, before heading home. Highlights include the pushed up green cut into a steep side-slope on the short 2nd and the superbly undulating 12th hole, which bends along a bumpy ridge and around a large basin into a small fall-away green. The variety of valley holes and elevated tees is terrific, as are the bunkerless short fours at the 3rd and 4th.

Unfortunately during the early 2000's there was one major change, when an excellent short par four adjacent to a busy road had to be axed because of safety concerns. Although the subsequent shuffling of holes has been well handled, the walk from the 7th green along this gem to the 8th tee is most upsetting. - - - 6 [2004]

Toronto GC, Mississaugua. Harry S. Colt, 1912, with revisions by Martin Hawtree.

One of the only courses in North America actually designed by Harry Colt himself [instead of his partner C. H. Alison, who handled the firm's work here after the Great War], the Toronto course was an understated gem until the recent revision that gave it more teeth. The par-34 front side is an interesting choice: almost any other architect would have stretched one of the three long two-shotters into a par-5 to achieve a more conventional par figure, but it's a more challenging course for the good player because Colt did not. The most memorable stretch of holes is from the 9th through the 11th, although the more subtle contours of the approach to the 6th and the fairway of the 8th were admirably utilized. A weak 18th hole has never helped the course's reputation. 6 – 6 7 [2004]

Uplands G & Ski C, Thornhill. Stanley Thompson, 1922.

Once a hangout for Toronto's best players, it looked like Uplands would disappear completely after half the course was sold off in the 1980's for a housing scheme, but somehow nine of its holes have survived. The club's new sideline as a cross-country ski site in winter testifies to the challenging nature of the terrain.

The course is much too narrow, with restrictions on clearing big trees and a lack of funds to maintain it, but its adherents still revel in the challenge. The 220-yard 8th [the original 17th] is one of the most difficult par-3's I've ever seen, all carry over a stream valley to a small green shelved into the side of a steep hill, comically overgrown by trees to boot. Not even Pete Dye would build a hole that severe today, but most architects could learn a thing or two from the simplicity of the 1st hole, the daring of the short 4th, and the undulating fairway of the 5th. 4 - - - [1991]

Weston G&CC. Willie Park Jr., 1920.

I'm not well versed on Willie Park's body of work, but I enjoyed his use of the rather severe terrain here -- in fact, the tee shot along the ridge at the par-4 5th looked like the first piece of a golf hole I would have found on the topo map. The rolling property requires you to place the ball off the tee to get a good stance for your next shot -- the 6th and 12th holes being other fine examples. 6 – 6 - [1991]

Wyndance GC, Uxbridge. Greg Norman, 2007.

This modern course is part of the large ClubLink chain of affiliated private courses, and one of the most popular of the group because of its difficulty. A good portion of the course is laid out in the bowels of a restored quarry, and though there are no severe rock faces as with some of the famous quarry courses in the U.S., there are lots of big, sharp slopes to the sides of the holes, generally used to threaten the golfer instead of to contain him.

Walkability takes a back seat to drama here. Four of the better holes on the course [the 3rd through 6th] sit away from the quarry, separated from the rest by a 200-yard belt of trees. Then on the back nine, the routing jumps back and forth so that the quarry wall will be a factor on the right side of one hole and the left of another. Sacrificing a smooth flow of play for "balance" in the hazards is usually a poor trade, but only those who choose to walk will notice. 5 - - - [2014]

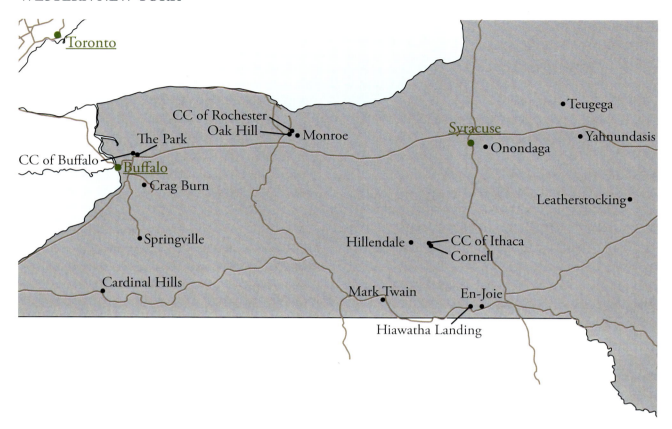

CC of Buffalo, Williamsville. Donald Ross, 1926.

Prior to visiting, I had seen pictures of the par-3 6th hole, with its tees along the rim of a quarry and a long, narrow green set on a bluff with steep drops to all sides. But I was surprised at the quality of the rest of the course, recently restored by Ron Forse. The set of short holes is outstanding from top to bottom – the 8th or 16th would be the best par-3 at 90% of golf courses in America – and the two short par-4's at the 5th and 10th each have a brilliant, unusually shaped green. The longer holes are not as distinctive, but the par-4 11th with its second shot over the edge of the quarry is daunting, and the long par-4 finisher coming back up behind the clubhouse is quite unexpected after everything out front was so flat. 6 - - - [2014]

Cardinal Hills GC, Randolph. Architect unknown.

The original nine holes date from the 1920's, and though tightly packed onto the sloping site they have quite a bit of character. Unfortunately, the more recent holes, which comprise the middle of each nine, are laid out across an open hilltop and are as basic as they come. 3 - - - [1994]

Robert Trent Jones GC at Cornell University, Ithaca. Robert Trent Jones, 1941-54.

My alma mater's course is no great wonder, but the design grew on me during my school years, leaving me to wonder if I don't underrate some of Mr. Jones' other work. The modest 350-yard gap between the middle tees and the back tees made an astonishing difference for a short hitter like myself. It was ideal for squeezing in a few holes before dark and getting one's mind off school – except that golf season is done by October! 4 - - - [1986]

Crag Burn GC, East Aurora. Robert Trent Jones, 1969.

Laid out on the site of an old farm well out in the Buffalo suburbs, Crag Burn is a fairly low-profile version of Trent Jones' work, with fescue between the holes giving it a less manufactured appearance. Scott Verplank recommended the course because of the par-5 2nd; I didn't love that hole as much as he did, but there is plenty here to like. 5 5 - - [1986]

En-Joie GC, Endicott. Ernie Smith, 1927, with revisions by Dr. Michael Hurdzan.

Host course to the former PGA Tour stop, the B.C. Open, this was a popular course among the contingent of pros who liked a tight, tree-lined course where the results were not just a putting contest. But it was really the tournament's friendly atmosphere that was the draw, not the golf course. It's been totally redone in recent years, so I won't bother repeating my dated rating of the course. NR [1984]

Links at Hiawatha Landing, Apalachin. Brian Silva, 1994.

One of the many faux links built in the 1990's, this one is in the Susquehanna River flood plain. It's okay if you like that sort of thing, but personally, I hate when inland courses use the "links" label. 4 - - - [1994]

Hillendale GC, Ithaca. Original nine holes from 1938, expanded to 18 by Mary Novickas and Darlene Sommer.

When I visited this course in my college days, it had ten holes, with an alternate finishing hole for those who played around twice; the ownership has recently expanded it to 18 holes. 2 - - - [1980]

CC of Ithaca. Geoffrey Cornish, 1958.

My mother learned to play golf on the old Country Club of Ithaca, a Tillinghast course that was destroyed to create Cornell's North Campus dorms. The university

There are few short holes more intimidating than the 6th at the Country Club of Buffalo

The par-5 4th at Monroe begins with a beautiful left-to-right diagonal tee shot.

graciously offered to pay the Country Club to have Geoff Cornish build a brand-new facility a couple of miles up the road … which has to be one of the worst trades any club ever made. 3 - - - [1981]

Leatherstocking GC, Cooperstown. Devereux Emmet, 1909.

Nobody loves baseball history more than I do, but when the sport's Hall of Fame becomes a bit too stuffy after a half day indoors, you must head to Leatherstocking, as baseball legends have been known to do. The short, old-fashioned layout touches both the lake and the hills across the road heading north out of town. There are some cool greens, a few leftover cross bunkers, and a dramatic par-5 18th hole reminiscent of Pebble Beach, with its tee on an island 100 yards out in Otesaga Lake, and the green around the shore by the hotel. 6 - - - [1980]

Mark Twain GC, Elmira Heights. Donald Ross, 1937.

Credit to my brother Dave Doak for this find, a hidden gem laid out on a hillside and operated by the town of Elmira. There are some wonderful holes and some wild greens, and it was in very good shape for a municipal course when I visited many years ago. I was a bit surprised to see Mark Twain's name associated with Elmira – he of the quote that golf was "nothing but a good walk spoiled" – but it turns out that my parents' favorite writer died and was buried here. 5 - - - [1994]

Monroe GC, Rochester. Donald Ross, 1924

Built concurrently with Oak Hill's two 18's, the neighboring Monroe is more of a family-oriented club and not nearly as busy, but it's the best piece of ground for golf in Rochester. It's a wonderful routing: from a corner clubhouse location, most of the front nine plays on a north-and-south orientation and the back nine more east-and-west, but the two finishing holes and the sensational par-4 17th play diagonally back to the northwest corner. The highest part of the ground is the far east end, and both nines tack their way uphill to get a piece of the drama coming back in. The 4th with its diagonal tee shot, the short 13th, and the long 14th are also fine holes. 7 - - - [2014]

Oak Hill CC, Rochester. East course by Donald Ross, 1924, modified by Robert Trent Jones, 1953, and by George & Tom Fazio, 1975.

Ross's original routing took full advantage of the winding creek through the middle of the property, but the Fazios re-routed some of those holes in the 1970's, after a former USGA president complained that there weren't enough holes where one could make a double bogey. They tore up one of the best holes in the country [Ross's par-4 6th] as part of a scheme to make the course tougher. Even 35 years later, the newer holes stick out like a sore thumb: the sinuous rock wall along a pond at the short 15th is the worst of it. On my recent swing through upstate New York I had it as the fifth-best Ross course I saw. 6 7 7 7 [2014]

Oak Hill CC. West course by Donald Ross, 1924.

In contrast with the more famous East course, the West has never been manipulated in the name of championship play, so the fine green settings and its more consistent character stand out. The property has some quite abrupt green sites and fairway landing areas, especially on the front nine. Many members say the back nine of the West is the best nine holes at the club … and if I was a member, I think I'd play more of my golf here. But by comparing it to the East course they are probably overrating the West, too. 6 – 5 6 [2014]

Onondaga G&CC, Fayetteville. Walter Travis, 1919.

Probably the best-conditioned course between Oak Hill and Westchester County, Onondaga sits up on a hill, operating from a gorgeous stone clubhouse. It's a good routing, but fans of Travis' quirky green contours will prefer Yahnundasis, as these greens are more reliant on tilt and speed for their challenge. 5 - - - [2014]

The Park CC, Williamsville. C.H. Alison, 1928.

The golf course at The Park Club starts out at an immediate disadvantage: you walk through an architectural marvel of a clubhouse to get to the first tee, and it would be hard to outshine that building. The course is a bit of a cousin of Milwaukee Country Club, with a river winding through the property and a couple of holes routed across to the other side, but the land is gentler and the golf holes are not as striking. 5 - - - [2014]

CC of Rochester. Donald Ross, 1914.

Laid out on gentler terrain than Oak Hill, this is a pleasant, well-maintained parkland course, but a much more typical country club offering, without any of the memorable holes that set its neighbors apart. Everyone in Rochester speaks quite highly of it today; it was a mess of trees when Masa and I saw it, and I know that they've been cleared way back now. 4 – 5 - [1980]

Springville CC. Original layout from 1922, with modifications by Roger Bugenhagen.

When I saw this course there were two crazy, sporty holes descending into the narrow tree-lined Cattaraugus River gorge; these were apparently eliminated in a redesign shortly after my visit. Most of the rest of the property is flat and forgettable, though the course does have an old-school feel to it. 3 - - 3 [2015]

Looking back up the hill on the par-4 11th at Teugega.

Teugega CC, Rome. Donald Ross, 1920.

This charming course received Donald Ross' full attention; he spent a lot of time here the year after his first wife passed away, wooing the daughter of a local member while working on Monroe and Oak Hill. A clever routing gradually introduces the best of the golfing land. The back nine, in particular, is fantastic and features some of the most distinctive holes in the Ross portfolio: Darius was partial to the unique half-pipe par-3 15th green and the sharply undulating 16th, while Tom preferred the strong par-4 11th and the long par-3 that follows it. Though somewhat dated and not maintained to big-city standards, Teugega remains architecturally untouched – a perfect destination for Ross devotees, and an educational journey for those who mistakenly believe that the likes of Oak Hill and Oakland Hills are truly reflective of his design style. 6 - - 6 [2007]

Yahnundasis GC, Utica. Walter Travis, 1924.

I didn't think this was as good a golf course as Teugega or Onondaga, as there are a few boggy flat holes mixed in on the back nine. But there are some crazy-wild Travis greens and enough undulation in the property [even where it falls in awkward spots] that his fans will find features to remember, such as the undulating 4th fairway and the difficult par-3 11th. Your golf ball might need a parachute to stay on the green if you've got to putt from the left side of the 18th green to the right, over the sort of mound for which the phrase "buried elephant" was coined. 5 - - - [2014]

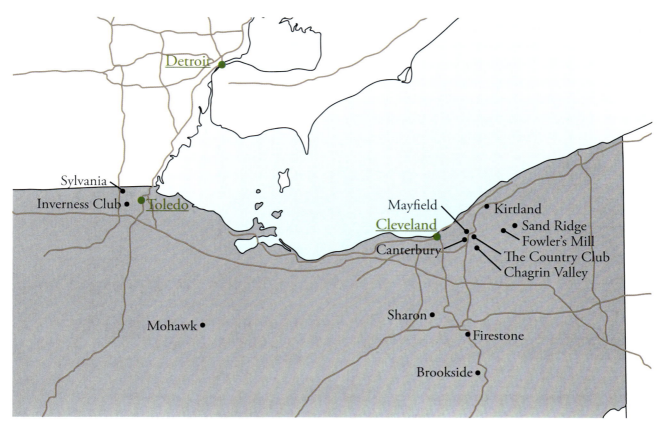

Brookside CC, Canton. Donald Ross, 1922.

Ross's fine parkland course over rolling terrain belongs in the conversation about the most difficult sets of 18 greens in America. There was a point at which the club insisted on maintaining the greens so fast that the contours were just silly, but with a combination of a bit of softening and more sensible speeds, they've come down off the ledge now. The other noteworthy feature is one of the most difficult sets of par-3 holes I've ever seen, without a drop of water involved. 6 - - - [1990]

Canterbury GC, Cleveland. Herbert Strong, 1922.

Herbert Strong's work is not as ubiquitous as many other Golden Age architects, so his designs often feel unfamiliar. Imagine playing holes like the 15th with its abrupt rise and the long 16th in the days of hickory clubs: modern courses are all soft by comparison!

Another favorite is the long two-shot 4th, routed along a ridge top. It's a shame a few more of Strong's designs aren't as well preserved as this one. My former associate Bruce Hepner has done a lot of work here getting the details right. 6 7 7 6 [2015]

Chagrin Valley CC, Chagrin Falls. Stanley Thompson, 1925.

As one of the Canadian architect Stanley Thompson's few U.S. projects, I was hoping for a real hidden gem here, but the site is a bit too steep for that: for every strong downhill par-4, such as the 12th, three others have to tack their way back up the next slope. It's a beautiful place late in the year, though, with a spectacular variety of fall colors on display. 5 - - - [1989]

Firestone CC, Akron. North course by Robert Trent Jones, 1960.

Built around a large reservoir, the

expansive property of Firestone North gave Mr. Jones ample opportunity to show off his favorite heroic holes like the par-5 16th with its approach over water, and the par-3 after it, 225 yards to a peninsula green. In contrast to its famous sister, it is an underrated course hiding in plain sight. 6 – 6 5 [1981]

Firestone CC. South course by Bert Way, 1929, redesigned by Robert Trent Jones.

Of all the courses that are overrated because of their association with professional tournaments, the South course at Firestone might be at the top of the list. The back-and-forth routing produces a bunch of monotonous par-4 holes, with flanking bunkers that may catch a ball, but never cause a second thought. Even after fifty years of TV exposure, the only hole anyone remembers is the long par-5 16th. - - 5 4 [2007]

Fowler's Mill GC, Chesterland. Lake/River nines by Pete Dye, 1971.
See the "Gourmet's Choice," pp. 16-17. - 6 - - [2015]

Inverness Club, Toledo. Donald Ross, 1920.

The charm of Inverness is that like Merion, it packs so much golfing interest into such a small property. The routing of the back nine is much like the presentation of targets in a shooting gallery, yet the big contours of the land fall in a different place on each fairway, so that no two holes are much alike. Indeed, from a quick glance at Google Earth you'd think the 1st and 10th holes were a B-movie two-headed monster, but with one green up and the other down, they couldn't play more differently. It's one of the best sets of par-4's in the game ... but a pity that only one of the par-3's is actually Ross's. The starting holes, altered in the name of keeping the course relevant for tournaments, get off on such a wrong foot that it's hard for newcomers to stay engaged for all the great holes that follow. 8 8 7 7 [2015]

Kirtland CC, Willoughby. C. H. Alison, 1921.

Ran nominates the back nine at Kirtland as the best nine holes in America that most people have never heard of; I can only vouch for not having heard of it. The 10th starts with a tee shot down into the Chagrin River valley 100 feet below, and four of the next five holes play across the river at some point, before you start working your way back up ... a funicular between the par-3 17th green and the 18th tee atop the bluff preserves the walkability of the course. The front nine isn't nearly as dramatic, but the 440-yard 9th has been put up as the single best hole on the course, as the golfer tries to avoid a deep right front pit by using the left-to-right slope of the approach to access the angled green. - 8 7 - [2015]

Mayfield CC, Cleveland. Bert Way and Herbert Barker, 1911.

The marriage of the very old Mayfield and the much younger Sand Ridge is straight out of the movie "Harold and Maude," but it saved two fine courses from bankruptcy. Many of Mayfield's holes are laid out in the bottom-lands along a stream, but it is the up-and-over holes to bridge the gaps between the valleys, like the 2nd and 9th, that make the course fascinating, and others like the 13th with its green site between two enormous mounds are simultaneously fun and stout. This is one of the few classic Golden Age designs where no one has done a proper restoration; I guess there's just not enough potential work for any designer to portray themselves as a "Bert Way expert." 6 6 - - [2014]

Mohawk G & CC, Tiffin. Donald Ross, 1919.

If you're ever driving from Columbus to Toledo, stop in to see the back nine here, laid out through a series of 15-foot ridges and valleys. If only Inverness could trade its Fazio holes for the 14th through 16th! 5 - - - [2016]

The 10th at Kirtland is the start of a terrific back nine.

Sand Ridge CC, Chardon. Tom Fazio, 1998.

Many moons ago, this course beat out both Victoria National and my own Lost Dunes for a *Golf Digest* Best New award, but that was mostly about conditioning: once superintendent John Zimmers moved to Oakmont, people started to wonder where all the great holes were. Only the heavily bunkered par-5 3rd was exciting enough for my collaborators to mention specifically. - 6 5 5 [2015]

The Sharon GC, Sharon Center. George Cobb, 1965.

This all-male club has some of the biggest greens I've ever seen; but absent interesting contours to define the strategy of the holes, it just makes for a lot of boring approach shots, little in the way of short game interest, and too many long putts. 5 - - - [1981]

Sylvania CC. Willie Park, Jr., 1916.

The ground here includes some of the most wonderful, tumbling landforms we've seen far from water, yielding a course with more interrupted fairways than anywhere this side of Pine Valley. Much of its quality is crowded out by trees today, but if fairway width is restored and the ball starts bouncing around this landscape, you will hear much more from Sylvania in years to come. - 6 - - [2012]

The Country Club, Pepper Pike. William Flynn, 1930.

Spread out over rolling parkland terrain, this relatively unheralded layout is one of the best in Ohio, and Ran prefers it to Flynn's Philadelphia courses. This one mercifully hasn't been overplanted with trees, and the wider fairway corridors allow golfers to access the strategy of the holes. Flynn remains an underrated designer, and his attention to detail shows on outstanding holes such as the par-3 9th and the par-4 15th and 17th. 6 7 6 - [2011]

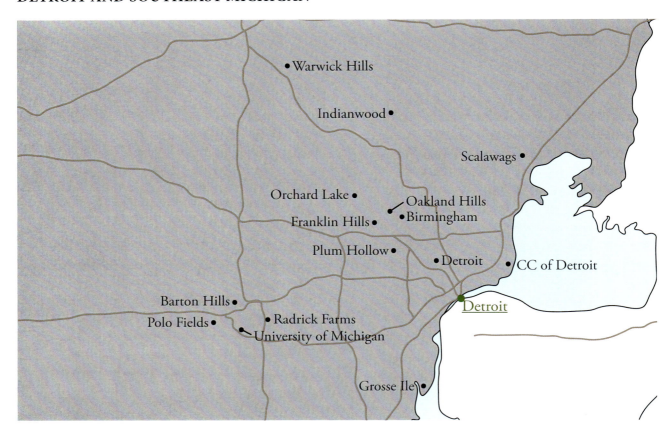

Barton Hills CC, Ann Arbor. Donald Ross, 1922.

Four miles north of Michigan Stadium, Barton Hills is built across fine rolling property that gets steeper as she goes. There's a great set of short holes, from the long and skinny 5th to the half-punchbowl 8th to the 16th across a deep valley to a difficult green. In fact, these are some of the most interesting greens I've seen, with a lot more hand-made wrinkles than most Golden Age survivors. Ron Prichard's restoration took the course up to 7,100 yards par 70, and with its deep restored bunkers and their gnarly fescue faces, it is a stern test of golf. 7 - - - [2016]

Birmingham CC. Wilfrid Reid, 1929, from two earlier nines by William Connellan and Tom Bendelow.

Ran tells me I wouldn't recognize this course and I don't doubt it, if the trees I remember on the par-3 11th are no longer there.

My former associate Bruce Hepner has just finished working here, trying to accentuate the "clamshell" knobs at the edges of greens like the 1st, 4th and 17th. Highlights include the 401 yard dogleg right 5th whose fairway bends enticingly around a depression before cascading onto the green and the bruising uphill 9th which finishes at a sprawling green with the attractive Tudor clubhouse as a backdrop. The sweeping view from the elevated first tee over the Rouge River will be glorious once their newly instituted fescue program takes hold. 4 6 - - [2016]

CC of Detroit, Grosse Pointe Farms. H.S. Colt and C.H. Alison, 1912-20.

Our work at the Country Club is one of the more successful renovation projects I've been involved with. Keith Foster had already redone the bunkering for the whole course, so our job was to re-contour all 18 greens to create as much variety as we could while sticking to the elevated green pads that Alison had left [but subsequent work had destroyed]. Factor in the magnificent clubhouse and huge trees and the polo field that the course circumnavigates, and it's got a lot more character than other flat courses do. 6 – 6 - [2011]

Detroit GC. North course by Donald Ross, 1916.

If there is a better side of Detroit to be on, this isn't it, but somehow Detroit Golf Club has survived the city's exodus in stride. The full-length North course once had a wonderful set of greens, but multiple rebuilds have eroded some of their character. 5 – 5 - [2007]

Detroit GC. South course by Donald Ross, 1916-36.

The par-68 South course, retouched by Bruce Hepner rather than rebuilt, has most of the coolest features nowadays. 5 – 5 - [2007]

Franklin Hills GC, Franklin. Donald Ross, 1926.

The central hazards that dominate play off the 2nd tee, the severe 9th green with its pronounced hump and the tiny 323 yard 13th that plays to a pulpit green will set tongues wagging. But the staunch traditionalist will be equally mesmerized by the understated tie-ins at grade from the fairways to the putting surfaces at holes like the 10th and 18th which represent Ross at his most graceful. The ebb and flow of demands make it more fun to play on a regular basis than the constant beat down administered at nearby Oakland Hills. 7 7 - 7 [2016]

Grosse Ile G & CC. Donald Ross with William Connellan, 1920.

South of the city on the way to Toledo, Grosse Ile occupies a surprisingly rolling site on an island in the Detroit River. The course is known for its difficult greens, nearly all of

The 15th at Indianwood (Old) displays a character different from others around Detroit.

The 2nd at Orchard Lake, following Keith Foster's restoration work.

which have a steep back to front pitch, sometimes augmented by hog-backed ridges that separate the left and right hole locations. This place is aching for some good restoration work, as they've lost needed hole locations at the margins of the greens, and the landscape plantings are getting in the way of golf. 5 - - - [2016]

Indianwood G & CC, Lake Orion. Old course by Wilfrid Reid and William Connellan, 1925.

It's a bit of a stretch to call Indianwood a "Detroit" course since it's an hour north of the city, but if it were closer to town it would be swamped with members. The setting is quite different than the suburban parkland courses – it's more like Shinnecock Hills than Oakland Hills, with lots of tall grasses dominating the roughs and a bit more up and down to the terrain. The greens, however, are quite repetitive, with most of the first 17 draining in to the center and out the front entrance. The huge and undulating 18th green in front of the clubhouse

is another story, but it's too late to save the day. 6 7 6 - [1989]

Indianwood G & CC. New course by Bob Cupp and Jerry Pate, 1989.

The New course is about as different from the Old as Oscar was from Felix; there are a few arresting holes, but the supporting cast is just too severe for most golfers to enjoy, with abundant wetlands crowding several fairways. Low handicappers might prefer it, but only because they know they won't lose as many balls as their opponent. 5 6 4 - [1989]

Oakland Hills CC, Birmingham. South course by Donald Ross, 1917-23, with Open doctoring by Robert Trent Jones and Rees Jones.

The South course is widely known for being the "monster" that Ben Hogan slayed in the 1951 U.S. Open, but Trent Jones' redesign stole the thunder of a wonderful Ross layout over one of the finest of parkland properties.

Holes like the par-4 10th and 11th would be standouts anywhere, with or without a major championship to call attention to them. Still, what really makes Oakland Hills a monster is not all the fairway bunkering, but the greens, which present as difficult a combination of slope and speed as anywhere in the world. My "9" here assumes that they'll eventually strip out some of the redundant bunkers added in recent years. 9 8 – 7 [2008]

Orchard Lake CC. C. H. Alison, 1926.

Not many outside of Michigan had heard of this Alison design until Keith Foster's 2012 restoration, just after Darius visited. With trees thinned and fairway width restored, there is a renewed appreciation for the human-scale undulations that define the golf here. It might not have the diversity of hazards of Kirtland or Milwaukee, but there are no dull holes either. The thoughtfully bunkered finishing holes would make any course proud, and the transformation to fescue roughs completes a handsome picture. - 7 - 6 [2013]

Plum Hollow CC, Southfield. C. H. Alison, 1921.

Based out of an office in Detroit, Hugh Alison was a busy man in the Midwest in the early 1920's. The terrain here is a bit similar to Inverness in Toledo, with a series of deep swales running across the course. There is a difficult set of short holes, but the par-4 13th is the one you'd most like to take home. 5 - - - [1981]

Polo Fields GC, Ann Arbor. Bill Newcomb, 1995.

The only memorable feature here are the back-to-back horseshoe-shaped greens at the 17th and 18th, Newcomb's tribute to the Alister MacKenzie-designed University of Michigan course. One such green might be good luck, but two in a row are ridiculous. 3 - - - [1995]

Radrick Farms GC, Ann Arbor. Pete Dye, 1965.

Radrick was Pete Dye's first 18-hole commission, built for the University of Michigan just before Pete's inaugural pilgrimage to Scotland, when his major influence was his contemporary Robert Trent Jones. He's said he wishes he had this rolling piece of farmland to work with again, but perhaps we're lucky as it's one of his few early works that is well preserved. 5 - - - [1989]

Scalawags GC, Chesterfield. Reggie Sauger, 1986.

Included only for the sake of completeness, you would never want to play here, even if you were drinking. 2 - - - [1986]

University of Michigan GC, Ann Arbor. Alister MacKenzie and Perry Maxwell, 1931.

The U of M course was restored in 1994, and is about to be restored again by Mike DeVries; perhaps this time they will get it right. Years of serving as the parking lot for Michigan football games took their toll on the layout, but there is more of MacKenzie here than at the more famous Ohio State courses, thanks to Maxwell's involvement. 5 – 5 5 [2011]

Warwick Hills G&CC, Grand Blanc. James Harrison, 1957, with modifications by Joe Lee.

Architect Harrison was a student of Donald Ross, and his design has a certain charming simplicity, though the two loops of parallel holes result in "paired" holes on the front and back sides that mimic each other, instead of adding variety to the course. Back in the late sixties, this was considered one of the most difficult courses on Tour, but before the Buick Open ceased to be, you had to be twenty under par in order to get on the first page of the leader board. If they'd handed out crystal goblets for every eagle at Warwick, Buick would have gone out of business two years sooner. 4 - - - [1986]

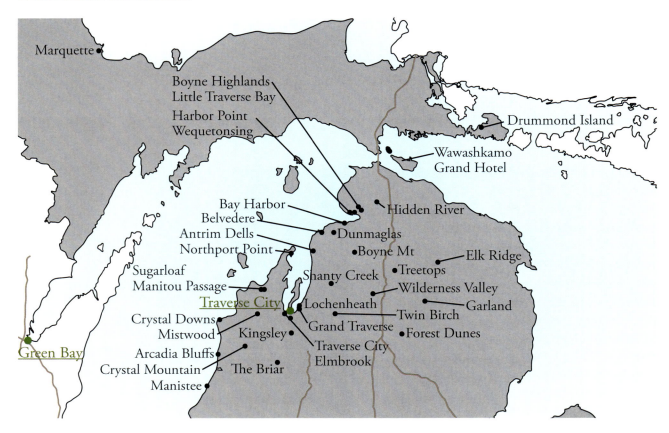

Antrim Dells GC, Ellsworth. Jerry Matthews, 1973.

    This popular public course is of simple design: nearly every green is guarded by bunkers front left and front right. 3 - - - [1987]

Arcadia Bluffs GC, Arcadia. Rick Smith and Warren Henderson, 2000.

    Built atop a sandy bluff 100 feet above Lake Michigan, Arcadia has been the most successful public course in the state since it opened for play. The scenery is spectacular, but the course is too difficult when the wind gets blowing, which in this location is a regular occurrence. The routing has been a source of confusion from the beginning: the sequence has been changed twice, but every version has had long, awkward green-to-tee transitions. I thought I might be biased against the course since it was built right in my back yard, so I was surprised to see that I gave it a higher grade than my co-authors. 6 – 5 5 [2007]

Bay Harbor GC, Petoskey. 27 holes by Arthur Hills, 1996.

    If there is ever a battle between old money and the nouveau riche, it could be fought across Little Traverse Bay, between the classic wooden boats of Harbor Point and the gaudy yachts moored at Bay Harbor. The golf is a mixed bag. There are some excellent holes on the Links nine, which play from the clubhouse down toward the harbor and back: the par-4 3rd and par-5 7th are standouts. But the much-touted Quarry nine is a bit of a mess, aside from the par-3 17th, with some exciting features used in awkward ways. And the way the 27 holes are laid out, in order to use the Links and Quarry nines together to get the best holes rated, you have to take a one-mile cart ride out and back from the clubhouse to get to the Forest nine, which is really just a front for the real estate. 5 – 5 - [1998]

The Belvedere Club, Charlevoix. William Watson, 1925.

A charming little course laid out over farm land, Belvedere is one of the best surviving examples of the work of the unsung William Watson -- he hated to be called Willie -- who sent George Thomas drawings of the 1st, 11th and 16th holes for his book on design. The little rolls around the greens and the surface drainage in those chipping areas are a work of art. For many years the club hosted the Michigan Amateur, and all of the long-time participants were sorry to see the event start to move around the state instead. They won't find many venues as fun as this one. 6 – 5 - [2010]

Black Forest GC at Wilderness Valley, Gaylord. Tom Doak, 1991.

With a construction crew of three [Gil Hanse, Mike DeVries and me], we set out to fulfill owner David Smith's mandate: he said he never wanted to hear anyone complain the course was too easy, and I'm sure he never has. The dramatic bunkering here is modeled after the great California courses of the 1920's, and lends a lot of character and contrast in the middle of the dense trees. But the difficult greens and the density of the surrounding forest give players fits. I still wonder how good this course might have been if I'd taken my foot off the gas a little. 5 7 - - [2013]

Boyne Highlands GC, Petoskey. Heather course by Robert Trent Jones, 1966.

Boyne USA have always been the big boys on the block in northern Michigan, and their expansion of Boyne Highlands and participation in Bay Harbor cemented that reputation. Trent Jones' original 18 holes are now back in one piece as the Heather; the par-5 9th is a serious three-shotter, but three of the one-shotters are just straight carries over ponds to squarish greens. 5 – 4 - [1989]

The 15th at Arcadia Bluffs shows how narrow and steep the course can get.

Boyne Highlands GC. Moor course by Bill Newcomb, 1970.

The restoration of Jones' original Heather course also grafts together Bill Newcomb's two additional nines, and reveals them as a weaker design. The par-3 holes are awful, while several of the long holes tempt you to make a 200-yard goal between trees to cut a dogleg down to size. 4 – 4 - [1989]

Boyne Highlands GC. Donald Ross Memorial by Bill Newcomb and Steven Kircher, 1989.

The most interesting course in the Boyne empire features replicas of Ross holes at Pinehurst and Inverness, but also from lesser-known gems like Wannamoisett. By trying to recreate the subtlety of Ross' greens, the course has more character and short game interest than most of what you can find in northern Michigan. However, Ross would stab his eyes out if he saw the routing, which starts with a quarter-mile ride from clubhouse to first tee, and numerous other 150-yard green-to-tee "transitions." 5 – 5 - [1989]

Boyne Mountain GC, Boyne Falls. Alpine course by Bill Newcomb, 1970.

Like the ski resort that is also part of Boyne Mountain, this course [like its younger sister] starts with a 1.5-mile golf cart ride to the starter's shack on top of the mountain, from where the golf holes zigzag down to the bottom like ski runs. The original Alpine course is straightforward but includes a fair amount of variety. 4 - - - [1986]

Boyne Mountain GC, Boyne Falls. Monument course by Bill Newcomb, 1985.

A monument to excess, Boyne Mountain's newer course is one of those modern designs that throws in all sorts of clashing features like bulkheaded bunkers, Church Pews imitations, and an island green at the par-4 18th. Today it comes off as gimmicky and overdone. 3 - - - [1986]

The Briar GC, Mesick. Oran Bishop, 1991.

Located at the headwaters of a trout stream, this is the only course I'm aware of where the developer actually went to jail, for repeated violations of wetlands regulations. You may feel like you're doing time if you play here. 2 - - - [1989]

Crystal Downs CC, Frankfort. Alister MacKenzie and Perry Maxwell, 1932.

See the "Gourmet's Choice," pp. 12-13. 10 8 9 8 [2012]

Crystal Mountain Resort, Thompsonville. Betsie Valley course by Bill Newcomb, 1977.

This ski, golf and spa facility is the epitome of a family-friendly resort, whether your kids want to train for a pro career at the best golf school in the state, or just hang out by the pool and arcade and enjoy the northern Michigan summer. But the resort succeeds on ski revenue, rather than interesting golf. At least the Betsie Valley course is walkable, as long as you don't mind finishing a good hike from the clubhouse. 3 - - - [2009]

Crystal Mountain Resort. Mountain Ridge course by Bill Newcomb, 1995.

I actually preferred the styling of the newer Mountain Ridge course to its older sibling, but the plot is ruined by the half-mile cart ride before you arrive at the first tee. I guess it didn't matter since the last three holes are routed up and over the mountain, so that no one could ever think of walking it. 4 - - - [2009]

Drummond Island GC. Gerry Gabel, 1960.

This isn't The Rock, which Domino's founder Tom Monaghan carved from the granite foundation of the island; I went up to look at that site, and told him I thought he was wasting his money. This nine holes was built around the island's airstrip, on a flat stretch of ground that had just enough soil to line every fairway with pine trees. 1 - - - [1987]

Crystal Downs CC
8th hole - 550 yards

Great three shotters are the rarest
holes in golf, and the 8th hole at my adopted
home club in Michigan manages to pull off
the feat without relying on fairway bunkers
for its interest.

Undulation is the name of the game
here. From tee to green, the hole climbs
more than 50 feet back toward the pro shop,
but it seems less because the dip just past the
driving zone takes your attention off the slope
of the fairway beyond. You can see the green
from the tee, to the right of a large maple
tree, but you have to play around the tree to
the left. If the wind is against, only the most
solid tee shots will clear a wildly undulating
bowl in the landing area: the rest will have
to assess their stance and see how long a club
they are comfortable hitting, knowing that a
safe play may mean they can't get home with
their third.

Though there are no formal hazards
on the second shot, placement is key. The left
side of the fairway is much lower than the
right, making it more difficult to judge the
approach to the smallest green on the course.
The green sits on a saddle, with any shot
short or long leaving a recovery played over
one's head to a sloping target.

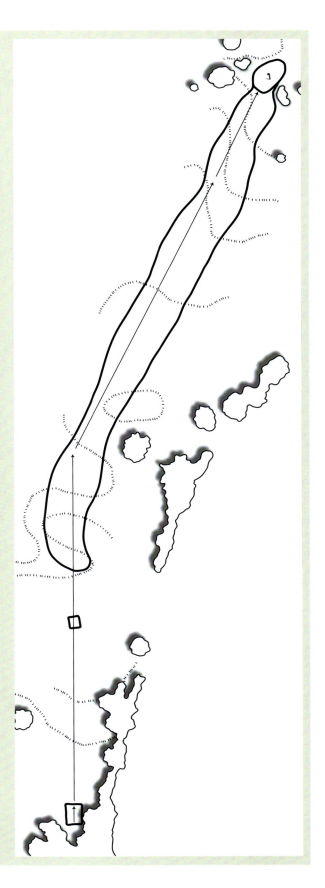

Dunmaglas GC, Charlevoix. Larry Mancour and Dean Refram, 1991.

One of the most difficult courses in the state, Dunmaglas was designed by the accomplished club professional Larry Mancour. The severity of the property combined with his straight and narrow golf game makes for a combination of interesting and difficult holes. The top of the course commands tremendous views of Lake Charlevoix, Lake Michigan, and the Fox Islands, but they abandoned plans to build a clubhouse up top, so you start down by the road and climb quickly uphill on holes that weren't built to be starters. If it were a ski run [and it's close], it would have a double-black-diamond rating: really good players may love it, but higher handicaps should shy away. 5 - - - [1991]

Elk Ridge GC, Atlanta. Jerry Matthews, 1991.

There really are elk wandering around the north-eastern corner of Michigan; the land east of I-75 is a bit removed from the beaten track of tourism. The clearings are so narrow here that on my inaugural round, a friend hit a tree on the left side of the first fairway with his opening tee shot, and the ball ricocheted across and hit a tree on the other side of the hole before it came to rest! If you manage to steer through the forest safely, your day might still be ruined by the 150-yard carry over water to the last green. 4 - - - [1990]

Elmbrook GC, Traverse City. Vern Nelson, 1964.

The typical townie daily-fee golf course, Elmbrook doesn't pretend to be anything special architecturally, but the property has just enough undulation to hold your interest in the game, particularly on the upper end of the course. Unfortunately, management's idea of interesting design are the fairway bunkers shaped like the Great Lakes on the 3rd hole. At least they didn't build ponds! 3 - - - [2006]

Forest Dunes GC, Roscommon. Tom Weiskopf and Jay Morrish, 2002.

One of the best designs from Weiskopf and Morrish, this course flew under the radar for a few years due to financial problems that delayed its opening, but it is finally on firm footing and beginning to attract national attention for its design as well as its immaculate conditioning. The mixture of wooded holes and sandy, open natural areas is appealing to almost everyone, and the greens contouring shows much more flair than Weiskopf's usual fare, especially at the short par-4 12th and 17th holes. 7 - - - [2013]

Forest Dunes GC. The Loop by Tom Doak with Brian Slawnik, 2016.

From the time I first saw the appendix to Tom Simpson's book, where he illustrated three reversible holes for an estate course, I've always dreamed of someday building a fully reversible 18 ... but I never thought I'd get the chance until our client Lew Thompson said he wanted a course that would make people want to stay at his facility and play for multiple days.

The fact that the par-3 17th on the Red routing reminds Ran so much of one of his favorite holes at Westward Ho! [the bunkerless 16th] tells you that building a reversible course is more about playing interest than esthetics. Some will try to rate the clockwise and counter-clockwise routings for the course, and miss the point: I see it as a single course with radical variety. One day you're playing a par-3 with a fallaway green like the Redan; the next you're playing a long par-4 up into the back end of the same Redan green, with a super-difficult chip if you bail out to the left with your second shot. The only certainty is that you'll have to play it at least twice to understand what's going on, and probably a lot more. 7 7 - - [2016]

The Loop at Forest Dunes
6th hole (Red course) - 122 yards
12th hole (Black course) - 381 yards

These two holes utilize the same green on alternate days, and illustrate how a good green design is always of interest even when the nature of the hole is completely different.

Playing the Red [counter-clockwise], the 6th is the shortest par-3 on the golf course, playing over a dip filled with woody ground cover plants, to a wide, shallow green that falls off at the rear.

The next day, you'll be playing clockwise around The Loop, and the green presents itself lengthwise for the approach to a beautiful short par-4. You'll have to thread the tee shot between flanking bunkers while allowing for a left-to-right slope, in order to leave a straight-on approach to the green. Playing short of the deep fairway bunker on the right leaves a more difficult second shot flirting with trees on the right and a bunker tightly guarding the right front of the green.

Garland Resort, Lewiston. Ron Otto, 1980.

I don't know how many holes owner/developer Ron Otto wound up building here; I think the course I played was later broken in two. Otto was a big believer in giving the public what he imagined they wanted – lots of water, pretty trees, minimal bunkering, and easy pickings. Gorgeous lodge, forgettable golf. 4 - - - [1986]

Grand Hotel GC, Mackinac Island. Golf from 1901, redesigned by Jerry Matthews, 1987-94.

The Grand Hotel is one of Michigan's great tourist attractions; the golf course has always been an afterthought. The idea that they have to allow golf carts on the course, when the entire island is off-limits to cars and other motorized transport, is cringe-worthy. If you get this far north, go play Wawashkamo instead. 2 - - - [1988]

Grand Traverse Resort, Acme. The Bear by Jack Nicklaus, 1984.

Developer Paul Nine complained to Jack Nicklaus that he wasn't making the golf course tough enough to attract attention to his new resort, and Nicklaus kicked it into high gear. Holes like the 4th and 5th, with their skinny angled greens defended by water front and right and deep bunkers on the other side, guarantee a six-hour round for the big convention groups that shell out to play here. I played here a few times when I moved to Michigan, and that was enough. 4 - - - [1995]

Harbor Point GC, Harbor Springs. Richard Lee and David Foulis, 1896.

The Harbor Point development is a collection of magnificent "cottages" on a private peninsula that forms the harbor of Harbor Springs. Sadly there was no room for golf on the point; their course, a mile to the west, is among the dullest I've played. 3 - - - [2004]

The tee shot on the 7th at Kingsley gives a good sense of the steep terrain.

Hidden River G & Casting Club, Brutus. Bruce Matthews III, 1998.

This is a great name for a golf course: do you get the impression that you'll be playing alongside the river? In fact, the name is meant to be taken literally. You only see the river on the ridiculously long cart ride from the 3rd hole to the 4th [and back again after the 9th], because a wide buffer was mandated to prevent the possibility of chemical runoff affecting the fishery. Even where the contours offered a chance to play along the edge of the upper ground and look down to the river, the designer shied away from the property's most interesting features. A great-looking bunker that's completely out of play at the par-3 15th epitomizes what might have been, but isn't. 3 - - - [2013]

The Kingsley Club. Mike DeVries, 2001.

The Kingsley Club is one of the more polarizing of modern designs. Its fans believe it is one of the great courses on earth, on par with Crystal Downs and unfairly judged because it's new; its detractors think it is over the top. I'm not too surprised that we all see it somewhere in between.

It is certainly a great-looking course – hilly and sandy, with a very open front nine and a few more trees present on the back – and it is one of the best-conditioned courses I've played, with wonderful fescue fairways and bent greens. The heavy contour in the fairways is more than any course I can think of. There are some great moments, like the long par-4 15th, my favorite hole on the course in spite of a green that causes regular train wrecks: at least there you have a place to play safe. Not so at the short 9th. Maybe that's okay for match play, but matches are not so dramatic when one player or another finishes in his pocket too often. Like many modern courses, it would have been much better if a friend of the architect had whispered to him to tone it down a bit, instead of jazzing it up even more. 7 7 6 7 [2015]

Little Traverse Bay GC, Harbor Springs. Jeff Gorney, 1991.

Like Boyne Mountain, this course starts at the top of the hill with panoramic views of the bay, but the first and eleventh holes are par-4's plummeting straight down to the base of the hill, and it's a death march back up to the clubhouse to end each nine. If you're not a walker, it's a well-maintained course with some reasonably interesting greens and fine views; but if you like to walk, don't even think about it. 4 - - - [2013]

Lochenheath GC, Williamsburg. Steve Smyers, 2001.

The centerpiece of a real estate development on East Grand Traverse Bay, the Lochenheath course has had a couple of iterations, as a couple of holes were sold off for real estate after a change of ownership. There are some good, big holes with Steve Smyers' manly bunkering, like the par-3 3rd and short par-4 4th, but there were also a couple of greens where a short approach would return your ball 40-50 yards back down a slope in front of the green, which is about the most frustrating brand of golf imaginable. 4 - - - [2005]

Manistee G&CC. Tom Bendelow, 1901.

This nice small town country club course touches Lake Michigan in the middle of the front nine, but only for a glimpse. 4 - - - [2009]

Manitou Passage GC, Cedar. Arnold Palmer, 1997.

The name has changed a couple of times, but this remains a fairly boring layout off the back side of the Sugarloaf ski hill. Palmer was personal friends with the original developer and so lent his name to the project, but I don't believe his design company was much involved. 3 - - - [2009]

The 6th at Greywalls plays from a tee atop granite boulders to a green surrounded by them.

Marquette GC. Greywalls course by Mike DeVries, 2005.

Greywalls is extreme golf, extremely well done. Some would dismiss the routing as unwalkable, but I walked and carried my bag without too much difficulty, as long as you discount the mile-long cart ride to and from the present clubhouse, and the 100-foot elevation difference from the 1st tee down to the 18th green.

Right from the tee of the par-5 opener, you are introduced to a wide course with oblivion beyond, featuring roller-coaster grades in many fairways and wild contours in half the greens. The short par-4 5th has one of the steepest uphill tee shots I've ever seen, and the par-3 6th requires a steep hike to both its tee AND its green, after crossing the deep valley that separates the two, while the 1st and 7th [and 18th] holes plummet down the fall line of the hillside like gnarly mogul runs. The back nine is a little more predictable than the front, with several long, parallel holes, but the green sites are well chosen and only the par-4 14th seemed unnecessarily difficult. After everything that has come before it, the downhill par-5 18th, with its flat green, seems an odd conclusion. 7 - - 6 [2014]

Marquette GC. Heritage course by William Langford and Theodore Moreau, 1926, expanded to 18 holes by David Gill.

Marquette Golf Club is one of the busiest clubs I've ever seen, cramming 30,000+ rounds into a short golf season, and the Heritage course was not nearly enough to handle it all. Langford had laid out 18 holes but only nine of them were built to start, and for some reason his routing for the back nine was disregarded when the time came to expand. There are only a couple of wild greens left that hint at what might have been. 4 - - - [2014]

Mistwood GC, Lake Ann. Jerry Matthews and Ray Hearn, 1993.

A well-used public course on the west side of Traverse City, Mistwood helped put my own High Pointe out of business; it's on the side of town where more of the golfers live, and they run a nice operation. The site is generally flat, except for one nice valley, which they dammed up to form the irrigation pond. 3 - - - [2001]

Northport Point GC. Tom Bendelow, 1913, with some bunkering by Bruce Hepner and Brian Slawnik.

Hardly anyone in Traverse City knows this course exists; it's a private club for home-owners on the point, an exclusive summer enclave that flies below the radar. The course would be a great spot to play nine holes every morning or afternoon. 4 - - - [2008]

Schuss Mountain GC, Bellaire. Warner Bowen, 1968.

One of the older resort courses in northern Michigan, it has its share of fans from an era long past, when the resort's small night club was hopping. The course itself is entirely forgettable. 3 - - - [1986]

Shanty Creek Resort, Bellaire. Legend course by Arnold Palmer and Ed Seay, 1986.

Shanty Creek was one of the big three resorts in northern Michigan in its heyday of the early 1990's, along with Grand Traverse Resort and Treetops, all of them demonstrat-ing today how far the appreciation of good golf architecture has come. The Legend runs down through deep wooded valleys and across a stream or two, but there aren't any holes where you really have to think. I've heard Tom Weiskopf's Cedar River course is better, but I've never gotten back here to check it out. 5 - - - [1988]

Sugarloaf GC, Cedar. Old course by C. D. Wagstaff, 1966.

Sugarloaf is the course for which the definition of a 2 on the Doak scale was written. The course was an adjunct to a nice family ski hill, but the ski hill closed, and somehow the golf course stays half busy. 2 - - - [1987]

Traverse City G&CC. Tom Bendelow, 1915, with revisions by Bill Newcomb.

Nobody got my joke in the first edition of this book that Noah stopped to play golf here during the Flood – the course sits atop a sandy bluff just south of downtown, so it shouldn't ever get wet. Its main attraction is "location" -- just five minutes from downtown, it's easy to skip up there for lunch or for a quick nine holes, which should never be underestimated in trying to figure the prospects of a course's success. Bendelow's original layout was the nine holes in the center of the property, which play back and forth between trees; the terrain on the outskirts is more interesting, but they haven't done a lot with it. 3 - - - [1986]

Treetops Resort, Gaylord. Robert Trent Jones course, 1986.

The fine teaching professional Rick Smith started here as the director of golf and wound up as the co-owner (!) -- not to mention as the architect of record of Treetops' third and fourth courses, which we haven't seen.

I will start by admitting a bias: I can't imagine liking a place that would officially call its courses the "Robert Trent Jones Master-piece" and the "Tom Fazio Premier" courses. The Jones course is harder than it looks … and therefore hard to enjoy. Steep banks down to trouble keep sneaking up on you, and the "signature" par-3 6th is just a straightforward hole with a 110-foot drop from tee to green. [People talk about 100-foot drops from tee to green all the time, but they are usually overesti-mating the fall by half: an actual 100-foot drop, like this one, is a crapshoot to judge and not so much fun to play.] The one course I really should see here is Threetops, the resort's par-3 course that has several steep, dropping holes but everyone thinks is good fun. 5 - - - [1986]

Treetops Resort. Tom Fazio course, 1991.

The Fazio course is on a beautiful site with deep wooded valleys, but the most memorable holes are a couple of short par-4's with overcooked greens, and it seemed that many of the opportunities for real drama were passed over. It was here that I first heard the Fazio dogma that hiding the cart paths from the golfer's view was the most important aspect of golf course design – and if you pay attention, you can find perfect valleys that were passed up for fairways because there was no place to hide the cart path for such a hole. 6 6 - - [1997]

Twin Birch GC, Kalkaska. Ron Cross, 1968, expanded to 18 holes by Joe Reske.

The facility describes itself as a "player-friendly design," which means that they don't require you to think too hard out there, but at least it is usually in reasonable condition and affordable to play. 3 - - - [1987]

Wawashkamo GC, Mackinac Island. Alex Smith, 1898.

If you're visiting Mackinac Island, this is the course to play. Hidden away on an old farm in the center of the island, Wawashkamo is one of the oldest courses in the state, and a really special little place, almost perfectly restored to its 19th-century roots by the former superintendent, Larry Grow.   Its teeny greens make approach play and chipping difficult, whether you are playing with rented hickory clubs or your own high-tech stuff.
5 - - - [1988]

Wequetonsing GC, Harbor Springs. Golf from 1896.

The old-money answer to Little Traverse Bay, Wequetonsing has a similar setting overlooking the bay, but with its clubhouse down low and much handier to town. They didn't bother to build a clubhouse to look like Augusta National, since one or two of the members here are also members there.
3 - - - [1987]

Wilderness Valley GC, Gaylord. Valley course by Al Watrous, 1971.

The sister course to my Black Forest, this is a short and playable eighteen laid out by the long-time professional at Oakland Hills, whose most famous result as a player was his runner-up finish to Bobby Jones in the 1926 Open Championship at Royal Lytham. His foray into golf course design was not as illustrious.
2 - - - [2007]

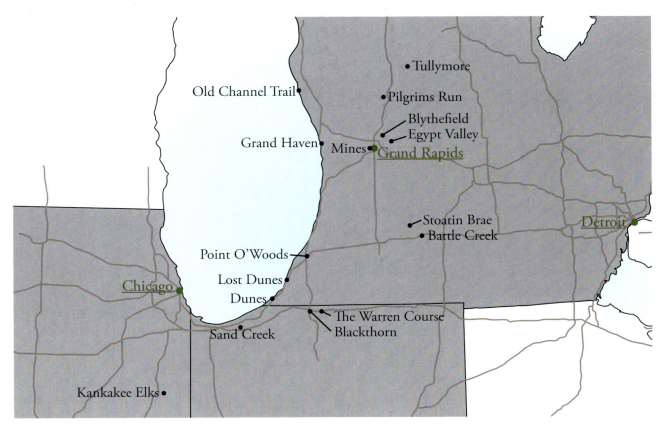

Battle Creek CC. Willie Park, Jr., 1919.

The "Cereal Capital of the World" is no longer a boom town, but it was big enough in its day to warrant an excellent country club course. Laid out over gently rolling terrain, its primary quality is a wonderful set of greens, including the difficult 18th with a seven-foot false front ... and not much flat space beyond! 6 - - - [2012]

Blackthorn GC, South Bend, IN. Michael Hurdzan and Dana Fry, 1994.

This affordable public course has 19 holes in total, including a 266-yard betting hole, known as the Blarney Hole, in play to settle deadlocks or simply allow a little extra fun. The left-bending par-4 opener can be played as the 2nd if you want to start with the Blarney and continue from there.

It's a good routing, working around wetlands across uneven terrain. Better holes include attractive par threes at the 3rd and 13th,

and undulating par fives at the 4th and 18th. It's a local favorite in the South Bend area, but probably not one we'd travel to see. - - - 5 [2011]

Blythefield CC, Belmont. William Langford, 1928.

Blythefield was one of the first Langford courses I saw, and a pretty dull affair it is. The club wouldn't listen to my thoughts on revisions; maybe their forefathers didn't listen to Langford, either. The holes down by the Rogue River are the most memorable, but only the long par-3 13th makes use of the river. 4 - - - [1992]

Dunes GC, New Buffalo. Dick Nugent, 1991.

Mike Keiser's first foray into golf course development is the nine-hole Dunes Club, conceived to prevent the small plot near his summer home from being developed with houses. At first it was just a lesson

The home green at The Dunes Club epitomizes its simple but challenging design.

in cost-efficient construction – the tiny clubhouse keeps costs at bay, so that it can survive on the dues of fifty members – but why not also try to make it like Pine Valley, with sandy wastes outside the fairways, and free-form tees with no tee markers? It's a bit narrow for my tastes, and the greens contouring does not show the same level of sophistication as the rest of the design, but it is still comfortably one of the best nine-hole courses in America and a wonderful example of how simple golf can be. 7 7 – 7 [2015]

Egypt Valley CC, Ada. 36 holes by Arthur Hills, 1990.

Created as part of a land-swap deal so that the club's former property [near downtown Grand Rapids] could be developed, Egypt Valley is symptomatic of the type: the club ethos completely changes when someone else is footing the tab. They moved from a walkable, forgiving 18 holes to a big, hilly, carts-only

layout way across town. Does any club really benefit from such a deal? I'm not sure which of the two courses I saw, but I don't want to meet the sister. 4 - - - [1993]

Grand Haven GC. Bruce Matthews, 1965.

Grand Haven's success has been the foundation for two subsequent generations of Matthews as architects. A well-regarded public track through pine trees close to Lake Michigan, it has some good two-shot holes and an interesting set of greens, but the clearings are some of the narrowest I've seen. Many holes are just 30 yards from tree line to tree line, which isn't enough for me. 4 - - - [1986]

Kankakee Elks CC, Saint Anne, IL. William Langford and Theodore Moreau, 1926.

A modest club in a blue-collar town, the Elks course is an audacious design, chock full of Langford's bold greens and abrupt fairway hazards in spite of a fairly low-lying site. Unfortunately, as with many Langford designs, the wide scale of his fairways and features has been compromised by over-planting, so that key parts of the strategy are no longer available for play. 5 - - - [2015]

Lost Dunes GC, Bridgman. Tom Doak with Tom Mead, 1999.

Less than a mile inland from Lake Michigan, this modern-looking course in an abandoned sand quarry was one of my first designs to attract attention. It is my most difficult set of greens, with a variety of hole locations that require different avenues of attack on different days. The key to scoring is not to leave yourself an impossible lag putt up and over the internal contours, even if it means missing the green short or wide. Two huge ponds come into play on eight of the last eleven holes, yet the most memorable features of the course are the "dry" holes like the long par-4 2nd with its green tucked behind a gnarly mound on the left, the short par-5 4th with its wicked back shelf, and the long par-4 11th [pictured below]. I'd worried that the noise from Interstate 94 would turn off golfers, but that's never been a factor. My co-authors wish the playing surface was bouncier, but that's hard to pull off in this humid, sandy bowl. 7 6 7 6 [2012]

The Mines GC, Grand Rapids. Mike DeVries, 2005.

Built through a hilly collection of old mine works on the west side of Grand Rapids, The Mines is a rollicking little track that has proven quite popular, though it is much more severe in spots than one would script for a public golf course. The very first hole swoops sharply downhill on the second shot to a difficult green, and within a couple of holes you realize that hole is the rule for the course, not an exception. It's just unfortunate that it is too hilly for most people to walk. 5 - - 5 [2013]

The two-tiered 11th green at Lost Dunes sits back in a dramatic natural bowl.

Old Channel Trail GC, Montague. Woods nine by Robert Bruce Harris, 1926.

There is also an 18-hole course here by Jerry Matthews, but the only reason to see the place are the unique, overgrown grass bunkers that Harris left behind; I've never seen hazards quite like them. I'm baffled why they didn't try to copy the style on their newer course; it would have been easy to do, and a lot more interesting than what they got. 4 - - - [1989]

Pilgrim's Run GC, Pierson. Design committee with Mike DeVries and Kris Shumaker, 1998.

The program for this course sounds like a complete disaster – six of the developer's friends were entrusted to design three holes each, with the help of a young architect and superintendent to build them. Fortunately, most of the committee leaned heavily on the talents of their helpers, resulting in the best course we've seen in the Grand Rapids area. On Ran's recent visit, the course was crawling with children out learning the game ... it's refreshing to find a course with architectural interest that is affordable enough for golfers to engage. 6 6 - 5 [2016]

Point O'Woods G & CC, Benton Harbor. Robert Trent Jones, 1958.

One of Trent Jones' most respected works, the Point was a staple of the top 100 lists for many years, based on two strengths: it was a vivid contrast to the Chicago parkland courses that most of its members called home, and as host club for the Western Amateur, it held the young and strong at bay for 30+ years. But all courses known for their difficulty eventually cede the title to newer models. The par-5 2nd with its skinny green defended by water is still a tough target for those who want to get in red figures early. But the signature par-3 9th hole, 210 yards over water, is no longer a hole that strikes fear into scratch players' hearts. 6 – 6 - [1998]

Sand Creek Club, Chesterton, IN. 27 holes by Ken Killian and Dick Nugent, 1976.

Featuring sandy wastes on a few holes [notably the par-5 16th], this modernist design made a splash in the early 80s, when low-maintenance design was touted as the wave of the future. But between the flat site and the surrounding homes, it's no Pine Valley. 5 - - - [1985]

Stoatin Brae GC at Gull Lake View, Augusta. Renaissance Golf [Eric Iverson, Don Placek, Brian Schneider and Brian Slawnik], 2016.

The first course designed and built by my associates, without my involvement, is the sixth course owned by the Scott family at Gull Lake View resort. In contrast to its heavily wooded cousins, the new course is on a wide-open site atop a bluff, with big views in spots of the Kalamazoo River valley and downtown Battle Creek.

After some fairly open holes at the beginning, the course kicks into another gear at the par-5 6th, and then the short-par 4 8th features a skinny green with fall-offs to both sides. Holes 10 through 14 make an elegant loop around one another at the north end of the course, and the run home is full of very good holes, too. Pick of the litter are the three par-3's on the back nine, as good a set as any of my own. 6 - - - [2016]

Tullymore Golf Resort, Stanwood. Jim Engh, 2001.

Set among attractive marshes and lakes, Tullymore is an unconventional resort course noted for its skinny greens. Unfamiliar with Jim Engh's work, Darius found his style jarring here in the woodlands of the Canadian Lakes region. The deep, grass-faced bunkers are lost visually in the lush landscape and the shadows from the trees, so that fairways and greens seem to lack definition.

The 11th at Stoatin Brae, almost ready for its close-up.

Tullymore's heroic par threes are some of the toughest anywhere, demanding all-or-nothing tee shots over hazards into difficult targets. The most severe is the 12th, where from the back tee you need to drive more than 250 yards across a swamp to have any chance of reaching a hidden Dell green. More appealing are holes like the 17th, with its concave target lined by deep traps, and the back nine par fives, which all sweep left but use hazards and narrow greens more effectively than some of the earlier holes. The reachable par four 3rd, for instance, has a tiny green that would tempt most to play an aggressive shot were it not for the tall oaks and large frontal bunker that force an awkward layback and conspire to destroy any semblance of strategy for the vast majority of players.
- - - 4 [2007]

The Warren Course at Notre Dame, South Bend, IN. Bill Coore and Ben Crenshaw, 1999.

One of the things I admire most about Bill and Ben's early work is how immune they seemed to worrying about winning awards. The Warren Course is a perfect example: their goal was to build an intimate, easily walkable course which wasn't too difficult for the students and faculty, but one which could accommodate collegiate events. Driving by, you'd assume it's just another old country-club layout on a flattish site, but holes like the 13th constitute great flat-land architecture, and the three finishing holes really amp up the drama. The greens are purposefully contoured and well bunkered, making this a closer cousin to Winged Foot than any modern design I can recall. 6 6 - 6 [2016]

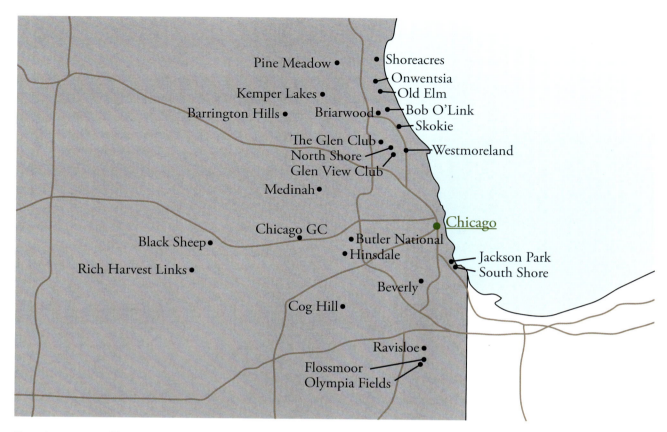

Barrington Hills CC. George O'Neil and Joe Roseman, 1921.

An overlooked small gem in the Chicago district, Barrington Hills is a rock-solid layout with a rare set of rolling greens as the foundation of an excellent test. There's nothing flashy about it, and no signature hole to hang its hat on, but there aren't many courses in Chicago with more day-to-day interest than this one. 5 - - - [1996]

Beverly CC, Chicago. Donald Ross, 1916.

Beverly is one of the courses that I sorely underrated in the original edition of this book; it was so choked by trees back then that it was hard to appreciate the undulation of the property and how well it was used in the design. A severe 30-foot drop-off running across the property on the front nine was once the shoreline of a larger Lake Michigan, and most of the back nine is laid out over the top of the low, rolling dunes formed by the older lake. The most memorable holes are the par-5's – the 2nd has a fine tee shot from the escarpment, the 7th requires you to drive back up the hill, and the long 11th is a true three-shotter with an undulating fairway and a wicked back-to-front green. Together, they must be one of the best sets of par-5 holes in the country. 7 7 5 - [2012]

Black Sheep GC, Sugar Grove. David Esler, 2002.

The first new course designed by David Esler, Black Sheep is a men's club with 27 holes built across an open, rolling cornfield, yet it's an appealing venue with great intimacy and flow. The bunkering is rugged and extensive, but it's quite consistent in rewarding the golfer who can play close to a hazard with a better line to the green. Darius' recommendation is to skip the nearby Rich Harvest Farms and try to play here instead. - - 5 6 [2007]

Bob O'Link GC, Highland Park. Donald Ross, 1916, with revisions by C. H. Alison.

One of its members described the atmosphere of Bob O'Link as "a fraternity house with a golf course," and that's probably as much of the reason it's famous as the golf course itself. Classic parkland in character, it benefits from an expansive property so that the holes never feel packed in together, but the longer holes rely too much on bunkering to make up for the lack of terrain features. They've just completed a major renovation here, but we haven't seen that part. 6 – 6 - [1989]

Briarwood CC, Deerfield. C. H. Alison, 1921.

Alison's work is never bland, but this course is on a smaller property than most, and doesn't really have the same sense of expansiveness and scale. It's also got a lot of big trees of the kind that start to interfere with play, but are too big to take down. 4 – 5 - [2003]

Butler National GC, Oak Brook. George & Tom Fazio, 1974.

Before political correctness made it *verboten* for an all-men's club to host a public event, Butler National had 17 years as host of the Western Open, and it was never conquered; in fact the Tour erected grandstands on certain back tees so as to hide that the pros weren't even playing it from all the way back. After the Tour left, its reputation started to wane, so Tom Fazio was retained to strengthen it even further! I haven't seen the latest iteration, but I suspect a tougher Butler National might be too much for me. 6 – 6 6 [2007]

Chicago Golf Club, Wheaton. Charles Blair Macdonald, 1895, modified by Seth Raynor. 1925.

One of the five founding clubs of the U.S.G.A., and the only one west of Philadelphia, Chicago Golf is one of the most exclusive of old-school clubs, and America's closest

The clubhouse at Chicago Golf Club, viewed from the 18th hole.

The fourth at Flossmoor is an underrated short par-4 on an underrated course.

cousin to Muirfield. A few of the holes closer to the clubhouse are intact from Macdonald's original design, including the long 1st and the par-3 10th over a pond, but the intimidating 220-yard Redan and the Punchbowl 12th and a lot of the most dramatic holes are the product of Raynor's 1925 reconstruction, done with his mentor's blessing but not with his involvement. Sadly, with a small membership and no unaccompanied guest play, it is one of the most under-utilized great courses in America, and often appears to be deserted. 8 8 9 8 [2012]

Cog Hill GC, Lemont. No. 4 (Dubsdread) course by Dick Wilson and Joe Lee, 1964.

   With four courses in all, Cog Hill is a wonderful public golf facility, and Dubsdread has always been its attention-getting flagship. But that reputation took a big hit after ownership tried to strengthen the course to attract a

U.S. Open deal, and Rees Jones's changes were so poorly received that the course lost its place as annual host to the Western Open, instead. In truth, it was never a classic design – even Tiger Woods, who won here five times, said the greens were much too big for a U.S. Open type course. It's still a tough test for any and all comers, but it doesn't have as much variety as it used to have. 6 – 6 5 [2007]

Flossmoor CC. Herbert Tweedie, 1899, with revisions by Harry Collis.

   Without doubt, the ability of man to intelligently bunker a course greatly improved throughout the Golden Age. Once symmetrical, artificial and poorly placed, bunkers became works of art that enhanced the landscapes. The same is not necessarily true for the evolution of greens. Greens built around 1900, such as the ones here, closely adhered to the ground and its natural tilt, instead of being routinely built up in the back to receive indifferent approaches. Personally, I have a lot of time for these old fashioned greens and the ones at Flossmoor are some of the most appealing of this genre. Look no further than the first hole. The green is an extension of the fairway, is angled to the right and falls toward the rear. Golfers get near this par 5 green in two but routinely take three to get down. Add other, lay-of-the-land, tilting greens like those at the 3rd, 4th, and 12th to the elevated ones on knolls like the last three, and you have an unheralded course of character. - 7 - - [2012]

The Glen Club, Glenview. Tom Fazio, 2001.

Created from the runways of a naval air station, The Glen Club is a well-funded attempt to put the right product in the right market, despite its lack of natural attributes. That it has worked out well is a fair indication of the lack of variety available to public golfers in Chicago. 5 - - - [2001]

Glen View Club, Golf. Herbert Tweedie, 1897, revised by William Flynn, 1922.

Host to the U.S. Open of 1897, and home club of pro Jock Hutchison and amateur legend Chick Evans, the present Glen View course is the work of William Flynn, who expanded it in the 1920's. The front nine sits up on a low, forested bluff, while the back nine sits down in the valley of the North Fork of the Chicago River, requiring water carries on every hole except the 15th and 16th. 6 - - - [2012]

Hinsdale GC. Donald Ross, 1913.

This is a nice old club, but neither the greens nor the bunkering have even an inkling of the character typical of Donald Ross' work. The class of the course are the short holes, especially the 13th with its steeply sloping green, and the long 16th with the "Andy Gump" bunker off its right shoulder. 4 - - - [1995]

Jackson Park GC, Chicago. Tom Bendelow, 1899.

Built on the grounds of the Columbian Exposition, Jackson Park lies close to the University of Chicago, and provides affordable golfing opportunities for south side residents. Perhaps its proximity to the home of President Obama will someday lead to its refurbishment. 2 - - - [2013]

Kemper Lakes GC, Hawthorn Woods. Ken Killian and Dick Nugent, 1978.

Here's the corporate approach to giving the golfer what he wants: fast greens, high-end maintenance, lots of water hazards, and a premium price. The bottom line says it's been a winning formula in Chicago, but the course leaves me cold – the lines of the fairways and bunkers look like they came straight out of a blueprint machine, and the challenging finishing holes have too much water in play for their own good. 5 – 4 - [2000]

Medinah CC. #3 course by Tom Bendelow, 1928, remodeled by Rees Jones.

There is no other golf club in America comparable to Medinah, with 54 holes of golf serving three different constituencies of its membership. Put them all together with the huge, Moorish-inspired clubhouse – with a rotunda bigger than some state capitols – and it's quite an impressive collection.

I've never been a fan of course #3, which has often had to reinvent itself after Cary Middlecoff or Lou Graham cast doubt on its ability to produce the most worthy champion. [Tiger Woods' two PGA Championship victories finally put an end to their inferiority complex.] It's a relentless test through the trees, lacking in finesse holes or interesting contours, and these weaknesses were never addressed in the renovations, because being perceived as big and strong is its whole reason for existence. [The drivable 15th, added by Rees Jones for the Ryder Cup, was a tentative step in the right direction.] Suffice to say that my co-authors have yet to inquire about using my honorary membership to go play #3. 6 – 5 5 [2012]

Medinah CC. #1 course by Tom Bendelow, 1925, redesigned by Tom Doak with Brian Schneider, 2014.

I rarely do redesign projects, because it's hard to get all the members on board, so I was surprised to be chosen to work on Course One, after half of it was destroyed to build the infrastructure for the 2012 Ryder Cup. Course One had been handicapped by a long, narrow routing along the creek that feeds Lake Kadijah, but we were able to remove trees in the mid-section of the course and play diagonally into the corridors of other holes, preserving the best of the old course [like the run from the 7th through 9th] while adding the short game interest that the big course lacks. I've never done work at any course which has been so well received by the membership. 6 - - - [2014]

Medinah CC. #2 course by Tom Bendelow, 1925.

Medinah's second course is the facility that every big club wishes it had – a whole golf course that caters to family play, so that the big course(s) aren't tied up by beginners who are in over their heads. Bendelow's design here is almost intact, and I hope it retains its character through its refurbishing, as it would be a shame for his work to completely disappear from the club. 4 - - - [2012]

North Shore CC, Glenview. C. H. Alison, 1924.

In the 1970's and 80's, North Shore was considered among Chicago's elite courses, because they had managed to stretch it to 7000 yards and earn a token spot on the *Golf Digest* 100 Greatest list. But, the loss of many elm trees exposed the dearth of other features on the property, and the course has struggled to regain its status. 5 – 5 - [1995]

Old Elm Club, Highland Park. Donald Ross, 1913.

An all-men's club for the older generation, this is a course perfectly suited to its membership. The shortness of the course is seen as an asset rather than a handicap. The open green fronts accommodate 4-wood approaches by the oldest of members, while the undulations of the fairways and greens are enough to keep better players on their toes. The bomb and gouge set may not be impressed, but they aren't likely to be invited here to begin with. 6 – 4 - [1994]

Olympia Fields CC. North course by Willie Park Jr., 1923.

In its heyday during the Roaring Twenties, Olympia Fields was the greatest golf community in America, including four courses, its own school system and fire department. Only two courses are left today, and the North is the more celebrated, as host to the U.S. Opens of 1928 and 2003. It has a good variety of holes on rolling parkland, with a handful of steep putting surfaces, and a standout hole in the big par-4 14th, with its second shot over a creek to an elevated green. Refinements for the 2015 U.S. Amateur were especially interesting: some greenside fronting bunkers were removed as superfluous. 7 8 6 6 [2015]

Olympia Fields CC. South course by Tom Bendelow, 1915, redesigned by Steve Smyers, 2007.

Only Ran has seen the Smyers revisions here, and he was most enthusiastic about the South course. This was always the best property at Olympia Fields, with Butterfield Creek winding across eleven of the 18 holes, and the drive-and-pitch 6th with its green perched high in the air never received the praise it deserves. The new South is now as strong a test of golf as its more famous sibling. 7 7 5 - [2015]

The Onwentsia Club, Lake Forest. James Foulis, Robert Foulis, H. J. Tweedie and H. J. Whigham, 1895, with revisions by Tom Doak.

Going in the front door of its fashionable brick clubhouse, you might expect great things of a course that hosted the U.S. Amateur and Open championships in its early years, but those were the days when a club's social standing meant much more than its golf course. The course out back was a 5700-yard layout that no one would restore, but we did what we could to add interest. 5 5 - - [2000]

Pine Meadow GC, Mundelein. Joe Lee and Rocky Roquemore, 1985.

This modern public facility looks like an old private club, because it was, so they were able to utilize the older trees and mature parkland as part of the new layout. It's one of the best public courses around Chicago, but there is nothing that an out-of-towner ought to see. 4 - - - [1988]

Ravisloe GC, Homewood. James Foulis, 1901, with revisions by William Watson and Donald Ross, and restoration by David Esler.

When I saw Ravisloe twenty years ago, it was a private Jewish club with a declining membership, and a course in disrepair. Opening to public play has transformed the financials and the condition of the course, to the delight of daily-fee golfers on the south side. The Mission-style clubhouse is one of the region's most distinctive. 5 - - - [1997]

Rich Harvest Farms, Sugar Grove. Greg Martin and Jerry Rich, 1998.

How can a private golf course which rates a 4 on the Doak scale be rated as one of the top sixty courses in America?   Either owner Jerry Rich is one hell of a guy, or *Golf Digest* panelists have lost their minds. Actually, it's probably both. - - 4 3 [2007]

If you've driven anywhere near these bunkers on the 6th at Olympia Fields (South), good luck.

Shoreacres
15th hole - 521 yards

Though Seth Raynor was beholden to most of the concepts his mentor C.B. Macdonald brought back from Scotland and England, one prominent exception was the idea of a sharp doglegged hole, inspired by one of the entries in the competition to design a hole for Long Island's Lido course.

His first use of the concept was the 15th at Shoreacres. A deep ravine running through the property is used to enforce the dogleg. The closer one can play to the ravine off the tee, the shorter the second shot, whether the aim is to get home to the green, or simply to get across the ravine in two to set up a reasonable approach. A line of shallow cross bunkers on the far side of the ravine force an intermediate decision for the average member, while the narrow end of the first fairway gives a good angle for attacking the green with a long third shot, if one is forced to lay up after a poor drive.

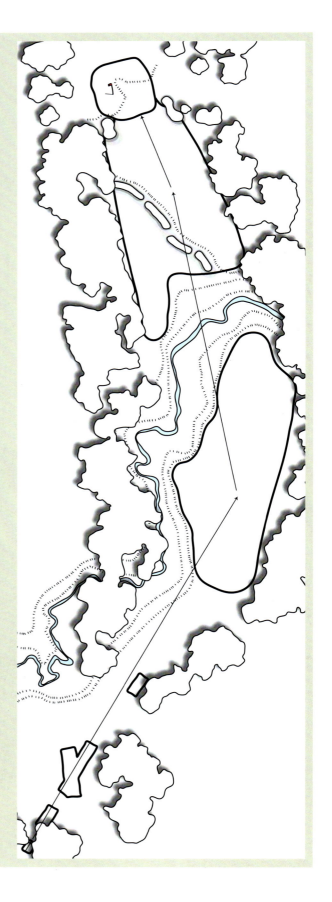

Shoreacres, Lake Bluff. Seth Raynor, 1922.

One of Raynor's finest layouts, Shoreacres is a must-see for fans of his work. The clubhouse sits on the shore of Lake Michigan, but the golf course is out back, routed around several deep ravines whose sharp banks meld perfectly with Raynor's construction style. In addition to the usual template holes – including an especially good version of the Road hole at the 10th – there are some wonderful originals like the short par-4 11th with its fairway surrounded by the ravines, and the par-5 15th (at left). I had been consulting here for twenty years and thought the course was 95% restored, but in the final round they threw off the gloves and took it to 120%, with bold grassing lines that invite approaches to skid off the greens into trouble. At 6,521 yards it will never host championships, which is one reason it will always remain a delight. 8 7 8 7 [2015]

Skokie CC, Glencoe. Tom Bendelow, 1904, remodeled by Donald Ross and William Langford.

The product of several different designers and multiple renovations, Skokie is a good parkland course with some difficult greens [courtesy of Ross] and some unusual bunkering [courtesy of Langford]. There is a fine set of par-5 holes, each of which puts pressure on the second shot, but the showstopper is Langford's 220-yard 12th hole, across water to a high platform green. Chicago clubs have certainly stepped up their game: when Skokie was rebuilt by Ron Prichard ten years ago, it was easily in the city's top five, but after a wave of other top-flight restorations, it now has to fight for a place in the top ten. 6 7 6 - [2007]

South Shore GC, Chicago. Tom Bendelow, 1906.

This nine-hole course, taken over by the city after the club failed in the Depression, owns impressive frontage on Lake Michigan, but utilizes little of it in the current configuration. For now, its main claim to fame is that the clubhouse was the site of the wedding of Barack and Michelle Obama. 2 - - - [2013]

Westmoreland CC, Wilmette. Joseph Roseman, 1911, revised by many.

I understand that Arthur Hills did a major renovation of Westmoreland in the early 1990's, so my rating of it is outdated. The previous iteration of the course was not especially interesting, with too many parallel holes. I hope they didn't tear up the long par-4 3rd, with its blind second shot and stop-light signaling system. 4 - - - [1988]

Blackwolf Run GC, Kohler. River course by Pete Dye, 1986-90.

The River is the course Mr. Dye always wanted to build – its middle holes go down into a wooded area that Mr. Kohler had held back from golf at the outset, starting with the par-4 5th from a high tee. The Sheboygan River comes into play early and often, and there is enough elevation change to provide high drama at the par-5 8th and 16th. Many have opined that the multiple-fairway 9th is one of Mr. Dye's best holes, but with a bunch of trees in play off the tee, for my tastes it is a bit of overkill. It's a major accomplishment to play to your handicap here. 7 7 6 6 [2007]

Blackwolf Run GC. Meadow Valleys course by Pete Dye, 1986-88.

The expansion of the original Kohler course from 18 holes to 27 to 36 split the original holes between the two courses. The strong back nine became the 1st and 11th through 18th holes of Meadow Valleys. The finishing stretch from the original back nine features some of the best holes on property, notably the par-3 15th; but the front nine are the blandest holes at Kohler. 5 – 6 5 [2007]

Blue Mound G & CC, Wauwatosa. Seth Raynor, 1926.

Blue Mound is about what you'd expect to find seeking out a Raynor course in Milwaukee, but it was a hot mess the first time I saw it, so credit to Bruce Hepner for helping the club clear out a forest of nursery trees and get the greens back out to where they belonged. The ridges and terraces in these greens are some of the wildest I've seen in the Raynor / Macdonald collection. The downhill Short 7th that drops down by the Menomonee River is distinctive, as is the crazy 8,000 square foot Punchbowl green at the long 8th back up the hill. 6 7 - - [2013]

Chenequa CC, Hartland. Tom Bendelow, 1912, expanded to 18 holes by Roger Packard.

Driving past this course on my way south from Erin Hills, the terrain was exciting enough to make me pull over and go for a walk. The two nines are separated by a considerable gap, which is good so that the newer holes don't infect the original nine. 4 - - - [1998]

Erin Hills GC, Erin. Mike Hurdzan, Dana Fry and Ron Whitten, 2009, with lots of editing by USGA executive director Mike Davis.

Set across gorgeous Wisconsin countryside, there have already been three versions to this young course. The first change was brought about by a change in ownership, and the second by the deal to host major events. What remains is an expansive course that's just a brute to walk, even though it's walking-only. Holes like the par-4 12th across exhilirating, tumbling land fully capture the property's potential; others like the 17th have been neutered.

Though we all believe a better course could have been built on this site, and we are concerned at the precedent being set by the USGA in stretching a course beyond 8,000 yards for "tournament flexibility," we suspect that Erin Hills will make for more interesting golf than many other U.S. Open sites. Ran gleefully predicts that the downhill 9th to its long, narrow green -- a "bye hole" in the original design -- will have the professionals screaming bloody murder in 2017. 6 7 6 6 [2013]

Green Bay CC. Dick Nugent, 1995.

A big and bold modern design, the Green Bay course was built on prime property, with dramatic elevation changes, mature hardwoods, and a looping river. Sadly, it was also built in the age of concrete cart paths, island greens and 650-yard par fives. I wish we'd seen what Donald Ross would have done with the same property. 5 – 3 - [1994]

The 17th green at Erin Hills [foreground], with the 12th and 10th in the background.

Kenosha CC. Donald Ross, 1922.

Just a couple of miles from the big lake, Kenosha's clubhouse sits up on a small bluff, with most of the course in the river flood plain below ... but it's more rugged and interesting than I made it sound. 5 - - - [1996]

Lawsonia Links, Green Lake. William Langford, 1930.

See the "Gourmet's Choice," pp. 24-25. 7 7 – 6 [2007]

Legend at Brandybrook, Wales. Ron Kuhlman, 1993.

I cannot remember the circumstances by which I was asked to have a look at this course, or the details of it. Perhaps it was all just a bad dream? 2 - - - [2003]

Milwaukee CC. C. H. Alison, 1929.

Overlooking the Milwaukee River in the city's northern suburbs, this rolling property is one of the best pieces of ground Alison had to work on during his residency in America. The front nine occupies higher ground, with an especially good stretch of holes from the 5th through 9th, and then the back nine brings the river into play on nearly every hole from the 10th to the 15th, before working back up to the clubhouse with three difficult holes to finish. A couple of unfortunate changes made ten years ago have now been expunged.

The club atmosphere is also special: the men's locker room is a place you could spend all day, and as soon as you walk out the door you step right onto the first tee, overlooking the fairway in the valley below. By the same token, at the end of the day, you've got to be very careful not to overshoot the 18th green: just off the back, there's a tightly-mowed bank that will carry the ball down onto the first tee, or if you're long and right, right through the door to the pro shop! 7 8 7 6 [2013]

Oneida G & Riding C, Green Bay. Stanley Pelchar, 1928.

Packerland's old-guard standard, the members swear by Oneida, with its large, deep greens flanked by long blobby bunkers. Even the two most interesting holes, the short par-4 7th and 15th, are both 90-degree doglegs to the left. 5 - - 5 [2015]

Ozaukee CC, Mequon. William Langford and Theodore Moreau, 1924.

I was only able to play nine holes here before we were put off by rain, but had the impression this could be a really good course if an architect could convince the members to cut some trees. [Unfortunately, I also got the impression that the architect would have to enlist Henry Kissinger to negotiate over the tree removal.] The greens are large and feature some difficult shelved hole locations, though my favorite hole was the "easy" short par-5 15th. 5 - - - [1991]

Pine Hills CC, Sheboygan. Harry Smead, 1928.

Formerly the Sheboygan Country Club, this semi-private club is worth a detour if you visit Kohler. There's a fine set of par-3's, and two gorgeous par-4's built around a swift-flowing stream. The contours of the land are wonderful, but the narrow, elevated greens detract from the feel of it a little bit, even as they add to the challenge. 5 - - - [1987]

Sand Valley GC, Rome. Bill Coore and Ben Crenshaw, 2016.

It's awfully early to write about this new resort; two of my favorite holes, the par-4 12th and 15th, hadn't even been seeded when I walked it this spring. But if the magazine panelists continue to give awards to big-scale courses, this one is sure to be a hit -- it feels like there's room for another 18 holes in the gaps! 7 - - - [2016]

Whistling Straits GC, Haven.   Straits course by Pete Dye, 2000.

Ran writes that "anytime you move this much dirt, the end result is likely to be polarizing," as if anyone else has ever tried to transform a property so completely. The Straits started out as a flattish bluff 90 feet above Lake Michigan; Mr. Dye and Mr. Kohler tried to turn it into Ballybunion, cutting all the way down to water level at the par-3 17th and using that material to build huge dunes further inland. [They eventually gave up trying to go high enough to hide all the trees beyond.]

While there are some terrific holes, the finishing holes of each nine are clunkers, and then there's the incongruous 5th, which was mandated by the Wisconsin Department of Natural Resources as a make-up hole for other work on site. It does achieve its goal of presenting a test for the world's best players, but that's not my idea of a vacation!   7 7 8 7 [2007]

Whistling Straits GC. Irish course by Pete Dye, 2002.

Set in the cornfield on the back side of the Straits course, this is a completely manufactured design that sometimes defies description, but also features some of the most visually dramatic holes you'll ever play. Every one of the par-5's is a roller-coaster ride -- it feels as if Mr. Dye was channeling Mike Strantz with his challenging second shots and long detours for the weaker player -- and the par-3 holes are just as arresting, with the blind short 13th barely taking the prize as most unusual. The par-4's are much less compelling, though the long 9th where you have to carry a small creek on both tee shot and approach is a beautiful exception. It's hardly an easy course, but you are more likely to leave with a smile on your face after the Irish course than after the Straits. 6 - 5 5 [2013]

The long, narrow green of the 3rd at Whistling Straits is far less intimidating looking back.

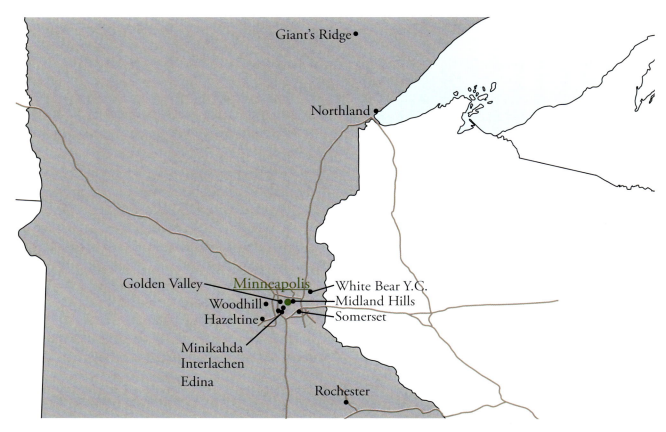

Edina CC. Tom Bendelow, 1924; remodeled by Tom Lehman and Chris Brands, 2011.

I saw this course long before the latest changes, so the rating is perhaps no longer valid. It was a good hilly property, but the tight acreage meant that there was no wiggle room to get the landing areas where one wanted them. Hopefully the two small blind water hazards have been eliminated. 5 - - - [1994]

Giant's Ridge G & Ski Resort, Biwabik. Quarry course by Jeff Brauer, 2003.

Reclaimed from a long-abandoned sand and gravel quarry, the Quarry at Giant's Ridge is golf at a Paul Bunyan-esque scale. The course is full of modern design memes, like par-5's with split fairways and big waste bunkers with sharp banks; there are also two or three holes where the approach narrows dramatically or requires a forced carry that punishes the short hitter. Hole for hole, I liked it, but they did feel like individual pieces arranged in a box, instead of a whole course that flows together: years of overgrowth block most of the views between holes, and the green to tee transitions are rarely easy. But holes like the short par-4 6th and 13th [pictured at right] are worth getting in a cart for. 6 - - - [2007]

Golden Valley G&CC. A. W. Tillinghast, 1914.

One of the best players I've ever known, Jody Rosenthal, grew up at Golden Valley, and seeing its slick and tilted greens, it's obvious why she was such a good putter. There is an odd mix of holes with only seven par-4's, five short holes that are much too close to the same length, and six par-5's – for some reason nearly every course in Minneapolis has five par-5's, even though it's exceedingly rare to find that many in other locales. The one excellent hole was the par-5 6th, reachable in two with a drive to the left and a long second over a stream seventy yards short of the green. 5 - - - [1993]

Hazeltine National GC, Chaska. Robert Trent Jones, 1965, modified by Rees Jones.

     Founded by a former USGA president with the intention of creating a championship course, Hazeltine has seen several redesigns, and for this year's Ryder Cup the course has been renumbered, as Rees Jones' signature par-4 16th along Lake Hazeltine is a real bottleneck for gallery flow. Trent Jones' original fairway bunkers are now stacked three deep to try and deal with today's distances.   - - 6 6 [2007]

Interlachen CC, Edina. William Watson, 1911, remodeled by Donald Ross.

     With a great sense of history, Interlachen is little changed from that Saturday in 1930 when Bobby Jones skipped his second shot across the lake at the par-5 9th, on his way to the U.S. Open title and the third leg of the Grand Slam. There are some better holes than that, too – the par-5 4th, with another pond in play; the short par-4 10th with its uphill ap-

proach to a severe green; and the down-and-up par-4 18th with a severe false front at the green. Even with all that, I'm a bit surprised my co-authors liked it so much. 6 – 7 7 [2011]

Midland Hills CC, Roseville. Seth Raynor, 1919.

     Either this is one of the less well-preserved Raynor designs I've seen, or perhaps it was built just before he really got his design menu perfected; in either case, it's not one of his best efforts. The Redan 16th is on a grand scale, but some of the other templates are poorly executed. 4 – 4 - [1994]

Minikahda Club, Minneapolis. Robert Foulis, 1898, with revisions by Donald Ross.

     One of the most respected courses in the Twin Cities, Minikahda wasn't as impressive as I expected, though it has been restored again since I saw it. There are some very good holes in the middle of the course, including the

The 325-yard 13th at Giant's Ridge presents several options from the tee.

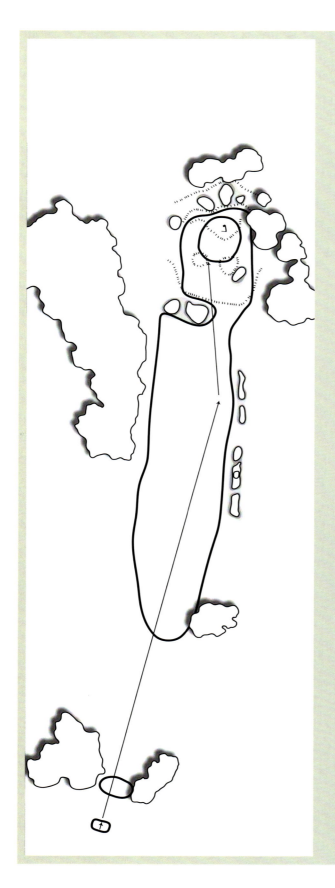

White Bear Yacht Club
12th hole - 383 yards

The English designer, Tom Simpson, wrote in his book that the center of the fairway should never be the optimum location for the tee shot. I have never seen a hole where this is more true than the 12th at White Bear Yacht Club.

From the tee one finds an inviting, wide and straight fairway. But the elevated green is nearly impossible to hold with a straightforward pitch, as nearly all of it runs sharply to the back toward a couple of deep bunkers. There is some room to land the ball short of the green and try to sneak it on, but there is very little room for error this way.

Instead, the trick is to play the tee shot out wide to the left or right [near a line of bunkers], and then play the second shot across the approach into a shoulder of green on the opposite side, which will funnel the ball back down to the hole. I feel badly that I may have spoiled the trick for others, but otherwise it's likely that golfers would dismiss the hole without discovering its secret.

short 3rd across a valley, and two of the par-5's, the 7th and 13th. I like the idea of a finish of four par-4's, but these are all of similar length, and you have to go back and forth across a road after the 14th and 17th greens. 5 - - - [1993]

Northland CC, Duluth. Donald Ross, 1927.

Set on a steep hillside just north of the city, the course's higher reaches provide majestic views of Lake Superior. It's a relatively unchanged example of Ross' work, and a bit reminiscent of Capilano in Vancouver in the way it tacks up a steep sideslope and then plunges down, although here the clubhouse is at the bottom. It's got a great set of greens, with a lot of tilt that's tough to read due to the big backdrop. It's certainly worth the drive up from St. Paul to play here. 7 - - - [1995]

Rochester G & CC. A. W. Tillinghast, 1927.

Overplanted with pine trees, this lesser-known Tillinghast design is a good routing that deserves a massive clean-up. The short holes are not what one expects from Tillie -- three of the four play sharply uphill -- but the par-5 holes are some of his best, including the sweeping downhill 4th, and the 6th which needs its cross-bunkers restored. The short par-4 13th is also a gem. It's a difficult course for women, thanks to several tee shots over deep valleys that leave no good place for a forward tee; the irony is that Tillie took the job after his daughter married a physician from the Mayo Clinic. Maybe she didn't play? 6 – 6 - [2016]

Somerset CC, Mendota Heights. Seth Raynor, 1919.

This club has always had a fine reputation in the Twin Cities, but as at Midland Hills, I found it not to be the best example of Raynor's work. It looked like a lot of the greens have been softened, and too many parallel holes spoil the broth. 5 - - - [1993]

White Bear Yacht C, Dellwood. Donald Ross and/or William Watson, 1912-15.

Our favorite course in the Twin Cities, White Bear Yacht Club is one of the last hidden gems in America – a great course that hardly anyone ever mentions. Likely part of the reason for its anonymity is that from the big par-4 1st hole to the blind tee shot on the 18th, it is a walk on the wild side, with fairway undulations that would require a small craft advisory, and greens that would make Perry Maxwell blush. It is not reminiscent of any other Ross course I've played, and there is some dispute that it was instead built by his contemporary, William Watson.

The back nine, in particular, includes a run of the wildest putting surfaces I've ever seen, from the par-3 11th, where the green flares up into a hillside at the back right, to the bruising 15th, its narrow green divided lengthwise by a shelf. I was told that at one point the committee decided the 14th was beyond the pale and brought Pete Dye out to advise: after looking at it for a few minutes in silence, he said, "Man, I wish I could get my guys to build greens like this," and there it sits to this day.

You're either going to love the course or hate it, but you should not miss it if you get to Minneapolis. 7 – 6 8 [2015]

Woodhill CC, Wayzata. Donald Ross, 1916.

Out in the western suburbs of Minneapolis, Woodhill is an excellent Ross layout over a woodsy parkland site, although there are two or three up-and-over par-4 holes that the fairness police might decry. The best hole is the par-4 7th, running downhill through a valley with a tight second shot made more difficult by an uneven stance. 5 - - - [1997]

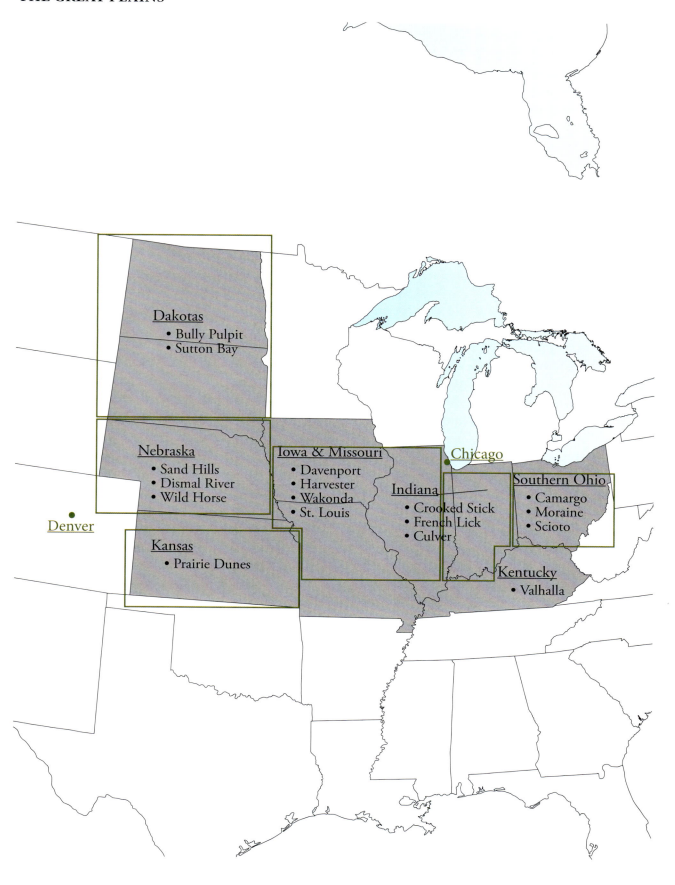

Dakotas
- Bully Pulpit
- Sutton Bay

Nebraska
- Sand Hills
- Dismal River
- Wild Horse

Iowa & Missouri
- Davenport
- Harvester
- Wakonda
- St. Louis

Chicago

Indiana
- Crooked Stick
- French Lick
- Culver

Southern Ohio
- Camargo
- Moraine
- Scioto

Denver

Kansas
- Prairie Dunes

Kentucky
- Valhalla

The story of golf in the midwestern U.S. is wrapped up in the life of Jack Nicklaus. Born and raised in Columbus, Ohio, Jack learned to play at Donald Ross's Scioto, and played his college golf over Alister MacKenzie's design for The Ohio State University courses. His role in the development and design of Muirfield Village cemented his position as a force to be reckoned with in golf course design.

Yet Nicklaus' interest in golf course design was nurtured by another midwesterner who just happened to be building one of his first projects in Columbus back in the first half of the 1960's. Born in Urbana, Ohio but headquartered in Indianapolis for many years, Pete Dye invited both Nicklaus and a young Tom Weiskopf out to The Golf Club [pictured below] during its construction, to get a sense of how long he needed to build the new course to stand up to the strongest players in the modern game. For the next fifty years, all three men would have an outsized influence on the development of new golf courses in America, and in the midwest specifically.

Mr. Dye's early style was influenced by the great courses he had seen growing up in the midwest: Donald Ross's undulating greens at Broadmoor Country Club in Indianapolis, Seth Raynor's stunning par-3's at The Camargo Club, and William Langford's bold grass-faced hazards at Lake Shore [now Maxinkuckee] Country Club, where his wife Alice's family had a summer home; his original design for Crooked Stick had little homages to all of these great designers. But in 1963, just before starting work on The Golf Club, Mr. and Mrs. Dye made a long golf trip to Scotland, and came back ready to shake up the establishment with the sleepered bunkers and abrupt contouring they'd seen in Scotland. The Dyes have built courses at all price points, from Indiana west to Des Moines and Nebraska.

The more western regions of the Great Plains have also had a profound influence on the post-modern age of golf course design. Perry Maxwell's Prairie Dunes, built on sand dunes near the Arkansas River in Kansas, was the prototype for Sand Hills Golf Club in Nebraska, and the minimalist movement in golf design that followed its success. Yet many of the designers who built these courses [including myself] trained on construction sites under Pete and Alice Dye. Their shadow looms large on the history of golf course design, and on its immediate future as well.

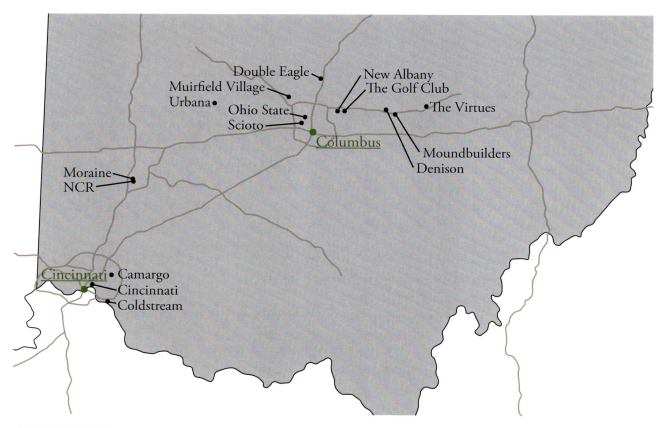

The Camargo Club, Cincinnati. Seth Raynor, 1926.

The premier course and club in Cincinnati, Camargo was a mess for twenty years after a bad facelift in the 1960's. Now fully restored, it shows up on the top-100 lists and deservingly so; the rolling farmland provides enough sharp breaks in elevation to make an excellent canvas for Raynor's deep bunkers and platform greens. Pete Dye believes it has the best set of par-3 holes in America, but I tend to remember the less familiar holes like the par-4 9th which dares you to play for a big kick forward on the drive, and the short par-4 16th with its wild "Maiden" green. 7 8 8 7 [2015]

Cincinnati CC. Robert White, 1895.

A funky, cramped course on hilly property, which has been changed many times over the years so that it doesn't really feel old or new. 3 - - - [1999]

Coldstream CC, Cincinnati. Dick Wilson, 1959.

For many years this was the token Cincinnati entry in the *Golf Digest* 100 Greatest Courses – a long and strongly bunkered layout on gently rolling wooded property. There's nothing very original about it, though, especially compared to what he had to work with up the road at NCR. 5 - - - [1994]

Denison GC, Granville. Donald Ross, 1924.

Formerly known as Granville Golf Club, this old course has been taken over by Denison University after a second round of financial difficulties. Sadly, earlier in their struggle to stay afloat, the club re-routed three holes overlooking the town to a real estate developer, and replaced them with three banal holes in between the houses -- thus losing the very thing that made the course special. 5 - - - [2016]

Double Eagle GC, Galena. Tom Weiskopf and Jay Morrish, 1992.

We'd all like to belong to a club like this, if we could find someone like John McConnell to subsidize it for us – 300 acres of nothing but golf, and a very small membership that assures the course is usually empty. The course came to prominence less for design than for its over-the-top conditioning – you could practice putting on the tees! The bunkering imitates the California style of San Francisco Golf Club and Riviera, but without the 3-D sweep that makes those courses so gorgeous. In hindsight, this might be the course where conditioning and flashy bunkering and rich owners became the driving factors in modern course ranking. 6 – 6 6 [2007]

The Golf Club, New Albany. Pete Dye, 1967.

Twenty years ago, I wrote that the highest praise for The Golf Club was that Pete Dye had been able to resist tinkering with it for all these years, but he came back recently to soften the 5% tilt in several of the greens. The original course was the epitome of founder Fred Jones' directive to "make it look like it's been there 200 years," and a wonderful study in how to create interest on a flattish site by employing some small, abrupt changes in elevation: the 10th and 13th couldn't be more flat, but an abrupt two-foot rise makes each a memorable hole. A quiet low profile hole like the 11th was never a standout, but the new work done around the green is a bit fussy. 8 7 8 7 [2016]

Moraine CC, Dayton. Alex "Nipper" Campbell, 1930.

When Ran played here in 1986, he assumed the course was in a town called Moraine as opposed to being laid over glacial landforms: it was more an arboretum than a golf course, and you could hardly see the contours of the ground. Eight years of working with Keith Foster have seen the growth

The inviting 7th hole at Moraine, before its recent renovation.

peeled back to reveal a rambunctious land-scape befitting of the club name. Stand on the tees of the downhill 326-yard 7th and 408-yard 16th and be amazed at the end result. The landforms and how Campbell captured them within the holes make it a cult course but it also measures 7270 yards with the long holes frequently uphill and the short holes downhill. This host site of the 1945 PGA Championship won by Byron Nelson is once again in the conversation for best course in golf rich Ohio. - 8 - - [2016]

Moundbuilders CC, Newark. Tom Bendelow, 1911.

A unique project, Moundbuilders was conceived to preserve an archaeological trea-sure. These are not "Indian burial mounds," but a Stonehenge-style observatory dating to around 250 A.D., with berms forming the shape of a large octagon and a smaller 350-yard circle, as well as an allee between the two that lines up on the moonrise on the shortest day of the year. As features of golf holes they've been well preserved for more than 100 years.

Bendelow's routing utilizes the mounds as driving hazards for many holes, and even locates the 3rd green inside a circular mound ring, but his shaping of greens and bunkers sadly doesn't respond to the unique landscape. Some of the best holes are on lower land near the river, including the par-5 11th with its blind green site. There are only three short holes but they are all exciting: the tiny 13th has a narrow green on a shelf, the 17th plays sharply up a slope to a difficult green at the precipice, and the 211-yard 9th plays right down the celestial alignment -- except trees block you from seeing through to the "observatory mound" beside the 10th fairway. 4 - - - [2016]

Muirfield Village GC, Dublin. Jack Nicklaus with Desmond Muirhead, 1974.

At Muirfield Village, Jack Nicklaus was not only the designer of the course but a driving force in its development, and he began this project as any developer should: he took his time to look for the right piece of property to build something special, a beautiful wood-ed property intersected by creeks [happily, in the era just before creek frontage became an environmental bugaboo]. Though the course is surrounded by real estate, Desmond Muir-head's land plan was crucial to the course's success, as the homes are sited well back in the trees, and just a single road crossing interrupts the golf.

Jack's biggest influence at the time was Augusta National, with his 12th hole modeled after Augusta's 12th, and all of the par-5's daring the golfer to flirt with water hazards to go for the green in two. But with the recent addition of a pond to the par-3 16th, the course now features water on three-quarters of its holes. However the most striking feature of the course is its perfect sightlines – how you can see the green surface and all the hazards around the green from each fairway. 8 7 7 [2014]

CC at Muirfield Village, Dublin. Jack Nicklaus, 1982.

Muirfield Village wasn't planned for 36 holes, so when demand suggested another course, an adjacent property with few of the same natural advantages for golf was drafted to serve. Here the focus is on real estate, with all but a couple holes surrounded on both sides by homes. 4 - - - [1982]

NCR CC, Kettering. South course by Dick Wilson, 1954.

Developed by the National Cash Reg-ister company, NCR must be one of the best pieces of property Dick Wilson ever had to work with. Its strength is in the longer holes, including the par-5 6th with its diagonal tee shot into a valley, and the 434-yard 12th. Greens like the 2nd and 14th, with their 9-yard-wide front pandhandles widening out at the back, are a trademark of Wilson's work. 6 7 5 - [2016]

NCR CC. North course by Dick Wilson, 1954.

Always on more open land than its big brother, this is an entirely different course on bigger, broader slopes. What's missing are fairway bunkers that punctuate the strategy.
- 5 - - [2016]

New Albany CC. 27 holes by Jack Nicklaus, 1992.

There is some good land here -- especially the 3rd through 5th holes on the West course. But spreading it out over 27 holes diluted the product in order to gain more frontage for real estate. I wonder if there is really that much demand in Columbus to live on a difficult course? 4 – 4 - [1997]

Ohio State University GC, Columbus. Scarlet course by Alister MacKenzie, 1938, with revisions by Jack Nicklaus, 2006.

It's interesting that MacKenzie's Ohio State University courses are more acclaimed than his work for the arch-rival University of Michigan, since Perry Maxwell was involved only with the latter. Ran is the only one of us to see the course post Nicklaus's 2006 work, and believes it is much improved. The large scale fairway bunkers work because they are only on one side, and a fairway like the 7th pivots perfectly to the left along the axis of the single 50 yard long bunker on the inside of the dogleg. That kicks off a really fine stretch over the club's best topography that lasts all the way through the 14th. The par-5 4th, with its skinny green turned 90 degrees to the line of play, challenges the collegiate golfer in a way MacKenzie would never have contemplated. 5 6 6 4 [2016]

Ohio State University GC. Gray course by Alister MacKenzie, 1938.

MacKenzie made no pretense as to which would be the superior course, as he reserved all the best land for the Scarlet course, save for the fine closing stretch on the 5,800-yard Gray. 4 3 4 - [2016]

Scioto CC, Columbus. Donald Ross, 1916.

Like everything else in Columbus, Scioto's reputation is based partly on its connection to Jack Nicklaus [it's the course where he grew up playing], as well as to Donald Ross and to Bob Jones' 1926 U.S. Open victory there. But Dick Wilson had his usual heavy hand in a 1960's remodeling, and we haven't seen the latest restoration. 7 7 7 6 [2007]

Urbana CC. Nine holes by Paul Dye, 1922; expanded to 18 holes by P.B. Dye, 1993.

This goat-hill nine hole layout was built by Pete Dye's father on a small patch of farmland, providing the foundation for Pete's interest in turf and in golf course design. The routing plan soldiers back and forth out of necessity, but the long 2nd and 8th holes stand out in my memory for their death-defying sidehill contours, and the mix of holes includes a very long par-3 and a couple of good short 4's, which have always been part of Pete Dye's design formula. It was a joy to go around the old nine twice, so I can't imagine how P.B.'s new nine will have improved on that. 4 - - - [1989]

The Virtues GC, Nashport. Arthur Hills, 1999.

The former Longaberger Golf Course is a big and broad public track that explores varied terrain, but golfers will require a cart to follow along. Whichever of Arthur Hills' associates was in charge must be a good player who favors a fade, since nearly all of the most distinctive holes [like the par-3 5th and 9th, the par-5 4th with its green by a pond, and the long finishing hole] have a left-to-right angled green with water or a sharp falloff to the right. The par-4 8th is interesting: you either make a big carry over native grasses to cut forty yards off the hole, or play way up a hill to the right where the fairway doglegs around a large picket line of oaks, leaving a much longer second shot to a green that juts out into a large pond. 6 - - - [2016]

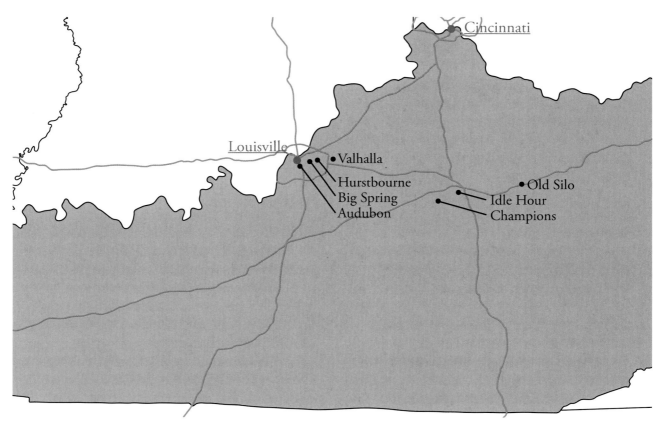

Audubon CC, Louisville. Tom Bendelow, 1908, with revisions by David Pfaff.

When Audubon opened, you could get to the club from downtown by train, and in the same manner, time has passed by this tree-lined parkland course. The par-5 7th down to a wooded corner is one of the few holes that made a positive impression. 4 - - - [2000]

Big Spring CC, Louisville. George Davies, 1923.

Recently renovated by Rees Jones, the Big Spring course occupies low ground near Bluegrass Creek, which loops into play most prominently at the par-5 7th and again on the short par-4 13th. 5 - - - [2000]

The Champions GC, Nicholasville. Arthur Hills, 1987.

If you are looking for a course that fits the image of open, rolling "bluegrass country," this one fits the bill. It's a good routing, with the development set well back from the golf, but the finicky shaping around the greens doesn't match the sweeping contour of the property. 5 - - - [1991]

Hurstbourne GC, Louisville. Chic Adams, 1966, with revisions by Keith Foster.

A country-club development from the outset, Hurstbourne's land plan gives the course plenty of breathing room, and it looked like a fine place to live and play. Keith Foster has done what he can to breathe some strategy into a very straightforward layout, most successfully at the par-4 10th where one plays diagonally over a straight creek from an elevated tee, and then back over the creek to a narrow green. 4 - - - [2000]

Idle Hour CC, Lexington. Donald Ross, 1925.

Only a couple of miles from the University of Kentucky campus, Idle Hour is the prestige club in the state, with a small mem-

The 13th at Valhalla plays to an island green shored up by limestone walls.

bership that plays only 12,000 rounds per year. Ross's layout was restored by Ron Prichard in 2003, with an emphasis on lengthening and strengthening the course: I had to wonder if Ross's bunkers were really as deep and taxing as these. The 317-yard 5th was my favorite hole, but the last five [the shortest of which is 434 yards] leave a lasting impression. 6 - - - [2016]

Old Silo GC, Mt. Sterling. Graham Marsh, 2000.

Marsh's first U.S. design has long been touted as Kentucky's #1 public course. But his design relied heavily on 80+ showy, large bunkers, so it sucks when a lack of funds and lack of care have you playing greenside shots out of dirt [if you're lucky] or gravel or casual water. It was an interesting course, with several greens that pitch away to the rear, and the best holes on each nine in a valley far from the clubhouse. But building so many bunkers where they're likely to silt up was a mistake. 4 - - - [2016]

Valhalla GC, Louisville. Jack Nicklaus, 1986.

Valhalla's selection to host two PGA Championships and a Ryder Cup was all about the Benjamins – the PGA of America owns the course outright now, after purchasing a bit more as part of each championship. It's a very difficult course, emblematic of that era of Nicklaus' career. The front nine is built in a flood plain along a wide creek, so that all of the greens had to be built up several feet to keep them from flooding; and most of the greens on the back side were given the same level of difficulty. It's a nasty course for those who aren't hitting perfect approaches: apparently, judging from our grades, that's not your authors' forte. But there's no doubt it has produced some of the most exciting championship golf in recent years, so perhaps we are underestimating its range and variety of holes. 5 – 5 5 [1998]

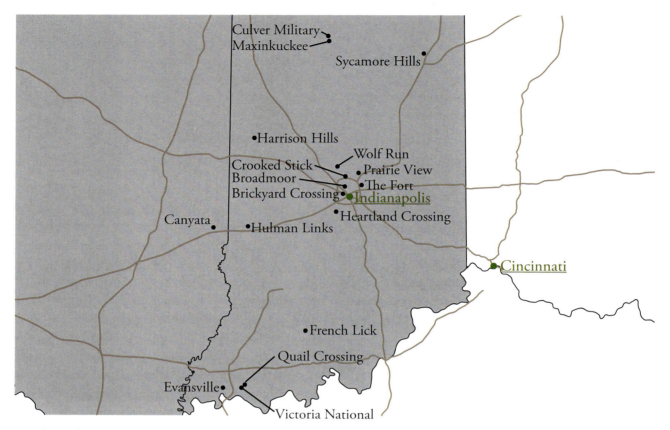

Brickyard Crossing GC, Indianapolis. Pete Dye, 1993.

Mr. Dye left no brick unturned in his complete remodel of the old Speedway Golf Course. There were once nine holes inside the famous oval; now that it's down to four it seems more of a gimmick that breaks up the continuity of the course. The exterior property has far more interest for golf, with a brook coming into play on the finishing holes. 5 - 5 - [1993]

Broadmoor CC, Indianapolis. Donald Ross, 1921.

Ross fortified this flattish property with more than 120 bunkers, but it is the wonderful set of greens that makes it worth a game. The gull-wing 13th and the penultimate par-5 with its diagonal ridge through the putting surface are prime examples that flat land is not a death sentence for fine golf. But you could take out 1,000 trees here before I started to miss them. 6 6 7 6 [2015]

Canyata GC, Marshall, IL. Michael Benkusky, 2001-04.

There are several privately developed courses in *Golf Digest*'s U.S. rankings whose appeal is grounded in exclusivity, but if it's true that less than fifty rounds were played at Canyata last year, it takes the cake. The course is a pleasant modern design with a mix of wooded areas and prairie-style views, and some big water features to add a bit of drama. But Top 100 courses need Top 100 golf holes, and we found none of those here. - - - 5 [2009]

Crooked Stick GC, Carmel. Pete Dye, 1964.

I'm surprised to be the only fan of Crooked Stick among the four of us. Perhaps I just remember the original course a bit more fondly than the others because I got a personal tour from Mr. Dye. He wanted to show me a deep, volcanic hollow hidden to the right of the 12th hole, as a peek into how much dirt he had moved to transform this cornfield into an interesting landscape.

The original course included greens modeled after the work of Ross, Tillinghast and MacKenzie, but these have been mostly homogenized through several reconstructions. Even so, the par-3 6th and 13th, with their greens set behind water, remain two of Mr. Dye's most iconic short holes. 7 6 6 6 [2015]

Culver Military Academy GC, Culver. William Langford, 1920.

For years, people have said this would be a terrific place if they'd only restore it, and now they've done so, with Bobby Weed overseeing the work. Langford's style is closely akin to Macdonald and Raynor's, with tall green pads resulting in deep greenside bunkers, but for decades the bunkers were just grassed over. Twenty-seven holes were originally planned here, but only nine were built -- and what a nine it is. Ran declares it is now the best golf course in the state! 5 8 - - [2016]

Evansville CC. Bill Diddel, 1922.

They call themselves THE family club in southern Indiana, and if you happen to be looking for such a thing, it's just fine; but the golf course is nothing to go out of your way to play. 4 - - - [1995]

The Fort GC, Indianapolis. Pete Dye and Tim Liddy, 1998.

Built on the old Fort Benjamin Harrison military reservation, this property enjoys more natural movement than one typically associates with a state famous for cornfields, as holes like the twisting par-5 11th and the uphill finisher across a valley demonstrate nicely. The nearly-drivable par-4 2nd is a classic Dye hole, luring you to to take a chance that you shouldn't. In this part of the country, most of Mr. Dye's courses are either private or quite expensive, so the modest green fee here is a bargain for Indiana golfers. - 6 - - [1999]

French Lick GC. Donald Ross course, 1921.

One of Ross's boldest designs, this resort course featues deep bunkers and an audacious set of greens, laid out across rolling topography punctuated by several ravines. It has all the makings of a cult classic: some contend that you can get away with a few too many loose drives, but we don't see it that way as the greens provide such a strong defense. There is not one, but a pair of 230-yard "short" holes, which must have been truly fearsome in 1932 when Walter Hagen won the PGA Championship here. If French Lick enjoyed year-round golf traffic like Pinehurst, you would never stop hearing about it. – 7 - - [2012]

French Lick GC, West Baden Springs. Pete Dye course, 2009.

The opposite in every respect to the Ross course, Mr. Dye's latest opus sits atop Mt. Airie, with commanding views over the Hoosier National Forest. The fairways are narrow ribbons, with steep drop-offs to one side or the other, if not both. Some of the golf shots to be played are invigorating -- the par-3 4th and par-5 14th are the two most interesting golf holes. But otherworldly shaping like the "volcano" bunkers at the 2nd will be a turn-off for many, and those who play it from anywhere close to the 8,100-yard back tees are likely to suffer humiliation, which doesn't encourage repeat play. It's probably lucky for everyone involved that the course was reviewed by the guys who don't believe in handing out zeroes on the Doak scale. – 6 6 6 [2015]

Harrison Hills CC, Attica. William Langford, 1924; expanded to 18 holes by Tim Liddy.

We were not even looking for a golf course the day Tom Mead and I drove past Harrison Hills on our way home from southern Indiana, but the minute we saw the wild mounding on today's 16th hole, we made an emergency detour to check it out. At

The mounded approach to the 16th at Harrison Hills caused me to pull over my car.

that point the club was still only Langford's original work, which was the wildest nine-hole course I have ever seen. Most of the foundation remains intact, except for the old par-5 3rd, where you were tempted to drive over an L-shaped property corner to a ridge-top fairway. Tim Liddy's companion holes are well done, but no one could compete with the boldness of the original nine. It's a true shame that the golf business insists you have an 18-hole course in order to be taken seriously, especially when the problem is that people don't have enough time to play 18 holes often. 6 - - - [1997]

Heartland Crossing GC, Madison. Steve Smyers and Nick Price, 1998.

Steve Smyers' courses are always big and bold, and that's the case here in the heartland, too, but it seems less appropriate for a development course than for a place like Wolf Run. 4 - - - [1999]

Hulman Links, Terre Haute. David Gill and Garrett Gill, 1978.

Built on land donated by the estate of Indianapolis Speedway magnate Tony Hulman, this formerly first-class facility has been in dire need of TLC in recent years. The course is interesting, but has several features that aren't ideal for a public course: there are a lot of small bunkers speckled across the property, the otherwise wide fairways tend to tighten just where higher-handicap players might fall short of a green, and the narrow par-5 11th through a woods could require a small range bucket for some golfers to complete. 4 - - - [1995]

Maxinkuckee CC, Culver. William Langford, 1921.

These nine holes near the lake are where Alice Dye spent her summers as a youth, honing her golf game and her fondness for bold golf course features. It's flat land, but there are still five original Langford greens with near-vertical six- to ten-foot banks down the sides and back, which may help to explain why no one in the Dye family thinks their work is all that radical. Anyone going to see the Culver course should stop by here, too. 4 - - - [2016]

Prairie View GC, Carmel. Robert Trent Jones, Jr., 1997.

A very good daily-fee golf course northeast of the city, though I didn't get too good a look at it. 5 - - - [1999]

Quail Crossing GC, Boonville. Tom Doak with Bruce Hepner and Jim Urbina, 1996.

One of my least-known designs, this daily-fee course is limited by some housing development and a major power line running across the property, but there are several greens that make it worth a stop. I'd thought that the 7th and 8th, around old quarry works, would be its best holes, but instead, two-shotters like the 4th, 12th, 13th and 16th are the heart of the course. 5 5 - - [1999]

Sycamore Hills CC, Fort Wayne. Jack Nicklaus, 1989.

A residential development on the western outskirts of Fort Wayne, Sycamore Hills is your better-than-average 1980s Nicklaus golf estate. It works because of an appealing collection of mature sycamore, oak and spruce trees and a naturally twisting river that runs through the property. As one would expect of this design team and this vintage, there are several ponds on the course as well as a number of holes routed along or across the river. Holes like the par-4 6th and 18th, where water is prominent from both the tee and the fairway, are among the most notable.

The greens are quite difficult, set across play and fronted by hazards that continually force golfers into an aerial approach route. Jack used to build those on every course; it was obvious that he's gotten more friendly on that count in his newer designs. - - - 5 [2007]

Victoria National GC, Evansville. Tom Fazio, 1998.

In a town where you wouldn't expect to find a lavish course, Victoria National earned its notoriety the old-fashioned way, by building a course so difficult that everyone would pay attention. The setting is unique; nearly every hole is lined on both sides by long ridges of grass-and scrub-covered coal tailings, or the deep pit lakes from which they were excavated, giving it the hole-to-hole isolation associated with Pine Valley. Any wayward drive from the back tees is an instant double bogey; from the white tees, the course is playable as long as the golfer's naivete holds out.

Several people have touted the set of dramatic short par-4 holes as outstanding, but they offer no relief for the weary, off the tee or on the approach. The par-3 holes with their abundant water and the long par-4's with their many demands are the standout holes on the course. Subtract your handicap from 15, and that's how many holes you can expect to play before you lose your cool, even if it's not a hot and humid summer day. 6 7 6 7 [2007]

Wolf Run GC, Zionsville. Steve Smyers, 1989.

Artistically, this is one of the best-looking courses of its era. Developer Jack Leer was building a men's club and told Smyers to make no compromises in the name of playability. He did a great job of mixing and matching the natural hazards, artificial mounding covered in fescue, chipping areas alongside the greens, and bunkers placed with reckless abandon. Unfortunately, it goes so far that it's difficult for someone like me (or anyone above a 4-handicap) to enjoy, which probably explains why Darius likes it better than the rest of us. It's difficult to finish with the same ball you started with, especially through the 240-yard 13th hanging off the shoulder of a bunker-strewn hill, and the long par-4 14th with its approach across a wide pond. 6 7 6 7 [2007]

IOWA and MISSOURI

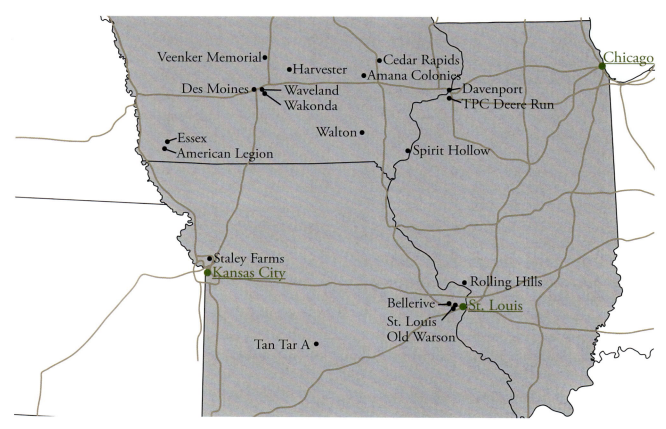

Amana Colonies GC, Amana, IA. William James Spear, 1990.

    Cut through a beautiful oak forest, the Amana course is not just for community recreation, but also for corporate entertainment. It's a beautiful setting, but experienced in carts due to the stretched-out walks and hilly terrain. Fairways are on the narrow side, but the finishing holes open up to fine views down a long pond, none better than the par-5 15th. 5 - - - [2006]

American Legion CC, Shenandoah, IA. Chic Adams, 1947.

    I played here with my wife's uncle many years ago. It's a fairly plain layout across a rolling field. 2 - - - [1991]

Bellerive CC, Creve Coeur, MO. Robert Trent Jones, 1960.

    Founded in the early 1900's, Bellerive moved to its present site in the western suburbs in 1960, and the new championship course hosted the U.S. Open just five years later. Compared to others of Mr. Jones' courses of the period, water hazards are a bit more scarce, with the greens of the par-5 holes defended only by sprawling bunkers. Rees Jones did some of his customary preparation for the PGA Championship of 2005, lengthening the course to 7,500 yards and enlarging the pond on the short par-4 2nd hole. - - 6 5 [2007]

Cedar Rapids CC, IA. Donald Ross, 1915.

    This vintage Ross course has a lot of variety, from severely hilly holes like the 2nd and 9th to flat and open holes near Indian Creek. Outstanding holes include the par-5 9th with its difficult second shot, a very good set of three par-3 holes, and above all the 346-yard 14th with its green set atop a 12-foot "burial mound." 6 - - - [2016]

Davenport CC, Pleasant Valley, IA. C. H. Alison, 1924.

See the "Gourmet's Choice," pp. 14-15. 7 - - - [2016]

TPC at Deere Run, Silvis, IL. D.A. Weibring, with Maury Miller and Chris Gray, 1999.

Nearly all the TPC courses are built into the land instead of on it ... there are no features of greens or bunkering derived from the natural terrain. The front nine plays mostly along high ridges, with views of the Rock River from the par-4 4th; the back side works its way down to the river at the par-3 16th. 5 - - - [2016]

Des Moines G & CC, West Des Moines. North course by Pete Dye, 1969-2014.

Mr. Dye built 36 holes here just before Harbour Town brought him to prominence, and the courses were relatively untouched until recently, when he and Tim Liddy renovated the North for the 2017 Solheim Cup. It's a big, brawny design, with vestiges of Dye's early style like the boomerang green at the par-3 12th, and several greens which tilt away from the line of play. 6 - - - [2016]

Essex GC, IA. Designer unknown, 1979.

They actually built eighteen holes here, but with only 977 citizens there wasn't much demand for the second nine. My ex-wife Dianna's introduction to golf was here, and was mostly about trying to get one of those old three-wheeled golf carts up on two wheels! 2 - - - [1993]

Harvester GC, Rhodes, IA. Keith Foster, 2000.

Forty-five minutes northwest of Des Moines, Harvester is an excellent modern course over rolling farmland, catering to out-of-town visitors. A 60-acre lake looms large on the two finishing holes. From the fine par-5 6th [below] to the lovely downhill 14th, there are good holes of every length. 7 - - - [2016]

Harvester's par-5 6th tempts players to carry a small pond in front of the green.

Old Warson CC, Ladue, MO. Robert Trent Jones, 1955.

Old Warson is a fine example of Trent Jones' work at the peak of his career; it's plenty long for Open qualifying to this day, and features his trademark large, undulating greens and sprawling white sand. The back nine is memorable, but the front is certainly no pushover. 5 - - - [1981]

Rolling Hills GC, Godfrey, IL. Golf from 1964; expanded to 18 holes by Gary Kern.

Not in Missouri but just across the river north of St. Louis, I had this course mistakenly listed as the "Alton Municipal GC" in previous editions of the *Guide*. I played it with my Uncle Gus and cousin Alan when I was 13, and remembered it distinctly for its weird finishing hole, a short par-4 which plays out and around a point of trees as a button-hook dogleg, so that you could also try to short-cut up and over the trees to the green. Thanks to the miracle of Google Earth, I found the course, because the hole is still there! For a 13-year-old kid interested in the field, it was a perfect example that there was good golf architecture and bad golf architecture, and the world needed more good architects. 2 - - - [1974]

St. Louis CC, Clayton, MO. Charles Blair Macdonald, 1914.

The old-money stalwart in St. Louis, C. B. Macdonald's furthest venture westward played host to the 1947 U.S. Open. It's a fine piece of hilly property: many of the fairway bunkers are invisible from the tees, but as one of the members I played with remarked, "You know where they are – anytime you hit a bad drive, you're in one." In addition to Macdonald's usual templates, the 9th and 13th are excellent three-shotters, and the par-3 3rd [a second consecutive par-3 hole] is one of the best Eden holes, with its steep back to front pitch that mimics the original. Elsewhere, there is great variety: from the short par-4

6th with its bold green contours to the Home hole that plays over a crater bunker, there is plenty to admire a century after the course was built. Ran considers this the most underrated of Macdonald and Raynor's courses, though I don't see how any of their work could qualify for that term any longer! 6 7 6 - [2008]

Spirit Hollow GC, Burlington, IA. Rick Jacobson, 2000.

Based on the name I'd assumed this was a Native American casino course, but instead it's part of a development project, and open to the public. [As at Harvester, they've built a small lodge to cater to out of town groups.] It's a big, modern layout; my favorite holes were the par-4 14th and 16th, but if they'd only switched the sequence of those holes, the course would have been more walkable. 5 - - - [2016]

Staley Farms GC, Kansas City, MO. Eric Iverson, 1998.

The one solo design by my associate Eric Iverson, Staley Farms is a development layout built over gentle farmland to the northeast of the Kansas City airport. The routing makes good use of the open spaces and trees and contours, but there are a couple of greens even I would have demurred on building. 5 - - - [2003]

Tan-Tar-A Resort, Osage Beach, MO. Hidden Lakes course by Bob von Hagge and Bruce Devlin, 1969.

I played this nine-hole course as a kid, and assumed the ridiculous green-to-tee transition from the par-5 4th hole to the 95-yard 5th was due to the severe topography. In fact, the land plan was the culprit; the client packed housing lots near the lakefront and forced the golf architects to deal with the leftovers. 2 - - - [1975]

Veenker Memorial GC, Ames, IA. Perry Maxwell, 1938.

Two friends volunteered that this was a better course before a re-routing in the 1970's, but what's left is still classic Maxwell, with lots of doglegs and some abrupt elevation changes. The longer holes are on the open parkland north of Squaw Creek, while the wilder holes are up on a sixty-foot wooded bluff along the south bank. The run of par-4's from the 2nd to the 5th is a tricky start, and the 590-yard 7th back over the creek is a beauty. A little t.l.c. would go a long way here. 5 - - - [2016]

Wakonda GC, Des Moines, IA. William Langford and Theodore Moreau, 1922.

All of Iowa's best courses were pretty hilly, but Wakonda is the hilliest of the lot. For years it was the premier club in the state, and the cool clubhouse still sets a tone, but the width of Langford's design is heavily compromised by trees. Even so, with its wild par-5's, severe greens and a great opening hole, it's got enough character to be worth a stop if you're ever in Des Moines. 5 - - - [2016]

The Walton Club, Fairfield, IA. Fred Speilmand, 1929.

Organized originally as a private fishing club, with a few golf holes for when the fish weren't biting, this short course has five short holes, three par-5's and only one par-4, so you could shoot just about any score on a given day. The 9th and 18th are separate holes, with the 18th requiring a daunting carry over the lake back to the clubhouse. 3 - - - [2010]

Waveland GC, Des Moines, IA. Warren Dickenson, 1901.

This famous old public course is wildly hilly; at the par-5 12th you might hit the green in regulation without seeing any of your three shots land! 4 - - - [2016]

The 17th at Wakonda sits beneath magnificent old oaks, but is crowded by more recent plantings.

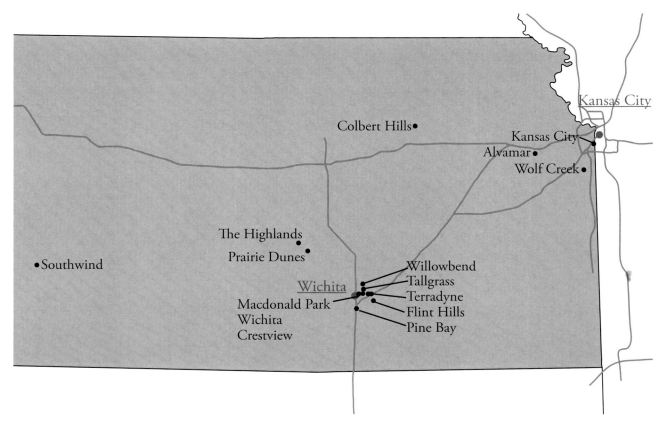

Alvamar CC, Lawrence. Bob Dunning, 1968.

This course near the headquarters of the Golf Course Superintendents' Association of America has achieved some notoriety, but I'm not sure why. The ground is modestly hilly, but the holes seemed quite dull. 4 - - - [1986]

Colbert Hills GC, Manhattan. Jeff Brauer and Jim Colbert, 2000.

Home to the Kansas State golf teams, I had expected this would be a prairie links, but the terrain is more severe than that. The land was donated for golf by a developer looking to build big homes, which loom over the course in spots. There are lots of forced carries with no recovery, and lots of big elevation changes that make it impossible to keep the ball under the wind. It seems built on top of the land, rather than spread over it. 5 - - - [2003]

Crestview CC, Wichita. 27 holes by Robert Trent Jones, 1969, with nine holes added by Robert Trent Jones, Jr., 1977.

I wonder if Trent ever spent time here, or simply flew over it and parachuted his plans down to earth? 3 - - - [1984]

Flint Hills National GC, Andover. Tom Fazio, 1997.

Set on an old ranch to the east of Wichita, Flint Hills might have been just another of the many big-budget Tom Fazio designs from this decade, but client Tom Devlin was engaged enough in the process to get one of Fazio's more appealing designs. The gently rolling property is divided into several smaller sections by thick, mature windbreaks of trees and long, narrow ponds, giving the course a look of maturity beyond its years.

The front nine is a bit of a yawn; the starting holes are out in an open field, and though the holes are challenging and the conditioning superb, only the short par-4 6th really gets our attention, shaped to encourage an aggressive play from the tee. However, the par-4 9th with its second shot up the end of a narrow lagoon is a dramatic end to the front side, and the par-3 10th across some murky wetlands serves notice that the back nine will be much more appealing.

The best stretch of golf is late in the round, and includes the par four 15th and 16th holes, and the lakeside par three 17th. The par-5 finisher might be a little too much: it plays along the big lake its whole length, with its green just across the water, but even if you've got the length to try to get home in two, a large cottonwood next to the fairway threatens to knock a pushed second shot out of the sky -- and maybe into the lake! - - - 6 [2007]

The Highlands G & Supper Club, Hutchinson. Leo Johnson, 1972.

Across town from Prairie Dunes, this development course had some good ground to work with, but saving most of the ridges for houses was a huge sacrifice for golf, and the good views for the houses mean bad views for the golfers, too. 3 - - - [1986]

Kansas City CC, Mission Hills. A.W. Tillinghast, 1925.

This is the course where the great Tom Watson grew up, and learned to deal with windy conditions. The parkland setting is reminiscent of the great courses back east, but the terrain is hillier than most of what you'll find in New York or Philadelphia, and the detailing of the greens and bunkers is not as artistically done. A well-used creek enlivens the proceedings on the back nine. Ran actually played three holes here with Watson at the height of his putting woes: watching him stiff a long iron to the tough back right hole location at the 14th and then miss the three-footer for birdie was brutal. 5 5 - - [1986]

Macdonald Park GC, Wichita. James Dalgleish, 1911.

Originally the home of Wichita Country Club, Mac Park was donated to the city when the club moved to a better neighborhood. It's just the sort of no-nonsense design you'd expect from an old Scots professional – though he wasn't one of the famous ones – and it's still one of the better offerings around Wichita, thanks to a couple of stream valleys that are used to great advantage on several holes. 4 - - - [1984]

Pine Bay GC, Wichita. Kevin Pargaman, 1986.

Laid out by a do-it-yourself developer, the opening hole here is one of the most dangerous I've ever seen, with a road way too close on the right, and houses left, along with trees that guard a late dogleg to the green. The last four holes of this affordable nine play around a pit lake, including two ninety-degree doglegs and an island green par-3. 1 - - - [1986]

Prairie Dunes GC, Hutchinson. Nine holes by Perry Maxwell, 1937; extended to 18 holes by Press Maxwell, 1956.

I'm still scratching my head how we left Prairie Dunes out of the Gourmet's Choice ... it was a staple of my original 31 flavors. Perry Maxwell's original nine holes [today's 1-2-6-7-8-9-10-17-18] were considered the best nine-hole course in America, and they are still probably the nine best holes out of the current eighteen, but the additions are tacked on in such a way that the difference is not so starkly apparent to most, and Press Maxwell's 12th green is a sight to behold. The native gunch off the fairways and around the bunkers does result in too many unplayable lies and lost balls, but the fairway undulations and the greens here are so special that nothing can detract too much from the result. 9 9 8 8 [2007]

Southwind CC, Garden City. Don Sechrest, 1980.

Southwind is frequently compared to Prairie Dunes for its windy, open setting, which is easy to say when no one has been there to dispute the description. In fact, there are only a handful of holes in exciting terrain, plus two large ponds; and the greens, as you'd expect, are no match for Maxwell's best. But if you're ever passing through Garden City, Kansas, it's worth a stop. 5 - - - [1985]

Tallgrass CC, Wichita. Arthur Hills, 1982.

This development course was an early success in Arthur Hills' career. When it opened, it turned heads, with lots of trees and native vegetation [even around the water hazards] giving it a look of its own. But it's a pretty weird design: there are several holes with cross-hazards at 200 or 230 yards where short hitters will have to lay back, and others with optional landing areas where taking the safe play may leave your second shot completely blocked by trees. Between that and the relentless encroachment of housing, and some long green-to-tee transitions for road crossings, it's not what it promised to be. 4 – 5 - [1984]

Terradyne GC, Andover. Don Sechrest and Craig Schreiner, 1987.

None of the courses which received the dreaded goose-egg rating in the original *Confidential Guide* felt they were deserving of the distinction, but the fact that a few of them are out of business today must mean something. Terradyne, though, is a thriving country club and development, so perhaps I missed the mark on this one. It seemed nothing more than a grab-bag of modern design elements all thrown together; the front nine, squeezed between I-35 and a row of housing, was particularly bleak. The short par-4 15th, with the direct line to the green right down the back of a row of houses, could get someone in real trouble. 0 - - - [1989]

Wichita CC. Bill Diddel, 1950.

Wichita's premier club is a fairly bland 1950's design, relocated to this site after the club abandoned its former home at Macdonald Park and donated it to the city. Mr. Diddel's greens have enough contour to require careful approach shots, but it was hard to concentrate on them when the B-52's were flying low across the course to land at McConnell Air Force Base nearby. 4 - - - [1984]

Willowbend GC, Wichita. Tom Weiskopf and Jay Morrish, 1987.

Not many of Weiskopf and Morrish's designs are pure daily-fee courses, like this one. Rock-lined artificial ponds are the main visual feature of the course, attempting to distract the golfer's eye from the 300+ houses in the development. The ponds come into play on seven holes, including the drivable par-4 9th and the par-5 finisher, but the most unusual hole is the par-4 10th: the direct line from tee to green is along a row of windbreak trees, with alternate fairways on either side of it, and the wide green makes it important to favor one side or the other if the hole is cut near either edge. 4 - - - [1989]

Wolf Creek GL, Olathe. Dr. Marvin Ferguson, 1972.

About an hour west of Kansas City, this all-men's club was nothing like I would have expected to find in Kansas. The drive from the first tee and the one-shot 11th are two of the steepest drops from the tee I've ever seen on a golf course [in Kansas?!], and there were also some fine strategic holes like the short 5th and the heroic par-5 7th. But of course it's too hilly to walk, and to me that's a big drawback at a club like this. 5 - - - [1981]

NEBRASKA

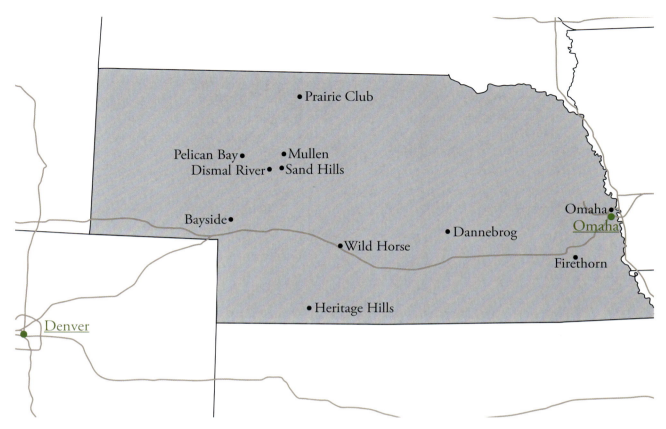

Bayside GC, Brule. Dave Axland and Dan Proctor, 2000.

     Dan and Dave are among the most talented guys in the business – see my review of Wild Horse, just ahead – but their client asked them for something totally different here, and they gave it to him [and to us!]. The front nine, on gentler land, relies on lots of bumpy contours around the greens for its challenge. The back nine, with rocky deep ravines and steep elevation changes, and big views of lake McConaughy, is one of the most extreme nine holes I've ever played. You'll need a cart to get around it, and you'll need to be careful where you drive it on the par-5 11th. It's well done if that is the kind of golf you're looking for, but it hasn't really appealed to the local golfers, and it quite likely kept Dave and Dan from building more courses across the state. 5 - - - [2002]

Dannebrog GC. Opened 1957.

     If you're taking the back roads to get out to the Sand Hills, be sure to stop and play this $4.00 nine-hole course right by the road northwest of Grand Island. It isn't the only sand-green course in the region, but none of the others have the 125-yard 2nd where the green sits in the base of an old grain silo, surrounded by a three-foot high metal wall. 3 - - - [2007]

The 2nd green at Dannebrog is one of a kind.

Dismal River Club, Mullen. White course by Jack Nicklaus, 2007.

For a great lesson that beauty is in the eye of the beholder, behold Jack Nicklaus' 18 holes at Dismal River, just a few miles upstream from Sand Hills. A difficult course in a severe and windy landscape, you might think it was built for great players, but they'd probably be the least likely guys to enjoy it.

New management has done well to make the course more playable, by beating down the roughs and softening many of the greens, and making significant changes to the 13th and 18th. Ran believes that Darius and I would be more accepting of the risks taken here had it been built by another designer; but if anyone else had built a hole like the 10th, I would have said they don't understand the game of golf at all. 5 7 - 5 [2015]

Dismal River Club. Red course by Tom Doak with Brian Schneider, 2013.

I've never been one to put special emphasis on the finishing holes of my courses, but the strong finish at Dismal River was an inevitable result of the topography -- once we went down to the river, the steepness of the surrounding hills made it hard to come back up, so why not finish at the river? The dogleg 13th and the finishing hole with its green set right above the river are probably the strongest holes of the bunch, both of them playing close to the steep bluff on the opposite bank; but the tee shots at the 14th, 15th and 17th are each wonderful in a different way.

I was sure when we started construction that the two long par-3's in the upper portion of the property would be among the most talked-about holes; instead, a lot of visitors have been more complimentary of the short par-4 4th. Ran enjoyed watching his approach feed off the bank at the par-5 8th, and then hoping his approach to the 9th would stop before it disappeared down the hill at the back. 8 8 - 7 [2015]

Firethorn CC, Lincoln. Pete Dye, 1985, with a third nine by Rod Whitman.

Developed by Dick Youngscap, who went on to bigger things in the sand hills, Firethorn was a rare project for Mr. Dye in the go-go 80's: a development course with a tight budget, on a good piece of property for golf. It's a good land plan, too: aside from the par-3 4th, the houses really don't affect the backdrops for the golf, a rare achievement when routing holes in an open prairie landscape.

Playing Firethorn for the first time drove home how severe Mr. Dye's take on golf really is. Lincoln is a very windy, dry climate in the summer months, and when the wind picks up and Firethorn bakes out, it's a beast. Pete's technique of routing the longer holes into the prevailing wind [in order to combat the length of the modern golf ball] is conspicuous here, but the water-laden finishing holes aren't nearly as inspiring as the holes in the middle of each nine. 6 6 - - [1993]

Heritage Hills GC, McCook. Dick Phelps and Brad Benz, 1981.

Instead of setting up perfectly from the tees and landing areas, with all the relevant features right in view, the holes at Heritage Hills seemed to look better from some completely different angle. If you could just move a few of the tees, there would be some pretty good holes here, but then you'd have to move the other holes and the housing lots, too. You can take a good picture of it, but it's not much to play. 4 - - - [1985]

Mullen GC. Opened 1934.

This nine-hole course for the locals still had oiled-sand greens prior to the development of Sand Hills Golf Club; the members of Sand Hills helped finance irrigation for grass greens and the maintenance equipment to take care of them. However, there would be a lot of better sites within a few miles' drive than the one they chose to build on. 2 - - - [1993]

Omaha CC. William Langford and Theodore Moreau, 1927, with revisions by Perry Maxwell.

Cut from rolling, wooded property on the north side of the city, the challenge of O.C.C. lies mostly in Maxwell's aggressively contoured greens, though the thick rough around them takes no prisoners. Keith Foster's fine restoration might have been even better if he'd widened the holes a bit to offset some of the tilt in the fairways. - - - 6 [2015]

Pelican Beach GC, Hyannis. Jack Dredla and Dan Proctor, 2000.

The golfing hub for a town of 250, this course began as a three-hole layout built on a shoestring, just to give the townfolk something to do on long summer days. The designer and shaper, Jack Dredla, really wasn't much of a golfer, but his three holes were a hit with the townsfolk, and a couple of years later he expanded the course to nine holes, with design help from Dan Proctor. The newer holes are a

bit jazzier, and most people would choose the par-5 9th as the cream of the crop, but for my money the best hole is Jack's bunkerless 4th, with an o.b. fence hard up against the higher right side of the fairway, and a green that wants you to stay right off the tee. 4 - - - [2002]

The Prairie Club, Valentine. Dunes course by Tom Lehman and Chris Brands, 2010.

One frustration with all the great new courses in the sand hills is that so much of it is off limits to the ordinary player. It's the reason The Prairie Club in Nebraska comes so highly recommended, with its strong public access business model. Plus the property in Valentine is really as good as anything else through this vast sandy region.

Lehman and Brands' design occupies a quite enormous stretch of dunes. Their routing is a giant loop across such a huge area, presumably to give holes a sense of seclusion and isolation, but instead the sense of intimacy and

The short 7th at The Prairie Club (Dunes Course) plays over a large "blowout" of open sand.

Sand Hills Golf Club
8th hole - 365 yards

This short par-4 is the closest thing
designers Bill Coore and Ben Crenshaw have
to a template hole: they've built a similar
green on most of their courses, usually on a
short par-4. A small, deep bunker eats into
the front of the green, creating two narrow
approaches, with the right side a bit higher
than the left, and a tier at the back can be of
use if you've somehow found the wrong side
of the green.

Getting to the left half of the green is
easy enough off a good tee shot, but to get a
line into the right entrance, the tee shot must
be carried or faded around the two fairway
bunkers to stay on the right side of the diagonal fairway. A short approach, or a miss into
the bunkers on the wrong half of the green,
will leave a very tricky recovery dealing with
the small, but abrupt, terrace in the green.

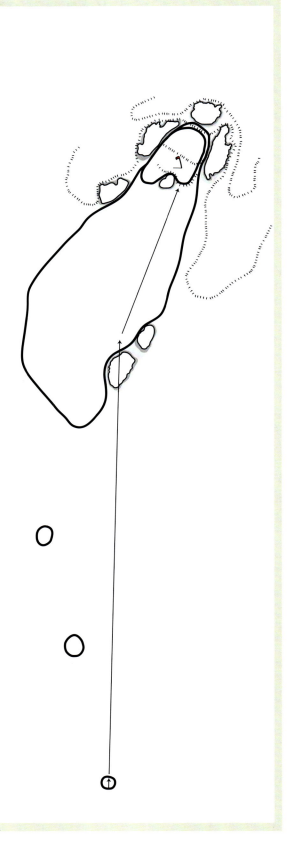

flow so important to a course like Sand Hills or Ballyneal was lost. There is a lot of climbing, when some of the gentle dune corridors in between look ideal for out and back golf.

On the positive side, the bunkering here is some of the most interesting and varied on any course we've seen, from tiny pots in the middle of the landing areas to huge natural blowouts in the dunes. The greens carry plenty of interesting contour, and those that are set down on the ground are great fun to approach and chip around. Among the better moments are the par four 2nd along an OOB fence, the approach shots across blowouts into the short 7th and mid-length 11th and the pair of excellent par-5's on the back nine. - - - 6 [2015]

The Prairie Club. Pines course by Graham Marsh, 2010.

By contrast to the Dunes Course, the footprint of the Pines is much smaller as the course wanders into the edge of a forest alongside the rim of the Snake River Canyon. It's a shame the canyon wasn't a more prominent feature of the design, due to boundary issues; exceptions include the green site at the 16th hole and the very pretty par three 17th.

Like Dunes, the core of this course is the sandy topography, which is just as bumpy and undulating through the trees as in the open. Marsh's fairways sit lower than Lehman's so his routing is more walkable. The course does change character when entering the trees, but holes on both sides employ sandy wastelands as hazards to help retain a similar style through the course. Aside from a pretty wild stretch from the 5th to the turn, the greens are reasonably calm, providing a good mix.

For those without access to the private clubs in the Sand Hills, the Pines and Dunes are good enough substitutes to attract the average golfer to this singularly beautiful region of America, and if one visits in the fall it's possible other doors will swing open as well. - - - 6 [2015]

Sand Hills Club, Mullen. Bill Coore and Ben Crenshaw, 1995.

See the "Gourmet's Choice," pp. 36-37. 10 10 10 10 [2015]

Wild Horse GC, Gothenburg. Dave Axland and Dan Proctor, 1999.

Fashioned by two of Bill Coore's longtime associates, Wild Horse was sort of a barn-raising project, funded by the local community leaders who also bought house lots along one side of the property. It is poorly described as a "poor man's Sand Hills," but the golf is first class, chock full of interesting shots compounded by the presence of the wind and the firmness of the ground. Cost considerations meant they had to keep the number and style of bunkers subdued, instead of going with the big blowouts that make the neighbor courses more exciting to look at, but difficult to keep under control. A bunkerless green like the 10th highlights the virtues of tight turf and the benefits of 'less is more' in design. Any golfer driving past on Interstate 80 should stop and play; indeed, the game would be better off if more developers made the same stop. 6 7 – 6 [2002]

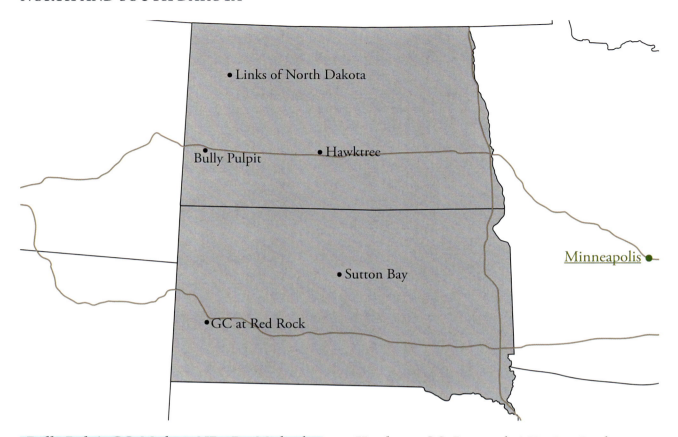

Bully Pulpit GC, Medora, ND. Dr. Michael Hurdzan, 2004.

The westernmost stop on the North Dakota Golf Trail -- it's only thirty miles from the Montana line -- Bully Pulpit is surrounded by the rugged beauty of the Badlands. Most of the course is a good, gentle layout in the river valley, but the golf amps up about five notches in the middle of the back nine, when you ascend into the hills for three spectacular holes, including the do-or-die par-3 15th from ridgetop to ridgetop a hundred feet above the rest of the course. At the same time, the decision to go up there prevents the course from being walkable for 99% of golfers, so ultimately those three holes are a mixed blessing. While I've given each of the courses on the Trail the same rating, Bully Pulpit was my favorite of the three. 5 - - - [2012]

Hawktree GC, Bismarck, ND. Jim Engh, 1999.

Born and raised in North Dakota, it only made sense for Jim Engh to go back home and build a course on this rugged site north of Bismarck. As with most of his work, it's too hilly to walk and a bit of a thrill to ride, and there are some fun holes like the par-3 3rd with its long, skinny green. The black-sand bunkers [filled with a local coal byproduct] are a conversation piece, and a bit weird to look at, but they play no different than a normal bunker. 5 - - - [2012]

Links of North Dakota at Red Mike, Ray, ND. Stephen Kay, 1994.

I know that Stephen Kay fell in love with this project and tried to help save it from a previous bankruptcy, and we must all admire an artist who sticks his neck out for his own work. However if you are expecting to find a Sand Hills type links course here, you will be disappointed to find that none of the greens feel like they sit on the natural landforms. The property feels more hilly than dunesy, and the one feature that would make it more attractive [Lake Sacagawea] was fenced off from use. 5 - - - [2012]

GC at Red Rock, Rapid City, SD. Ron Farris, 2003.

My friend Ron Farris who was on our construction crew at Long Cove has built a couple of projects in his home state of South Dakota, and Red Rock is the biggest production of the group. The steep elevation changes would have made it a tricky site to start with, but the need to make room for lots of housing lots exacerbated the problem. He's built some cool greens and a few fine holes, but there are just enough awkward corners that I can't recommend it highly. 5 - - - [2012]

Sutton Bay GC, Agar, SD. Graham Marsh, 2013.

With its clubhouse and accommodation set on an elevated ridgeline and a long view to the waters of Lake Oahe, Sutton Bay was immediately attractive to high worth American golfers looking to combine their love of the game with a passion for hunting and fishing when its original course opened in 2003.

Incredibly, a few years after opening the ground near the lake became unstable, and Graham Marsh's course started slipping down a shale ledge toward the lake. After several attempts at repairs only to see them crumble again, the hard decision was made to build a brand-new course and abandon the old one. The new course is set atop the opposite rim to the clubhouse, with a good 10-15 minute drive, down into the basin, to get from one point to the other.

Sutton Bay Mark II is clearly on much more stable footing, and though it lacks the abundance of water views that the original enjoyed, it has a better flow and is more pleasantly walkable. The old course really felt like

18 signature holes connected by cart paths. In terms of the routing, the course is arranged in two loops either side of a central comfort station. Holes nearest the edge of the canyon, like 17 and 18 enjoy the pick of the views, along with the short 5th at the far end of the course. As with Old Macdonald in Oregon, the views no longer come throughout the course, but they have greater impact when they do.

Surrounding farmland gives a hint of what this second site was to begin with, gently leaning and essentially featureless. It's not that way anymore, with an abundance of faux-dunes and buried elephants across the layout. Marsh certainly got more ambitious with his design and shaping this time around, and in places a little excessive. No question the 1st is an excellent starter, for example, but the same sort of humps and bumps are less effective on the next couple of holes. Same on the back nine where you have split fairway holes like the 12th that work very well and others, like the 14th, with completely redundant areas of fairway. The 14th does have an excellent green site, as does the almost drivable 11th, one unnecessary central bunker away from being outstanding.

For those who never played the old course, you can see the remnants from up atop the rim and make out certain features like green areas and tees. Mostly you'll see what appear to be fault lines, where the land slid away toward the water. Like many I was shocked to learn what had happened here, and saddened further by the sudden and tragic death of developer and CEO Mark Amundson in 2014. Hopefully the club has blue skies ahead. - - - 6 [2015]

THE MOUNTAIN WEST

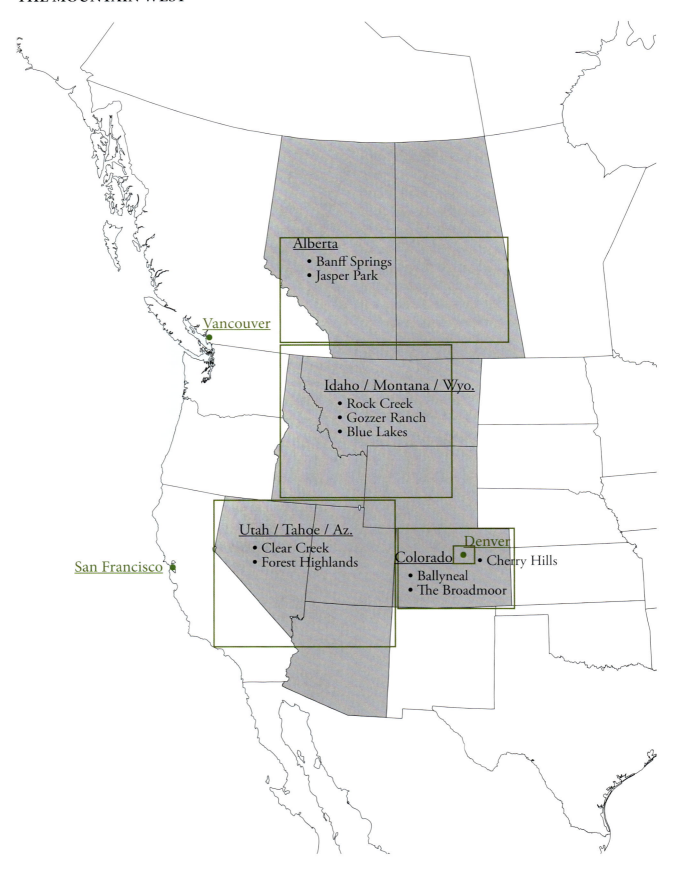

Vancouver

Alberta
- Banff Springs
- Jasper Park

Idaho / Montana / Wyo.
- Rock Creek
- Gozzer Ranch
- Blue Lakes

Utah / Tahoe / Az.
- Clear Creek
- Forest Highlands

San Francisco

Denver

Colorado
- Cherry Hills
- Ballyneal
- The Broadmoor

The working title of this section was the "Rocky Mountains," but it's become sort of a catch-all for those courses that fit better here than in the Pacific Northwest ... for example, Forest Highlands in northern Arizona, with its driveable par-4 17th hole pictured below.

Just twenty years ago, the mountains vied with the Pacific Northwest for the dubious distinction of being the most undercapitalized portion of the U.S. for golf. There were good reasons: the soils are mostly rocky, water is precious throughout the region, and the sparse population density makes it hard to justify the expense of solving the first two problems.

Yet, in the roaring second-home economy just a few years back, there was suddenly an economic case for building remote "destination courses," especially around towns that were a short hop by air from California, or Seattle, or Denver. States which had no great courses because of the population distribution during the Golden Age of design, saw their own Golden Age between 1990 and 2008. From ski-resort villages like Park City, Jackson Hole, Aspen and Vail, to lake towns like Coeur d'Alene and the Tahoe region, there are now courses sprinkled all over the mountain west.

Most of these courses were very expensive to build: fairways were capped with imported sand, and irrigation lines had to be trenched through rock. The only way to justify these costs was to develop the courses alongside real estate, and reserve access to them for those who bought in to the development. Most of this new breed remains private and off-limits to the average golfer, but we shouldn't complain because it's the only reason they exist at all. And with many of these courses struggling for business in today's economy, it's sometimes worth the effort to try and talk your way on to a 'private' venue, especially in the spring or fall.

But you don't have to know anyone to play the two great resorts of the Canadian Rockies, Banff Springs and Jasper Park, developed by the Canadian railways in the 1920's just as the parks were being formed. They had been atop my list of courses I wanted to see for more than twenty years, before I finally found time to take my wife last summer. After such a long buildup, I half expected to be disappointed by the reality; instead, I left wondering how in the world the two courses aren't fixtures in every list of the world's best. They are stunning golf courses that ought to have a place on every golfer's bucket list.

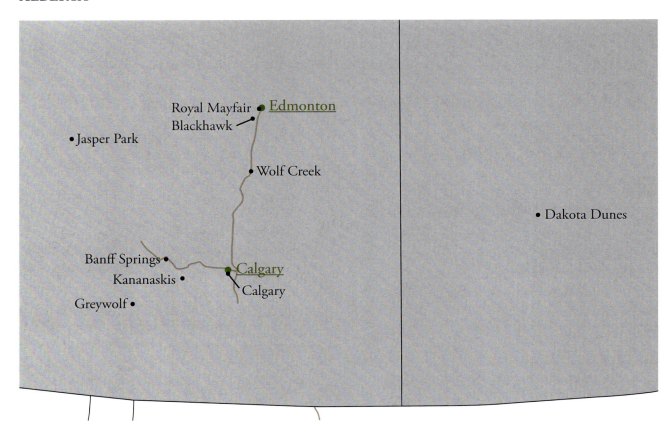

Banff Springs GC, Banff. Stanley Thompson, 1929.

    See the "Gourmet's Choice," pp. 8-9. 8 8 8 7 [2015]

Blackhawk GC, Spruce Grove. Rod Whitman, 2003.

    An understated layout beside the North Saskatchewan River, south of Edmonton, Blackhawk is a pleasantly playable layout set largely across a broad, wooded meadow. As at Cabot Links, the focus is clearly on width, approach angles and playing strategy. Whitman employs central traps beautifully on several holes, while building greens with deep sand hazards to one side and nasty run-off areas to the other. Better holes include the downhill par three 3rd, the multi-option 7th and water carry back nine threes at the 12th and 16th, the former with its green angled nicely to the left and the latter played to the base of a craggy hillside. - - 4 6 [2004]

Calgary G & CC. Willie Park, Jr., 1922, from a layout by Tom Bendelow.

    On the south side of the city, Park's Calgary layout features some dramatic ups and downs, with the clubhouse down close to the Elbow River and fourteen of the eighteen holes on the bluff above -- the par-5 1st is the most steeply uphill opening hole I've ever seen. The high ground is the better part of the course, though some holes are tight through trees without which there might be some fine views. The highlight of the course are its bullet-fast greens, with enough tilt and contour to give even the best putters fits. 6 - - - [2015]

Dakota Dunes GL, Whitecap, Saskatchewan. Graham Cooke, 2004.

    Laid out over rugged, peaceful prarie land, Dakota Dunes has the feel of a real links, except for all the cart paths that disfigure the landscape and occasionally come into play on the inside of a dogleg. The highlight of the

Jasper Park Lodge and Golf Club
9th hole - 231 yards

Stanley Thompson was known for his sometimes outrageous behavior, and he created a stir at Jasper when he unveiled the "Cleopatra" hole, a long par-3 playing 80 feet downhill, straight toward Pyramid Mountain across the valley. Legend has it that the hole was altered at the demand of his client [the Canadian Pacific Railway] for too closely resembling a woman's anatomy!

With its plateau green feeding to the rear, 12 feet above the bunkers that surround it to the sides and back, a tee shot that lands on the downslope before the green is called for, but a small bunker a few yards short of the green makes it hard to do. The better approach is to play 50 yards short and out to the right, over another bunker, where the remnants of one of Cleopatra's features will funnel a well-placed shot on down the hill into the heart of the green.

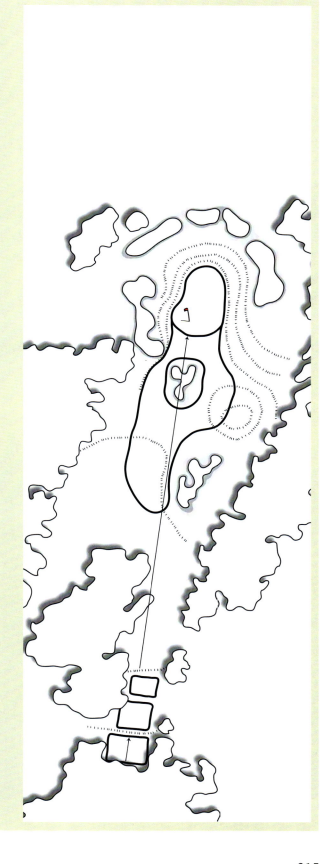

course is a fine set of par-4 holes, with green complexes that allow you to play a bouncing approach downwind, as long as you've played to the correct side of the fairway. The short holes are dramatic, but the signature 17th is very difficult to hold unless the wind is helping you, and then it's a bear to get home. Overall, it's a great holiday course and the best course of Saskatchewan. - - 6 - [2004]

Greywolf GC, Panorama, B.C. Doug Carrick, 1999.

One of the many beautiful mountain courses in this part of Canada, Greywolf is almost the equal of Banff scenically, though not architecturally. The cross-canyon 6th is every bit as memorable as the famous Devil's Cauldron hole at Banff, and the short par-four 11th and strategic right-bending 16th are also very good. Were there a little more width overall, and less climbing (or driving) between holes it would be terrific. - - - 6 [2004]

Jasper Park GC, Jasper. Stanley Thompson, 1925.

Few courses anywhere are so attractively bunkered and mounded as Jasper. Thompson already had splendid long views and the glacial Lake Beauvert to work with -- many of the holes here are aligned upon mountain peaks surrounding the course -- but the bunkers and mounds give the interior field holes like the 5th, 10th and 11th their own flair. And as usual, Thompson's set of short holes are full of variety, from the 240-yard 4th with its green backed by a rocky ridge, to the famous 9th diagrammed on p. 215, to the "Bad Baby" 15th on a peninsula across from the lodge.

It's a shame they can't cut more trees on the peninsula holes [14-15-16] to make the most of the views. Golf strategy is not the first priority of Parks Canada, but I guess we should be grateful that Canada had the foresight to allow the project to be built in

The 9th at Jasper Park.

the first place! And their management of the wildlife here is worth study: while some parts of the course are fenced off to protect the turf, a few are maintained as an open corridor for elk migration.

Yes, the mountain air makes the course play short for today's big hitters, but you're not one of them. Jasper is one of the world's most beautiful resorts. You should be here to relax, so enjoy the chance to actually post a good score if you can. 8 8 7 7 [2015]

Kananaskis GC. Mt. Kidd and Mt. Lorette courses by Robert Trent Jones, 1983.

Mr. Jones called this the most dramatic setting he had ever worked in, with 36 holes set along the Kananaskis River, at the foot of the two granite peaks after which the courses are named. In 2013, the massive Alberta flood destroyed both courses, but after much political maneuvering, work has begun to rebuild them for a 2018 reopening, with government funding aimed at restoring lost jobs. - - 5 - [2004]

Royal Mayfair GC, Edmonton. Stanley Thompson, 1922.

Set in the gorge of the North Saskatchewan River just west of downtown, Royal Mayfair is a pleasant course over gently rolling and heavily treed ground. Greens like those at the par-4 2nd, 6th and 17th give it a bit of character, but the bunkering is disappointing: it seems to sit on top of the ground instead of being built into the topography. 4 - - - [2015]

Wolf Creek GC, Ponoka. Old course by Rod Whitman, 1983-85.

Rod Whitman's first solo design is a spartan, neo-Scottish landscape, with most holes framed by low mounds, pot bunkers and the occasional waste bunker. The bulkheaded green out into the pond at the par-4 4th is its most incongruous feature, and an homage to Rod's mentor Pete Dye. - - 6 6 [2004]

Wolf Creek GC. Links course by Rod Whitman, 1990-2010.

Built in two pieces, with the back nine coming twenty years after the front [and after our last visit], the Links course is bigger and bolder than its older sibling, with wide fairways and several greens that are double the size of any on the original eighteen. The newest nine might be the most interesting of the lot, with big open sandy wastes between several pairs of holes; hopefully the housing at the perimeter won't spoil it. - - 5 6 [2004]

Elk grazing near a cart path at Jasper.

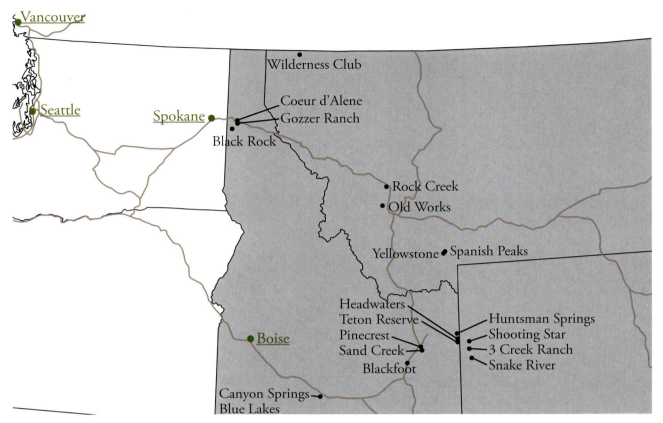

The Club at Black Rock, Coeur d'Alene, ID. Jim Engh, 2003.

I wish there were more designers who wanted to make golf crazy and fun, as Jim Engh does – but to create such an obviously fake landscape as this in front of such a beautiful natural background is just excruciating to my sensibility. If fake waterfalls are your kind of fun, that's up to you, but you'd probably be better off getting course recommendations from some other source. 0 – 3 4 [2009]

Blackfoot GC, ID. Original nine holes by George Von Elm, 1957-60, expanded to 18 holes in 1980.

The story of Blackfoot's construction by Von Elm, the 1926 U.S. Amateur champ, in the years before his death, is a beautiful example of how great players could give back to the game. Unfortunately, traffic noise from Interstate 15 spoils the ambience. 3 - - - [2015]

Blue Lakes CC, Twin Falls, ID. Francis James, 1949; expanded to 18 holes by Max Mueller.

Set in the bottom of the Snake River Canyon [made famous by Evel Knievel], Blue Lakes is crash-and-burn golf at a modest 6500-yard length. Fairways and roughs are lush, but the rocky native desert fringe presents many unplayable lies and lost balls. It's the sort of course where many golfers would be better advised to play the middle tees with a 5-iron, and keep the big dog under wraps. My threesome very nearly ran out of golf balls before we finished, thanks to a windstorm that whipped up on the last five holes.

In spite of its sometimes nasty disposition, Blue Lakes is a compelling course with a handful of world-class golf holes. The par-5 2nd, with its difficult green set atop a ten-foot hill with mowed rough on the bank of the approach, is a good one but very conventional compared to the short par-4 3rd, which snakes between hills and usually presents a blind second shot toward the towering I.B. Perrine Bridge arching overhead as it spans the canyon, 486 feet above the river. The two-shot 4th plays downhill and then back up through a narrow valley to a green framed underneath the arch of the bridge; the short par-4 5th features a beautiful diagonal tee shot over a series of bunkers; and the par-3 6th drops more than 100 feet to a difficult green set just before the bank of the river. Strangely, once you actually get down to the river, the holes are not nearly as exciting.

Moving to higher ground, the back nine is more sedate, and marred by several long transitions. The only standout hole is the 275-yard 11th, with one of the craziest greens I've seen: the sharp tier on the left side of the green is mowed at collar height, to keep balls putted from top to bottom from rolling off the reverse C-shaped green. 6 - - - [2015]

Canyon Springs GC, Twin Falls, ID. Max Mueller, 1975; expanded to 18 holes by Bob Baldock.

Right across the river from Blue Lakes, the public Canyon Springs is a much less risqué design, but you don't need to buy a dozen balls to finish 18 holes. The routing is a hodgepodge after some changes to the original holes; to get your bearings, you have to keep referring back to the big waterfall off the canyon rim just beyond the green of the par-4 13th [visible from across the river at Blue Lakes in the right-center of the photo below]. The best hole is the drivable par-4 10th, where the perfect tee shot is blind over a big rock, with a hint of draw to run down toward the green. It's far from a great course, but spending four hours down in the canyon is cool, unless a million followers paid to see you get across it. 5 - - - [2015]

The par-3 6th at Blue Lakes plays steeply downhill to the edge of the Snake River.

Gozzer Ranch Golf & Lake Club
12th hole - 323 yards

Set high above Lake Coeur d'Alene, Tom Fazio's Gozzer Ranch course is well known for its spectacular vistas of the lake, but the best of its holes is a short par-4 played away from the vista.

There are three routes to the green:

1) straight at it, requiring a carry of 260 yards from the back tee, and playing close to a natural area on the right to avoid a bounce left into the greenside bunkers;
2) long and right, offering an easy approach if one can drive clear of the lone pine tree in the native area, 275 yards from the tee; or
3) short off the tee, but close to the fairway bunkers on the left, so as to keep the pine from interfering with one's pitch to the green.

No matter which route is selected, correct placement of the tee shot is still critical to avoiding the pine tree and the bunkers one has chosen to bring into play.

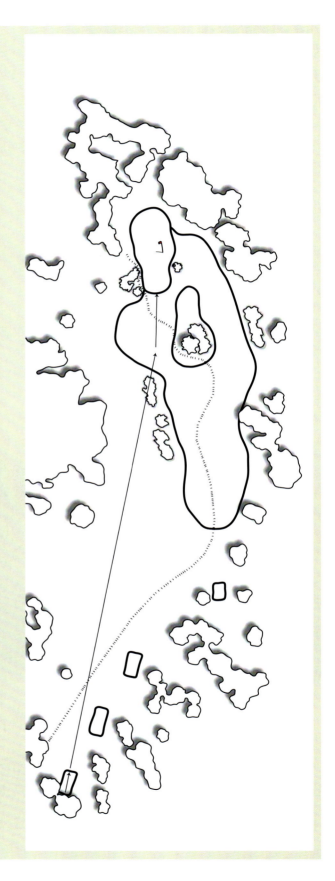

Coeur d'Alene Resort GC, ID. Scott Miller, 1991.

The world's first and only floating island green was a solution to a problem – there were barely 100 acres to build a course here, so they had to build one hole out in the lake in order to get up to eighteen! The rest of the course is crammed tightly together, and the decision to mow the grass short across the site means it is easy to bounce over into the wrong fairway if you are hitting your tee shots crooked. 5 – 4 - [2002]

Gozzer Ranch G & Lake C, Harrison, ID. Tom Fazio, 2007.

Thanks to a perfect dry climate and an excellent greenkeeper, the playing surfaces at Gozzer Ranch are a real joy. Tom Fazio has never struggled to build golf holes that would look good on a postcard, but high above Lake Coeur d'Alene, these are some of his prettiest compositions, as anyone who has seen holes like the 3rd, 15th and 17th can attest. It's the subtler features that separate this design from scores of other big-budget creations: the low profile 5th, the use of the natural contours at the par-5 8th, and the option to sling a ball left onto the 10th green are all about playing golf shots, which is something Mr. Fazio doesn't always concentrate on. - 7 6 7 [2014]

Headwaters GC at Teton Springs, Victor, ID. Byron Nelson, Gary Stephenson and Steve Jones, 2004.

The four-season Teton Springs Resort was the first development on the Idaho side of the Tetons, and though they didn't snare a great view of the jagged peaks, the setting up against a forested hillside is perfect for golf. [It is also the only course in the area that's open to outside play without contacts.] There aren't many holes where you can forget this is a housing development, and it will suffer as more homes are built, but there are several excellent two-shot holes, from the 6th with its green set against a

mountain meadow, to the long 11th where most of us would be wise to lay up short of a creek that crosses in front of the green, to the short par-4 15th where you can try to drive the green over a long narrow water hazard, a la the 10th at The Belfry. Good players will think highly of it. 6 - - - [2015]

Huntsman Springs GC, Driggs, ID. David Kidd, 2010.

In an aggressive transformation of dead-flat land, David Kidd moved more than 4 million cubic yards of earth to create the wild contours of Huntsman Springs, doing a re-markably good job keeping track of sight lines and playing angles in the process. The par-4 2nd recalls the 17th at Carnoustie, with a burn snaking across the landing area and here even wrapping around the green; the short par-4 3rd presents a different sort of challenge, as the intriguing carry over three fairway bunkers is a sucker play for many. The greens are large and complex – there is no better reminder of the need to tone down my own greens than to see another architect push the envelope a few times too many – but the course is full of strategy and the members should be inspired to keep coming back to learn its nuances. 6 - - - [2015]

Old Works GC, Anaconda, MT. Jack Nicklaus, 1997.

Touted as an environmental success story for golf, the Old Works course was created as part of the Superfund clean-up of the smelting plant that was the center of Anacdonda's economy. The front nine is inspired: mining relics are highlighted as features on several holes, and the black sand in the bunkers gives the course a unique look. Unfortunately, the Superfund agreement did not include an endowment to maintain the course indefinitely, and a lack of golfer traffic in this part of Montana has placed the future of the course in jeopardy. See it while you can – your tax dollars paid for it! 5 - - - [2004]

Black slag bunkers and old mining chutes highlight the unique landscape of Old Works.

Pinecrest GC, Idaho Falls. William Tucker, 1936.

    Idaho Falls' oldest municipal course was converted from a sand-green country club course with WPA money during the Depression, and became renowned as one of the finest public courses west of the Mississippi. The miracle of grass must have made quite an impression in those days; the layout is nothing special, although the pushed-up greens do have a bit of character. 3 - - - [2015]

Rock Creek Cattle Company, Deer Lodge, MT. Tom Doak with Eric Iverson, 2008.
    See the "Gourmet's Choice," pp. 34-35.
9 9 - 7 [2014]

Sand Creek GC, Idaho Falls. Chuck Deming, from an original plan by Billy Bell, 1980.

    Bell's concept for this course ventured into some 30-foot dunes at the south end of the property, but it took several years for the city to fund the construction of the course, and by then Mr. Deming had convinced them that building in the dunes would be too expensive. The course that got built is a solid municipal track in fine condition, and their heart is in the right place with a kids' course alongside the main 18, yet one glimpse at those dunes confirms it an opportunity lost. 4 - - - [2015]

The Club at Spanish Peaks, Big Sky, MT. Tom Weiskopf, 2007.

    On a pretty severe piece of property with beautiful surrounding mountain vistas, Tom Weiskopf did well to build an attractive set of holes here. However, only a few holes provide a genuine challenge or test for accomplished players: the par five 2nd, which falls steeply from the tee and then bends around a wetland, and the very strong set of holes from the 12th to 14th. - - - 5 [2009]

Tom Fazio's Shooting Star plays right up against the foot of the Grand Tetons.

Shooting Star GC, Teton Village, WY. Tom Fazio, 2009.

Adjacent to the Teton Village ski base, Shooting Star is the new king of the Jackson courses. All the housing is clustered up near the village, so Tom Fazio could create his golfing landscape in the south end of the meadow, with no homes to intrude. I happened to play it on a very windy day with a storm coming over the mountains, and it was great fun in those conditions, with Fazio's normal reticence to get in the golfer's face with hazards serving as a welcome relief. [The par-3 6th was all the driver I could hit, from 177 yards.] Perhaps we stopped playing at the right time, as the water-laden final four holes would have made a tough finish that day ... especially with the ball blowing off the greens. 7 - - - [2015]

Snake River Sporting Club, Hoback Junction, WY. Tom Weiskopf, 2014.

A few miles south of Jackson along the river, this star-crossed project languished without opening for several years after the financial crisis, but it has survived because the golf was too good to let go. Most of the course is in the flood plain, with only the two opening holes benched into the slope on the east side of the river; the drivable par-4 2nd is a fun introduction. Some of the holes on the front nine seem squeezed in, but in a good way, where the lack of width makes you think twice about hitting driver, or keeps a short par-3 short. The back nine is more manufactured, and a bit more predictable. 6 - - - [2015]

Teton Reserve GC, Victor, ID. Hale Irwin, 2004.

When it opened, this course was touted as the first fully reversible 18-hole layout in America, but the reversible parts currently go unmowed while the bank looks for a buyer. In truth, they should abandon the concept altogether: the visibility of features on the reverse layout is horrible, as if they never mentioned the possibility to whomever drew the grading plan. The normal routing is reasonably good, but the views of Grand Teton are blocked by a ridge. 4 - - - [2015]

3 Creek Ranch GC, Jackson, WY. Rees Jones, 2005.

Built in a flat meadow to the south of Jackson, the front nine at 3 Creek Ranch dances across the small creeks that gave the property its name, but the course doesn't really focus on the prime view of Grand Teton until the long 16th hole. They equip each cart with a radio in case of a bear sighting or other emergency, and I almost called for backup when I got to the 18th green and the clubhouse was nowhere in sight! 5 - - - [2015]

Wilderness Club, Eureka, MT. Brian Curley and Nick Faldo, 2009.

Montana is a beautiful state and, along with Rock Creek, The Wilderness Club gets closest to matching good golf holes with great scenery. Conceived as an exclusive residential facility, the course is now open to public play, and convenient for anyone visiting Glacier National Park. The small, contoured targets are certainly tougher than at most of architect Curley's Asian projects, and only accepting of very precise approach shots. A couple are a little cruel, such as the 4th with its sunken back tier, but most of the greens are quite fun and often have a safer side to miss.

The most memorable part of the course is through the early stages of the back nine. The 10th is an interesting short par four with a tall Pine in the middle of the fairway and an anorexic green set beyond a lake. The decision from the tee is whether to lay up short of the tree and leave a horrible angle across the water, or play further up the fairway and then pitch along the length of the green. The right bending 11th is more conventional, and with its push-up green complex bunkered attractively in the front. Next is a disjointed par five that plunges dramatically down alongside a pond, followed by a beautiful short hole at the 13th. - - - 6 [2015]

Yellowstone Club, Big Sky, MT. Tom Weiskopf, 2005.

A private golf and ski club begun with joining fees in the hundreds of thousands, The Yellowstone Club is set within the glorious expanses of the Big Sky region of Montana. Members can ski right to their doorstep and, in summer, basically drive out the garage and straight onto the course -- though you can ski far more days than you can play golf, here at 8,000 feet above sea level. Far from Weiskopf's best, the holes are nonetheless fun and often aligned to face distant peaks or look out toward the mountains. Many are quite steep: the opening par five, for example, is played down what feels like a ski run, the thin air and abrupt drop making it possible to flush your drive 400 yards down the fairway, as Darius enjoyed proving! - - - 5 [2009]

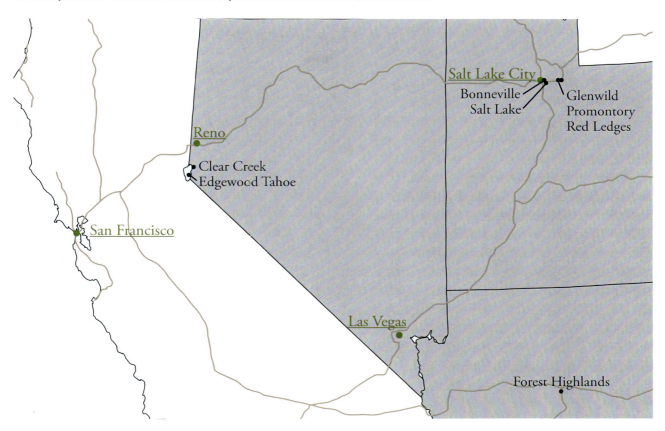

Bonneville GC, Salt Lake City. Billy Bell, 1929.

When you hear the name Bonneville you probably think "salt flats," but this fine old muni sits high up on the East Bench, looking out over downtown and the Great Salt Lake far in the distance. The upper portion of the property features several back and forth holes laid out sidehill over rolling ground, but the holes in the middle of the round play over, around and down through some canyons at the lower end of the course. The 5th hole needs a good grooming, but it's a wild par-5 with the second shot over a ridge to a half-blind two-tiered green that falls sharply away from the line of play. The par-3 6th and 9th are fine holes as well. 4 - - - [2015]

Clear Creek GC, NV. Bill Coore and Ben Crenshaw, 2009.

The combination of a mountain setting and a sandy site is quite rare, but that appealing mix is exactly what Coore and Crenshaw got to work with here. The steeply downhill 3rd isn't our favorite sort of golf, because it usually leads to a steep uphill climb later, but we admire how the routing edges the golfer back up the hill without ever feeling obvious. Highlights of the round include the dramatic 9th green with its false front, the views beyond the 13th, and the interior green contours at the tiny, downhill 17th [pictured on the next page]. - 8 - 6 [2011]

The par-3 17th at Clear Creek Tahoe plays over a boulder-strewn sand hazard.

Edgewood Tahoe GC, Stateline, NV. George and Tom Fazio, 1968.

The only golf course to touch the shore of Lake Tahoe, Edgewood was once a fixture in the top 100 courses in America, but the new wave of courses have shown how overrated it was. The shoreline of the lake curves so imperceptibly that it doesn't make for interesting holes along the edge. The big pines branch up so high that they play like telephone poles in the rough. 5 – 6 – [1986]

Forest Highlands GC, Flagstaff, AZ. Canyons course by Tom Weiskopf & Jay Morrish, 1986.

It sits among the San Francisco Peaks, not the Rockies, but the setting of Forest Highlands through rugged canyons and Ponderosa pines and rocky outcrops is what I visualized courses in Colorado would look like. With six par-3 holes, five par-5's, and two drivable par-4's, the Canyons course has one of the oddest mixes of holes I've ever encountered, but it

makes sense at 7,000 feet: the alternative would be an 8,000 yard course with 530-yard par-4's. With the altitude, the drivable par-4's of which Weiskopf is so fond are actually drivable for mortals here, and the 387-yard 17th is one of the best of that breed. 7 - - 6 [2007]

Forest Highlands GC. Meadow course by Tom Weiskopf and Jay Morrish, 1999.

Longer and more manufactured than its older sister, the Meadow sits upon a mostly flat and open landscape with large bodies of water and some heroic, modern design. Though it doesn't quite have the same appeal, it complements the Canyon Course well and makes the club an appealing 36-hole destination. - - - 5 [2007]

Glenwild GC, Park City. Tom Fazio, 2001.

Park City's combination of snow, sun and proximity to Salt Lake City has made the town a real estate developer's wet dream, and

Glenwild is the ritziest address in town for golfers. It's a core golf course wih huge homes around the perimeter, but since the course sits in a natural bowl it was not necessary to crowd the fairways with houses in order to get golf views. The front nine is pretty much Tom Fazio on cruise control, but the back nine starts out with a fine short par-4 and a par-3 set around a beautiful wetland pond, and really nearly all of the holes on the back side are quite good. The three-hole loop at the finish will leave you gasping for breath. 6 - - - [2015]

Promontory GC, Park City. Dye Canyons Course by Pete Dye, 2002.

Set on a hillside facing the ski areas, Promontory is another massive development with two 18-hole courses. Mr. Dye's course is aptly named, as the back nine is routed mostly down through the bottom of deep canyons between the hills. There are some silly back tees [the par-5 3rd goes back to 720 yards], but if you don't take the bait, the scale of the course is big enough that it's quite enjoyable. 5 - - - [2015]

Red Ledges GC, Heber City, UT. Jack Nicklaus, 2009.

Most Nicklaus courses of the post-Sebonack vintage are very difficult, thanks to the addition of undulating greens into his arsenal of length and bunkering. Add in big elevation changes and altitude, which caused him to stretch the scorecard even further, and you wind up with Red Ledges, which is one of the most difficult courses I've ever played. The par-3 9th is a lovely hole where the right-hand hole locations give you a choice between using the green's slope from left to right, or playing over an intervening pine tree. There are other beautiful settings for holes as well, but as the course climbs steeper up the hill on the back nine, missing a green becomes more and more costly. Overall, I found the course fifteen shots harder than Promontory the day after, from a comparable set of tees. 6 - - - [2015]

Salt Lake CC, Salt Lake City. Ralph Plummer, 1960, from a 1920 layout by William Watson.

The premier club in Salt Lake sits unfortunately close to Interstate 80 as it begins its grind up the hill toward Park City, so this is certainly not the place for a quiet round. Most of the front nine is a series of narrow, parallel holes up and down a big slope; golfers fighting a hook will not enjoy the stretch from the 6th through 8th. Then, suddenly, we are at the edge of a bluff on the tee of the heroic par-5 9th, a hole similar to the 17th at Kapalua, with the green hanging out over a deep ravine to the left on the second shot, and a safe lay-up fairway well out to the right. The back side begins with the other most dramatic hole, a long par-3 down into the valley below; after which the course follows the interstate down a valley and back, then turning awkwardly back up the hill for the second shot to the 18th. Despite its pedigree, it feels like a modern course, and it's a tough walk. 5 - - - [2015]

The 9th at Red Ledges, flag behind tree on right.

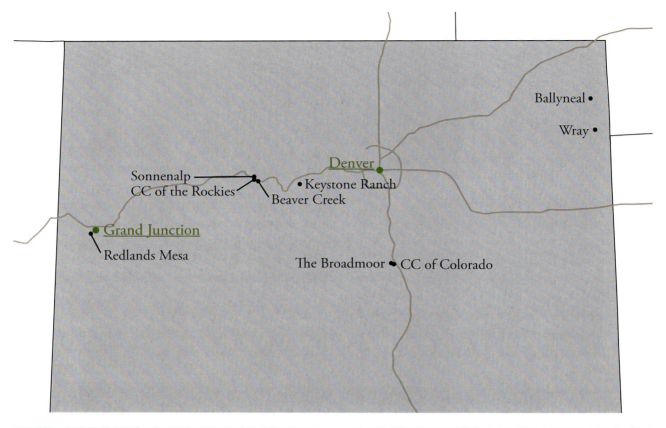

Ballyneal GC, Holyoke. Tom Doak with Bruce Hepner, 2006.

Set in "chop hill" sand dunes in the far north-east corner of the state, Ballyneal is a riot of contour from tee to green. The decision to never put out tee markers and just let members and visitors play from wherever they want set the tone for a course that exudes fun and inventiveness.

Several greens have outlandishly big contours; however the majority sit in bowls, so it's usually possible to corral a downhill putt [or a thoughtful approach shot] by playing off a backslope or sideslope, if you are clever enough to find it. The "E" green at the short par-4 7th, where you can putt around a bunker using a six-foot-high sideboard, the wasp-waisted 8th fairway, and the "Bowl of Achievement" which you can reach with a perfect tee shot at the 16th, are just a few of Ballyneal's most memorable features.

Because of the similar setting to Sand Hills, Ballyneal has to suffer comparsions with a course we all rated a perfect ten, but it is special in its own right: no other course in three volumes of *The Confidential Guide* has received nines across the board. 9 9 9 9 [2016]

Ballyneal GC. Short course by Tom Doak with Eric Iverson and Brian Schneider, 2017.

What could we do to enhance Ballyneal with an additional seven acres of turf? More than I imagined when Dave Hensley posed this question a year ago: we've built twelve par-3 holes in all, divided into two separate loops that use the same last five. There are tough little pitches, holes that would fit right in on the main course, and a couple that are too wild for anything but a satellite course. I'm confident it will fit right into the culture of this club and become a must-play part of the experience. NR [2016]

Beaver Creek GC. Robert Trent Jones, Jr., 1982.

I've always fancied the idea of a course routed along the line of a creek, so the opening holes at Beaver Creek were exciting to see, even if the creek sometimes comes into play in awkward spots. But after a few holes going steeply downstream, it dawned on me that the course would eventually have to come back up, and the rest of the walk was pretty daunting. Better to start a course like this at the bottom of the hill, rather than the top. 4 – 5 - [1984]

The Broadmoor Resort, Colorado Springs. East course by Donald Ross, 1918, with modifications by Robert Trent Jones.

The best holes at The Broadmoor are from Ross's original 18, but now they are separated over two courses as the result of the resort's expansion. The East course, set a bit lower on the mountain, is the choice for the prestigious amateur tournaments played here. It's a gentle design, but the contoured greens are perplexing to read against the mountain backdrop. 5 – 5 - [1984]

The Broadmoor Resort. West course by Robert Trent Jones, 1958-64, with a few holes from Ross' original 18.

Higher up on the hill than the East course, the West starts with a difficult uphill climb for its first six holes before settling into a better rhythm. 4 – 5 - [1984]

CC of Colorado, Colorado Springs. Pete and Roy Dye, 1973.

Between the lack of cover for the surrounding development and a few weird holes, this is not one of the Dyes' better courses. There are a bunch of interesting features – native grasses in the roughs, and the assortment of pot bunkers and waste bunkers and bulkheaded bunkers – but the golf holes just seem lost in space. 4 – 4 - [1984]

Keystone Ranch GC, Keystone. Robert Trent Jones, Jr., 1980.

Of the older generation of courses in the mountains, Keystone was my favorite. There's a wonderful variety of settings as the course works from pine groves to open prairie to lakeside and hillier holes. 5 - - - [1984]

GC at Redlands Mesa, Grand Junction. Jim Engh, 2001.

The project that vaulted Jim Engh to prominence, Redlands Mesa's stark, chiseled landscape was the perfect canvas for his deep bunkers and recessed greens. Jim is a very good player, so he has the confidence to design holes much narrower than I would envision. In a market with a short golf season, that's one way to give the course a fighting chance to prosper financially. 6 - - - [2003]

CC of the Rockies, Edwards. Jack Nicklaus, 1984.

With the exception of four holes along Vail Creek, most of this course is set in a fairly flat highland meadow. Built at the height of Jack's shelved-green, collection-bunker, double-green period, it must seem very dated now. 4 – 5 - [1984]

Sonnenalp GC, Edwards. Bob Cupp, 1980.

Formerly known as Singletree, this development is just across I-70 from the C.C. of the Rockies, but occupies a much hillier site that gives the course its character. Only a flatter stretch in the middle of the course held it back from being my favorite up here. 5 - - - [1984]

Wray CC. Architect unknown, 1970.

Set at the very western edge of the sand hills, I'd hoped to find a small-town hidden gem here, but the terrain is hilly rather than dunesy, so there aren't many memorable holes. No reason to make this detour. 3 - - - [2006]

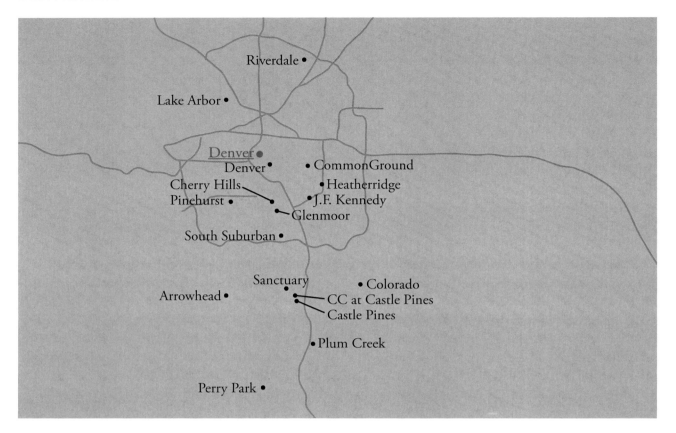

Riverdale •

Lake Arbor •

Denver •
Denver •   • CommonGround
Cherry Hills   • Heatherridge
Pinehurst •   • J.F. Kennedy
       Glenmoor

South Suburban •

Sanctuary   • Colorado
Arrowhead •   CC at Castle Pines
       Castle Pines

• Plum Creek

Perry Park •

Arrowhead GC, Littleton. Robert Trent Jones, Jr., 1972.

I used to believe that if you built a golf course in a beautiful setting, it would have to succeed, but Arrowhead made me reassess things. Set in the Red Rocks southwest of Denver, it is just far enough out of the city and a bit more affected by bad weather, so that it has never been a local favorite in spite of its stunning setting. In truth, they didn't make the most of the big rock outcroppings, either, staying back from them far enough that you are almost never afraid of hitting the rocks and they are rarely the backdrop for a golf hole, the one memorable exception to both rules being the par-4 4th hole. It's a cool place to take a picture, but if you want to see how the setting can really be used to maximum effect, go to a concert at the nearby Red Rocks Amphitheater instead. 5 – 5 - [1983]

Castle Pines GC, Castle Rock. Jack Nicklaus, 1981.

Developed by Jack Vickers as the Augusta National of the Rockies [with a few home sites tossed in to pay for the place], Castle Pines is one of the most beautiful sites Jack Nicklaus ever worked with, and it's a shame they didn't get more out of it. It's difficult and memorable and scenic, and the course is generally in immaculate condition; if that's your checklist for a great course, it passes in spades.

Artistically, though, it failed. The signature element of the design that made it different – the "collection bunkers" where a portion of the green sucks balls into a low pot bunker – were one of the most unnatural and gimmicky features on any modern course. Word has it that all of these have now been expunged. But that's why Jack's more subdued designs tend to be his highest-ranked courses, even though few have the scenic appeal of Castle Pines. 6 – 6 6 [1983]

The CC at Castle Pines, Castle Rock. Jack Nicklaus, 1986.

The development course at the north end of Castle Pines is the sort of course I kept hoping to find in Colorado: a rugged site with fantastic mountain views. At times it is a bit narrow through the trees, and there is one awful hole [the severely uphill 9th], but it's strategically interesting without having too many severe hazards. Scorecard trivia: the front nine was the first I'd seen to weigh in above 4,000 yards, though the altitude and many downhill holes make it play much less. 6 – 6 - [1985]

Cherry Hills CC, Englewood. William Flynn, 1922.

Flynn's original inspiration for Cherry Hills was the just-completed Pine Valley; there was lots of open sand between the holes and along the wide, shallow creek that slashes through the property from south to north. However as the city has grown up the course has evolved to a more suburban parkland experience. The creek is channeled to where it barely comes into play, and potential views of the Front Range are blocked by trees. There are some great holes, including the 9th, 14th and 16th, but it must have been much more exciting in the twenties. 7 – 6 6 [2014]

Colorado GC, Parker. Bill Coore and Ben Crenshaw, 2007.

Built in the rugged canyonlands just south of Denver, Colorado Golf Club offers plenty of exciting holes, but the encroachment of housing [which is hard to hide in this sparse landscape] holds it back from being the pure golf experience that we anticipated. Our favorite holes are the short par-4 3rd and 13th, plus the par-3 6th that invites a long draw into the green. The gurgling water feature at the 16th [set in a beautiful natural canyon] distracts from the quality of the golf. 7 6 6 7 [2009]

Playing among the Red Rocks at Arrowhead is an exhilirating day out.

CommonGround GC, Aurora. Tom Doak with Eric Iverson, Don Placek and Jim Urbina, 2009.

The home course for the Colorado Golf Association is a total redesign of the old Lowry Air Force Base golf course, and the fulcrum for many fine initiatives for juniors and caddies – a real model for public golf as a force of good in the community. Three of my associates had roots in Denver, so I let them be more active in the design of a course they would play a lot -- and Don's punchbowl 3rd green, Eric's offset green at the par-5 7th, and Jim's bunkerless par-3 14th are all holes I wish I had come up with myself. Though it exists for the local community, it's not too far from the airport, and worth a hit on the way in or out of town. 6 6 5 - [2015]

Denver CC. James Foulis, 1905, with lots of changes over the years.

Just south of the Cherry Creek mall, Denver Country Club is where the money is, but the course has gone through so many redesigns by everyone from Ross and Flynn to Coore and Hanse that there isn't much to hang one's hat on. Clearing back trees exposed the course to extra traffic noise. 5 – 6 - [2005]

Glenmoor GC, Cherry Hills Village. Pete and Perry Dye, 1985.

Trying to jam a golf course and 105 housing lots onto 190 acres was just the sort of job Perry Dye loved to sign up. He sent in Rod Whitman, who made a valiant effort, but without Tom Cruise doing his own stunts and a lot of special effects wizardry, it was an impossible mission. There are a lot of hard holes, and a few interesting ones, but the houses looming over your shoulders make it very hard to swing the club. 4 – 2 - [1985]

Heatherridge GC, Aurora. Dick Phelps, 1973.

Fist fights have been known to happen here between property owners and golfers, over errant drives into someone's backyard. I'll defend my own designs, but prefer to avoid fisticuffs over a bad swing. 1 - - - [1983]

John F. Kennedy Municipal GC, Aurora. Henry Hughes, 1969.

My own experience here was in the winter months, when the course was bleak looking but without any sense of claustrophobia. 2 – 2 - [1983]

Lake Arbor GC, Arvada. Gordon Revsink, with renovations by Orville Moody, 1972.

One of many courses in Colorado where the condos were built much too close together to squeeze golf in between, but someone tried anyway. A couple of holes are downright dangerous in the way they dogleg around houses, but it was in good shape for a well-trodden public course. 2 - - - [1986]

Perry Park CC, Larkspur. Dick Phelps, 1969.

This exclusive housing-development project is set in the Red Rocks, well southwest of Denver. The course is pretty short [especially when factoring in the altitude] and some of its wooded holes are very tight, but the 7th and 17th are both in the shadow of the rocks. The peace and quiet of the setting make the scenery that much better. 4 - - - [1984]

Pinehurst CC, Denver. Press Maxwell, 1958.

Positioned on a hilltop in the southwest part of the city, the Pinehurst course offers close-up views of the mountains and of downtown. The 230-yard 3rd and 600+ yard 4th holes are a great start, but the middle of the course runs tightly between small patio homes and changes the overall feel. Even so, Press Maxwell learned a thing or two about building cool greens from his father's construction crew, so the holes never become boring. 5 - - - [2015]

Plum Creek GC, Castle Rock. Pete and Perry Dye, 1984.

I was part of the construction crew when this course was born as the TPC at Plum Creek. After the course failed to meet the Tour's revenue projections, it was ditched from the fold – a sobering example of the perils of building courses specifically as tournament attractions. The golf is good and tough, but the location leaves it at the mercy of the strong winds that can blow along the Front Range, and the fairways and greens don't leave enough room for the members to handle that. If there's a wind coming up out of the south, you might want to stay in the clubhouse. 5 - - - [1985]

Riverdale GC, Brighton. Dunes course by Pete and Perry Dye, 1985.

Created from a gravelly, flood-irrigated onion field, Riverdale Dunes was the first course where I played a role in the design and shaping of greens, and it retains a loyal following among public golfers in metro Denver. The middle holes are my favorite part of the course: the 9th pays tribute to the Dell green at Lahinch, and the 13th to the Burmah hole at Royal Troon. There are plenty of interesting greens to make you think about where your approach should be coming from -- and it shouldn't be the rough, as the native grasses here extract a toll for sloppy play off the tee. 5 5 5 - [2007]

Riverdale GC. Knolls course by Henry Hughes, 1962.

When we built the Dunes course, they had to come up with a name for the older course at Riverdale; I suggested calling it the "Other," but they thought I was kidding. Tree growth has helped it some, but the concrete ditches that serve as water hazards are not very appealing. 2 - - - [1984]

Sanctuary GC, Sedalia. Jim Engh, 1997.

Few had heard of this course before it appeared in a *Golf Digest* Top 100 ranking list in 2007. Built by the philanthropic chairman of the RE/MAX real estate company, about the only way to play the course is to write a check to participate in one of several charity events held each year. Jim Engh's design offers spectacular views of the Front Range, but the routing constantly climbs and then falls and is dominated by some very strange high-risk/low-reward type architecture. The par five opening hole sets the tone: the tree-lined fairway looks like the kiddie pool at the bottom of a cartoon high dive, but it's hard to play a conservative tee shot when the ball has so much hang time to keep hooking or slicing. Each of the first five holes are downhill, as are at least another half dozen. Apart from the 5th, few of the par fours or fives offer any genuine incentive for aggressive play. The most memorable hole is the horseshoeing 12th, which is severe on the shorter hitter but cool for those able to contemplate a drive across the ravine toward the green.

Although the design negatives fail to detract from the honorable merits of the actual facility, they do provide further proof, if it were needed, of the infatuation some ranking panels have with exclusivity and great grass. - - 5 4 [2007]

South Suburban GC, Centennial. Dick Phelps, 1974.

A step above the average muni, this well-kept public course on the south side of town offers reasonably priced golf. Many of the holes dogleg, and dogleg too soon – I hit what I thought was a horrible slice off the 3rd tee, and wound up cutting the corner to within 75 yards from the green! But the greens have plenty of movement to keep golfers challenged. 3 - - - [1983]

THE PACIFIC NORTHWEST

Alaska
• Valley of the Eagles

British Columbia
• Capilano
• Sagebrush
• Victoria

• Vancouver

Washington
• Gamble Sands
• Chambers Bay

Oregon
• Bandon Dunes
• Pronghorn
• Waverley

San Francisco

The creation of Bandon Dunes Resort has had an impact on golf development worldwide, but none more stunning than in its own backyard.

Less than twenty years ago, Eugene CC in Oregon and Sahalee in Washington were considered the premier courses in the Pacific Northwest -- even though they were 5's on the Doak Scale. A fondness for tall trees and narrow fairways dominated golfers' minds, leaving little room in between for interesting design. Today, the bar has been raised, to the point that neither of those courses would be likely to make a list of the region's top ten courses.

It's hard to understand why this transformation was so long in coming. The maritime climate of the Pacific Northwest is perfect for growing cool-season grasses: in fact, much of the seed for other northern courses is produced in the Willamette Valley south of Portland. Meanwhile, east of the rain shadow of the Cascades Mountains, the cool dry nights of the high desert climate are Nirvana for bentgrass and fine fescues, as long as you have the water rights to sustain them.

The nicest thing about Bandon Dunes is that it is the embodiment of the outdoorsy, Oregon aesthetic that was previously lacking in American golf. If more of our younger citizens would see golf as outdoor recreation, the way the Scots see it, the game would boom again -- and because Bandon Dunes draws visitors from all across the nation, there's a chance more people will see the light that attracted all of us.

-Tom Doak

The undulating fairway of the 16th at Pacific Dunes is almost exactly as we found it.

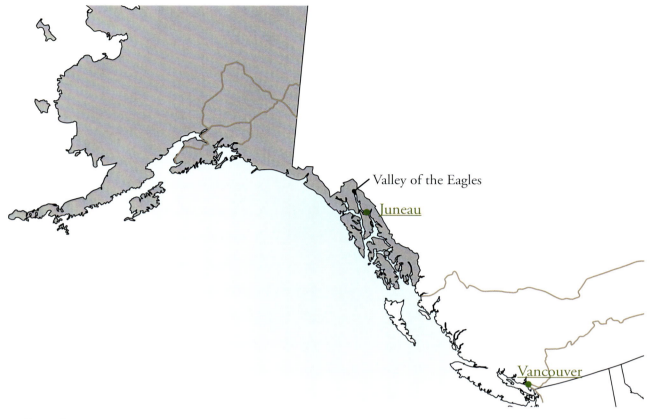

Valley of the Eagles

Juneau

Vancouver

Valley of the Eagles GC, Haines. Mark Miller, 2006.

Golf in Alaska? Well, there are a few courses in the state's bigger cities, and with 24 hours a day of sunlight at the peak of summer, there's lots of time to play. I had no interest in going just to say I had seen a course in all 50 states, but like everything else about Alaska, the journey is as important as the destination.

It's a miracle that owner Stan Jones was able to build a course here at all. The entire site was classified as a wetland, but the land has rebounded almost two feet due to the melting of surrounding glaciers, so the wetland is no longer wet. It's still very flat, but the course was still playable on my visit, even in a rainstorm. However, seasonal high tides put the whole course underwater for a few hours each month: the tides at the top end of the fjords fluctuate more than twenty feet from high to low!

With a resident population of 3,000, golf is a tough business proposition here. Cruise ship visitors help subsidize the cost of maintenance for the 40-odd local members, but the logistics of getting the cruise crowd from Skagway to Haines and back leave little margin on the green fee. Designer Mark Miller decided the only way to make ends meet was to build the course with artificial-turf greens! It's a bit harder to get the ball to check up on these greens than on real grass, but there is enough shape and contour that they play just fine for chipping and putting, as long as the resident grizzly bears don't tear holes in them.

Grizzlies? Yes, and eagles, too: the wide Chilkat River along the 6th fairway attracts thousands of bald eagles in the late fall when the salmon are running. Wildlife and fishing are the two best reasons to visit Alaska, but now golf has a toehold as well. 4 - - - [2015]

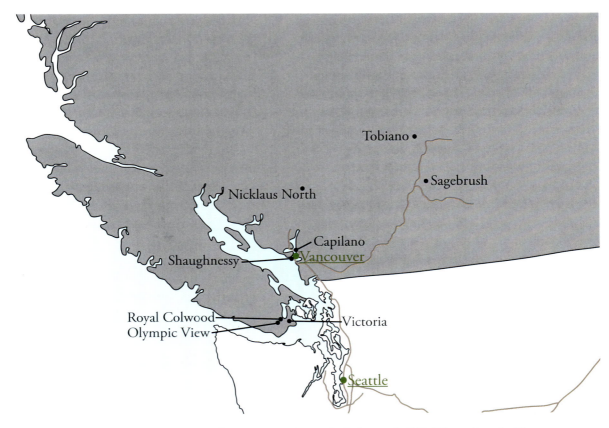

Capilano G&CC, West Vancouver. Stanley Thompson, 1937.

     With its spectacular setting high above the river and the city, Capilano captures the essence of Vancouver -- steep wooded hills and beautiful water views. Thompson did a shrewd job of routing holes on the difficult site, with the first six holes plunging dramatically toward the Lion's Gate Bridge and the next nine tacking back up the hill. The finishing holes are justly famous: the 15th and 17th play toward the mountain, and the par-5 18th with its green benched up below the clubhouse deserves to be better known. I didn't think the greens contouring or the par-3 holes were as well conceived as the routing, but there are many fine examples of design among the longer holes. 7 8 7 7 [2005]

Royal Colwood GC, Victoria. A. Vernon Macan, 1913.

     A parkland counterpart to the seaside Victoria Golf Club, Royal Colwood was also built by Vernon Macan and is noted for some quite aggressively angled green complexes. Like a lot of Golden Age golf courses, the key to scoring well here is to keep your ball below the hole and avoid having too many putts down or across the sharp putting contours. Although the par threes are very good, old photos show exposed sand between tee and green at the 7th, and make us think this course would benefit from serious restoration. - - - 5 [2005]

Nicklaus North GC, Whistler. Jack Nicklaus, 1996.

     Standard mountain golf here: you have views but are actually playing in a valley, with flat fairways. One level lie after another doesn't excite us, and the aggressive housing plan detracts from the joy of the setting. - 5 - - [1997]

Olympic View GC, Victoria. Bill Robinson, 1990.

At 6,500 yards, this public course is all about position, on fairways half as wide as courses being built today. Plenty of the playing corridors bend around fir trees or shoulders of hills, so the long bomber who can't shape the ball doesn't enjoy free reign. The most photogenic hole is the 417-yard 17th with a 40-foot waterfall behind the green, but the double dogleg 600-yard 13th is the card wrecker. - 5 6 - [1997]

Sagebrush Sporting Club, Quilchena. Rod Whitman, 2009.

Beset from the outset by financial and legal difficulties, Sagebrush was founded on a super-exclusive membership model but reborn in 2016, after a turbulent few years, as a pay-for-play public facility. The original developer's loss is the green fee golfer's gain, as this is a fine layout on a difficult hillside site above the unspoiled Nicola Lake, three hours' drive northeast of Vancouver.

Whitman's design here is spacious and strategic, and noteworthy for its rugged scar-like bunkering and fun, undulating greens. Some of the greens are enormous, including the 16th which is apparently the biggest single green in Canada. [Rod's double green at Cabot Links requires the qualifier.] The fairways are also huge and full of bumps, humps and all manner of exaggerated contours -- there are a few where the low side of the fairway is more than ten feet below the high side, so the golfer is asked to play far up the slope from where he wants his ball to finish. Although at times it seems you can hit the ball anywhere, the greens continually reward accurate driving with easier shots and preferred approach angles. Examples include the bending 3rd, the short par four 13th, played alongside a manufactured dam, and back nine par fives at the 14th and 16th. The short holes are also beautiful. - - - 7 [2015]

Shaughnessy G & CC, Vancouver. A. Vernon Macan, 1960.

Shaughnessy is a famous tournament course in Canada, built on a reasonably flat site near the mouth of the Fraser River. Aside from the opener and two back nine par threes, the holes basically run back and forth, adjacent to the water and with the wind an obvious obstacle. The other obstacles, being narrow fairways, thick rough and super quick, angled greens, are unfortunately what keep this course off the top tier in Canada. There is a sameness to much of the layout, both from the tee and into the small greens. The par threes stand out, perhaps because they aren't frustratingly narrow and penal. The shortish 16th and attractive 11th are also quite good.

It's not hard to see why the PGA Tour loves this venue: the club is terrific and the holes are so relentlessly demanding as to provide a pretty black or white verdict on who hit the ball the best. - - - 5 [2005]

Tobiano GC, Kamloops. Thomas McBroom, 2007.

An hour up the road from Sagebrush, but an almost polar opposite golf experience, Tobiano is one of many aesthetically affective, but architecturally empty, modern golf designs across Canada. The views out toward the surrounding lake are sublime, and some of the shots quite exciting to hit, but far too many holes are spoiled by unnecessarily narrow fairways, penal forced carries or extreme elevation changes. There are some nice holes through the early stages and the more subtle 14th and lakeside par three 15th both work reasonably well, but the overriding memory here is of some crazy steep golf and one par three, the 7th, which crosses a deep ravine to a shallow green that is almost impossible for average golfers to hit and hold. Tobiano is likely to appeal only to those who feel that difficulty is the ultimate gauge of quality. - - - 5 [2015]

Victoria GC, Oak Bay, Victoria. Golf from 1893; present layout by A. Vernon Macan, 1925.

With magnificent views across the Strait of Juan de Fuca toward the Olympic Mountains, this tightly packed course in the city's most fashionable suburb offers much more than the 6000 yards on the scorecard would suggest. The flavor of Scotland is all here, with abundant gorse and broom in brilliant yellow bloom each spring, occasional outcrops of rock on the holes nearest the coast, and wild small-scale contouring in greens like the 3rd and 7th. However, the city street that bisects the course and the lack of acreage makes it quite dangerous in spots, and at times the routing feels hemmed in, with two sets of back-to-back par-3 holes. It's a great place to enjoy a vacation round, as long as there's not too much crossfire. 5 – 6 6 [2005]

The 7th at Victoria Golf Club is one of four holes that play right down to the water's edge.

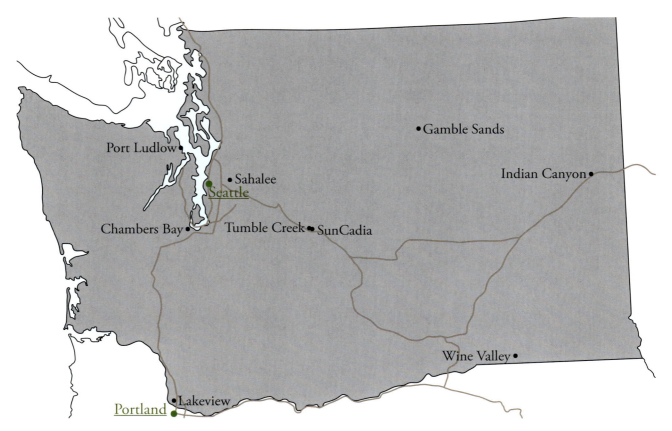

Chambers Bay GC, Tacoma. Robert Trent Jones, Jr., with Bruce Charlton and Jay Blasi, 2005.

Though our ratings of the course are not far apart, Chambers Bay proved to be a contentious course to reach a consensus for review -- none of which had much to do with its hosting of the 2015 U.S. Open.

Darius found the setting overlooking Puget Sound a beautiful venue for the game, and praised the course for many fun shots -- but questions the wisdom of 20-million-dollar municipal golf projects, and insider deals to host tournaments that will only encourage others to overspend lavishly.

Ran was most impressed with the very thing that received the most criticism from the Open competitors -- the all-fescue playing surfaces, which mean that the last 30 yards of run determines the fate of your shots. This elevates the course above slower-playing modern designs like Whistling

Straits, and into the class of Kingsbarns or Castle Stuart, where the greens have enough movement to justify the expansive fairways. [However Ran did question whether the severity of the interior contours on the 9th, 17th and 18th greens was necessary -- as I'm sure Dustin Johnson would grunt in agreement.]

My first take was positive -- I like that the course has an aesthetic and style of its own, instead of just trying to be another faux links. But on my more recent visit, I found myself agreeing with a friend who called it "a bit of a theme park." The course presents numerous opportunities to use banks at the edges of the greens to steer approach shots toward difficult hole locations, but surely others like me will tire of watching their too-short approaches come rolling back down into a deep bunker. As with many modern designs, Chambers is a full-length essay on the topic of "too much of a good thing." 7 8 7 7 [2015]

240

Gamble Sands GC, Brewster. David Kidd, 2014.

See the "Gourmet's Choice," pp. 18-19. 8 7 - 7 [2015]

Indian Canyon GC, Spokane. H. Chandler Egan, 1935.

Long regarded as one of the finest municipal courses in America, Egan's routing has to fight a fairly hilly site, and the steady traffic takes its toll on the grass. Perhaps my expectations were too high. 4 - - - [2004]

Lakeview Par-3 Golf Challenge, Vancouver. Duke Wager, 1988.

"The hardest par-3 in the Northwest" was a disappointment. I keep hoping to find a little course on rugged terrain with a couple of all-world short holes, but a green with a concrete bird-bath water hazard inside it was not what I had in mind. 2 - - - [1993]

Palouse Ridge GC, Pullman. John Harbottle, 2008.

Laid out over big, rolling terrain with the certain flavor of eastern Washington, the Palouse Ridge course is predictably difficult, as such projects are usually driven by boosters of the schools' golf teams, instead of by the university community as a whole. "Driven" is an apt term for the general layout, too, because it's hilly enough that relatively few players are going to tackle it on foot. The front nine is very up and down, but the last four holes are a fine finish, starting with the drivable par-4 15th. 5 - - - [2015]

The Resort at Port Ludlow. Tide and Timber nines by Robert Muir Graves, 1975.

Before the Age of Bandon, Port Ludlow was often heralded as the best golf resort in the Pacific Northwest. It's playable and pretty, but there are also blind water hazards and bad uphill finishing holes, and I find Graves' trade-

The elevated tee of the 5th at Chambers Bay gives a great view of Puget Sound beyond the green.

mark squiggly fairways annoying because they are inspired by a 2-D drawing rather than the contours of the ground. Leftover old-growth pine stumps add native character, but also the possibility of unplayable lies. A later third nine, the Trail, which was awarded a 0 rating in the last *Confidential Guide*, has been abandoned. 5 – 5 - [1992]

Sahalee CC, Redmond. Ted Robinson, 1968, with renovations by Rees Jones.

Now that it's no longer Washington's token entry in the top 100 lists, Sahalee is having trouble living up to its reputation, even if they did play a PGA Championship here. There are so many tall, skinny trees so close to the fairways that sometimes it feels like you are playing golf underneath an archway, instead of out in the open. There is no width for the course to offer strategic interest, and the contouring of the greens cannot make up the deficit. 5 – 5 5 [2007]

SunCadia Resort, Cle Elum. Prospector course by Arnold Palmer, 2005.

Just ninety minutes up the interstate and across to the dry side of the Cascades, Sun-Cadia is a beautiful facility for residents of Seattle, but the golf course is not going to attract visitors from afar. For some reason there were restrictions on installing any underground drainage here, so all of the contouring consists of mounding that tails down into the fairways and sends golf balls careening to the low side of the holes. 4 - - - [2005]

Tumble Creek Club, Cle Elum. Tom Doak with Brian Slawnik, 2006.

As the exclusive private side of the Sun-Cadia development, Tumble Creek may be the best-kept secret in the Pacific Northwest. We subdued our bunkering here to a more classic style, so perhaps there is not the wow factor of some of our other work, yet the huge vistas of the mountains and the Cle Elum River snaking

alongside the course are some of the prettiest I've worked with, and the big picture window views expose the course to strong afternoon winds. The par-5 4th required as much cut and fill as any hole I've ever built ... yet, uncharacteristically for my work, it became the star of the show. Ran correctly cites the two following par-4's and the short 11th as the best of the supporting cast, though he found the last five holes disappointing because they're set on very flat ground. 7 6 6 7 [2015]

Wine Valley GC, Walla Walla. Dan Hixson, 2009.

Rolling over the hilly terrain of south-eastern Washington, Wine Valley is a fine routing and its open feel and wide fairways make it fun and forgiving to play. The bunkering here is distinctive: extra-large pits are gouged out of big slopes, with the fairways tending to run in valleys underneath, or to climb around the low side of the hazards. The large greens are very well done, with all sorts of little twists and nuances that reward local knowledge; I enjoyed the first few, though by the end I was wishing they'd had some simpler ones in the mix. 6 - - 7 [2015]

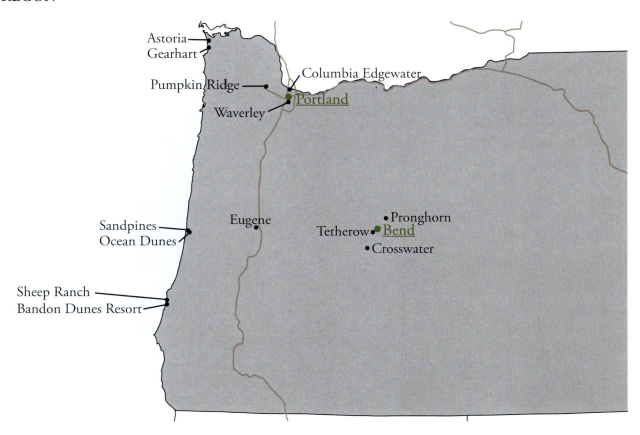

Astoria G & CC, Warrenton. George Junor and George Halderman, 1923.

The dune ridges at Astoria are unlike any I've ever seen in golf – a series of steep north-to-south ridges that are as much as 30 feet high, and so close together that the fairways running down the bottom of the valleys can be as little as ten or twelve paces wide. The short par-4 3rd is the first encounter with these narrow valleys, but several holes on the back nine are also laid out in the half-pipe formations. The small and tilted greens provide plenty of short game interest to compensate for minimal bunkering. However, the widespread use of golf carts here takes a heavy toll on the fairway conditions and has led to some VERY awkward paths, as you can see in the picture on page 245. If this was a walking-only course, as in the U.K., I would remember it even more fondly 6 - - - [2013]

Bandon Dunes GC, Bandon. David Kidd, 1999.

The first eighteen holes at Bandon Dunes Resort are still the favorite of many golfers who have been regular customers since the beginning. Abandoning the original 7300-yard back tees made the course the most playable and friendly of any at the resort when the wind is up, though the relentless clearing of gorse in recent years has taken away some of its character [and its teeth]. The routing is arranged to touch the coastline as often as possible, and the 4th and 16th holes are two of the most iconic on [literally, *on*] the West Coast. 7 7 7 7 [2011]

Bandon Preserve GC, Bandon. Bill Coore and Ben Crenshaw, 2012.

Catering to golfers who don't have enough time [or Advil] to walk another 18 holes, Bandon's 13-hole par-3 course is a blast. For many, playing with seven buddies at the end of the day is the most fun they've ever had

Bandon Trails
4th hole - 408 yards

The fourth at Bandon Trails is noteworthy because its principal feature is not a hazard but a contour in the fairway -- specifically, a long ridge, attacked a slight left-to-right diagonal from the tee.

The fairway is 85 yards across, but you can only see the right half of it, and it's clear that driving to the visible portion will leave a blind approach over the end of the ridge. But to get to the left side, you have to play carefully, as a hook or an overly-safe line to the left may see you run through the fairway into bunkers on the far side.

Whether the approach is visible or blind, the long green set at the narrow end of the valley is a daunting target.

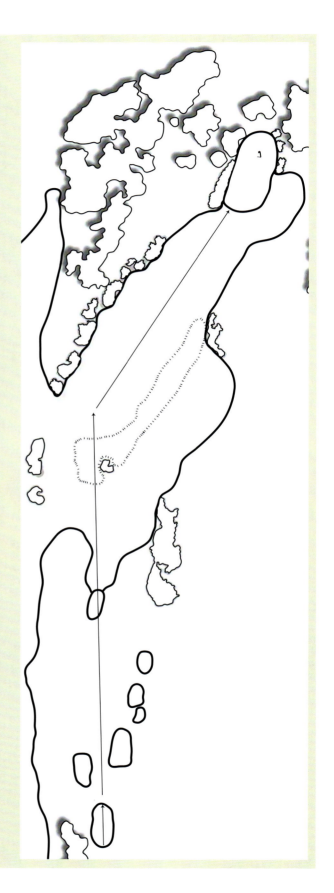

on a golf course. The downfall of such courses is usually the lack of a variety of shots – every hole is a short iron. But the Preserve is completely exposed to the wind, and the bumps and short grass at the edges of the greens encourage golfers to hit low running shots, sky-high pitches, and draws and fades depending on the strength of the wind. The course also descends closer to the beach than its big sisters at the resort, making a special setting for an hour and a half of golf. I'm just not sure what is the ceiling for a par-3 on the Doak Scale. 6 - - - [2012]

Bandon Trails GC, Bandon. Bill Coore and Ben Crenshaw, 2005.

The Trails is some of Coore and Crenshaw's finest work, a bit reminiscent of Cypress Point as the course transitions from dunes to glade to forest and back again, though it gets no share of the cliff edge that would have made it iconic. Many low-handicappers believe it is the finest course at the resort, although the polarizing short par-4 14th, even after two attempts to soften it, turns off quite a few. The difficult finishing stretch intimidates higher handicaps, so Trails is less busy than the other courses in spite of all its critical acclaim … making it a wonderful setting for a peaceful afternoon round. 8 9 8 8 [2012]

Columbia Edgewater CC, Portland. A. Vernon Macan, 1925.

This must have been a cool club in its early years, when the clubhouse was across the road right on the Columbia River, and many members arrived by boat – and before the take-offs at Portland Airport contributed so much noise. There is a surprising amount of roll in the fairways even though the course is down in the bottom lands next to the river, but the majority of Macan's interesting greens have been redesigned over time. Only the par-4 8th really stands out today. 5 - - - [2013]

The par-4 15th at Astoria plays through the valley in between two steep ridges.

Crosswater GC, Sunriver. Bob Cupp, 1995.

A course whose name perfectly reflects its character, Crosswater plays back and forth across the Little Deschutes River often enough to demoralize lesser golfers, but low-handicappers find it a compelling test of their long games, and homeowners could not find a prettier backyard playground. My only complaint is that a course in the mountains shouldn't be so flat. 6 – 6 5 [2005]

Eugene CC. Robert Trent Jones, 1960.

For many years Eugene was the #1 course in Oregon, but it was overrated then and it has been totally eclipsed over the past dozen years. Trent Jones famously reversed the routing of an original Chandler Egan layout here, to bring some ponds which had been in front of tees into play in front of his new green sites. The golf holes here don't look like they were bred for improvement, they just all look like clones. 5 - 5 5 [2007]

Gearhart GL. Robert Livingstone, 1892.

Purportedly the oldest golf course west of the Mississippi, Gearhart was laid out by Scots immigrants who had settled in this corner of the Oregon coast, and found familiar country for golf in these low, rolling dunes. Now separated from the sea by development, the fairways are tightly crammed together, four holes wide on a linear site, though there are good views to the coastal range heading south. 4 - - - [2013]

Ocean Dunes GL, Florence. Bill Robinson, 1961.

With its holes packed like sardines in high dunes to the east of Florence, this small development course offers a bit of enthralling golf on very simple terms, but straight hitting is essential, and good umbrella insurance coverage is strongly recommended. 4 - - - [1999]

Old Macdonald GC, Bandon. Tom Doak and Jim Urbina, with George Bahto, Brad Klein and Karl Olson, 2010.

Blocked out from ocean views by the high dune ridge just north of Pacific Dunes' famous 13th hole, the gorse-covered open plain that was the site for Old Macdonald was thought of as an inferior site when the project started, which gives you some idea of how spoiled we all have been by the property at our disposal in Bandon. The concern about the site led to a different concept for the course, in which we tried to adapt C.B. Macdonald's favorite holes from the U.K. [which are all from the links] to the true links site he never had. The massive scale of the fairways and greens means it is almost impossible to lose a ball, but there are plenty of obstacles to keep golfers entertained. Some critics deem our Redan green to be too exasperating, while others favorably compare the Alps 16th to the ones at Prestwick and National; such comparisons are inevitable on this type of course. As with Raynor's own work, the most interesting holes are the unscripted ones, like the blind short par-4 3rd and the uphill 7th. 8 8 8 8 [2012]

Pacific Dunes GC, Bandon. Tom Doak with Jim Urbina, 2001.

People ask me all the time which is my favorite of my own designs. When we finished Pacific Dunes, I never imagined anyone would ask me that question again. While the three holes that play right along the edge of the cliff are well documented, the bowl of dunes near the clubhouse is the best land for golf, teeming with great short par-4's like the 2nd, 6th and 16th holes. It was great fortune that we were able to find a routing that sprinkled those holes through different parts of the round, just as the course returns to the coastline multiple times. Even the less memorable holes here would be standouts somewhere else. 10 9 10 9 [2013]

Old Macdonald's 15th gives a sense of the vast scale of the course and its fairway undulations.

Pronghorn GC. Nicklaus course by Jack Nicklaus, 2004.

Building on top of volcanic rock is neither easy nor cheap, and kudos to Jack Nicklaus and his team for working with the natural contours and vegetation to create this beautiful and challenging course without breaking the bank. My only complaint was that the abundant short grass in the fairways and greens was cut so tight that it felt impossible to stop one's ball from running away off the green into trouble. 6 – 6 - [2005]

Pronghorn GC, Bend. Fazio course by Tom Fazio, 2006.

I can't imagine Mr. Nicklaus was too happy that his client turned around and spent the savings from the first eighteen to let Tom Fazio dynamite his way to a much more dramatic sister project. I would rank this course as a bit of a guilty pleasure; it is really much too opulent for my tastes, but the dramatic use of

sandy expanses up against the lava rock is superb and the mountain vistas are well exploited in the routing. The greens add a great deal of difficulty to the course, too. 7 – 6 - [2007]

Pumpkin Ridge GC, Cornelius. Ghost Creek course by Bob Cupp and John Fought, 1992.

The public side of the public/private Pumpkin Ridge development, Ghost Creek has "playability" written all over it, at the expense of character and interest. The decision to build smaller greens on the public side was a counter-intuitive choice, but since it's not a high-end muni, this is an effective way to challenge golfers while keeping the maintenance costs down. 5 – 5 - [1993]

Pumpkin Ridge GC. Witch Hollow course by Bob Cupp and John Fought, 1992.

On the private side of the development [separated from Ghost Creek by a two-headed driving range], Witch Hollow is far more

The par-3 17th at Tetherow looks west, toward the peaks of the eastern Cascades.

appealing to the eye, with a variety of bunkering patterns and a lot more native grasses at the margins of the course. All of that makes it tougher than its little sister, and to compound the difficulty, there are several long holes with wide and shallow greens guarded by a frontal hazard … a design feature Cupp learned from Jack Nicklaus, which doesn't play well for anybody with a handicap higher than four.
6 – 6 - [1993]

Sandpines GC, Florence. Rees Jones, 1993.

I don't know how an architect could go out to a sandy site on the Oregon coast and fail to be inspired by it, but it feels as though Sandpines was built by someone who had never been to the beach when he was a kid. Designing the last three holes around a man-made lake in the middle of the dunes was the ultimate cliché. 4 – 5 - [1999]

The Sheep Ranch, Randolph. Tom Doak with Don Placek, 2002.

A disagreement between the owners has kept this project dormant since we built it, but the concept of a free-form design where golfers can play from any green to any other was fascinating to explore. The fairways along the cliffs near Five Mile Point are more dramatic than any single spot at the nearby Bandon resort, and the lack of bunkers [and other golfers] leaves few landmarks to help judge distances, adding greatly to the challenge. For the rare golfer willing to throw away the scorecard and just go play the game, an afternoon with friends at The Sheep Ranch can be a transcendent experience. 6 4 5 - [2010]

Tetherow GC, Bend. David Kidd, 2008.

David Kidd lives adjacent to his course here, and perhaps the experience of playing it regularly is what led to his recent epiphany concerning more subdued greens design. Par is protected more fiercely than Darius would recommend on a residential development course, with many greens that repel approach shots rather than accept them. Apart from the gravel-pit 17th, with its mountain backdrop, the best holes are the longer, simpler par-4's such as the 4th, 5th and 12th, but other holes are chock full of confusing options. Masa was more fond of the quirkier holes, arguing that one would learn different ways to access the most difficult hole locations over time. - - 6 5 [2011]

Waverley CC, Portland. Jack Moffat, 1898, with revisions by Chandler Egan and Gil Hanse.

Though it's hard to imagine today, Waverley was so overgrown just a few years ago that when we were building Pacific Dunes, no one ever thought to tell me to go see it. Gil Hanse had the honor of restoring it, and his clearing work and expansion of short grass areas give the course an exhilirating feel. Everyone raves about the finishing holes: the 225-yard 16th plays sharply downhill toward the Willamette River just behind the green, followed by two entirely different par-5 holes playing along the river to the clubhouse. But there's more to it than the finishing act: the restored width and difficult green at the par-4 3rd captures the imagination early, and the 130-yard 9th played over a crater bunker is a fine short hole. 7 7 - - [2015]

The long par-3 16th at Waverley CC.

CLUBHOUSES - Most Stylish

Shinnecock Hills
Newport
Friar's Head
Indianwood
The Park Club
Medinah
Chicago Golf Club
Winged Foot
Farmington
Ridgewood

Veritable Museums

Garden City Golf Club
Merion
Oakmont
Baltusrol
The Country Club (Mass.)
Inverness
Royal Montreal

Most Comfortable

Myopia Hunt Club
Rock Creek
Cherry Hills
Glenwild
Milwaukee Country Club
St. George's (Ontario)
Gozzer Ranch
Redtail
Diamond Creek
Waverley

Most Understated

Bidermann
Northeast Harbor
Burning Tree
The Dunes Club
Oakhurst

The jewel box clubhouse at Newport Country Club.

Northeast Harbor's clubhouse is little more than a changing room and a covered porch.

Best Setting

Capilano
Crystal Downs
Prouts Neck
The Creek
Maidstone
Dismal River
National Golf Links of America
Sebonack
Sutton Bay

Best Pro Shop Setting

Crystal Downs
French Lick (Dye)
Bandon Trails
Cape Arundel
Roaring Gap

Best Relationship to Course

Merion (East)
Stonewall (Old)
Pine Valley
Old Elm
Newport

Clubhouses Most In Play

Milwaukee Country Club
Philadelphia Cricket Club
National Golf Links of America
Stonewall

Best Relationship to Town

Shooting Star
Harrison Hills
Cabot Links
Saratoga Golf & Polo
Chambers Bay

251

The late Tom Simonson manned the grill at Ben's Porch, overlooking the 9th fairway at Sand Hills.

Best Lunch

National Golf Links of America
Jasper Park
Sand Hills
Medinah
Deepdale
Cherry Hills
Mt. Bruno
Calgary Country Club
Sebonack

Best Halfway House

Sand Hills
Stonewall
Chicago Golf Club
Old Macdonald
Sagebrush
Shinnecock Hills

Best Entrance Drive

Pine Valley
The Creek Club
Blue Lakes, Idaho
Jasper Park
National Golf Links of America
Shoreacres
Lost Dunes
Bald Peak
Winged Foot

Best Club Accommodations

Rolling Rock
Sebonack
Rock Creek
Farmington
Sutton Bay
Pine Valley
Redtail
Dismal River

Most Hospitable Clubs

Prairie Dunes
Cedar Rapids
Mt. Bruno
Waverley
Dismal River
Bob O'Link
Cataraqui
Beverly

Best Non-Golf Facilities

Sutton Bay
White Bear Yacht Club
Piping Rock
The Creek
Roaring Gap
Grandfather

Best Small-Town Clubs

Battle Creek, Mich.
Harrison Hills, Ind.
Hooper, N.H.
Wild Horse, Neb.
Whitinsville, Mass.

Courses Worth Groveling to Play

Sand Hills
Crystal Downs
White Bear Yacht Club
Chicago Golf Club
Pine Valley
Merion
The Country Club, Mass.
Friar's Head
Shinnecock Hills
Myopia Hunt Club

If you ever do manage to talk your way onto Pine Valley, good luck hitting the green at the 5th!

RESORTS

Best Golf Resort - Accommodations

Banff Springs Hotel
The American Club, Kohler, Wisc.
Grand Hotel, Mackinac Island, Mich.
Keswick Hall, Va.
Jasper Park Lodge
The Greenbrier
The Sagamore Resort
Otesaga Hotel, Cooperstown, N.Y.
Inn at Bay Harbor

Best Resorts for Golf

Bandon Dunes Resort
Cabot Links
Banff Springs
Jasper Park
Destination Kohler
The Prairie Club
French Lick Resort
The Homestead Resort
Forest Dunes

Best Casino and Golf Resorts

French Lick Resort
The Greenbrier
Atlantic City Country Club /
  Atlantic City Hilton
Grand Traverse Resort

Favorite Places to Stay and Play

Jasper Park
Rock Creek
Bandon Dunes
Banff Springs
Ballyneal
Cabot Links
The Otesaga Hotel / Leatherstocking GC

Best Golf and Beach Combination

Grand Traverse Resort
Crowbush Cove
Bandon Dunes

note: Maidstone and The Creek Club have
  awesome beach clubs, but both are private

Best Golf Resorts with a Young Family

The Broadmoor
Kingsmill
The Otesaga Hotel
Banff Springs
Crystal Mountain Resort
Grand Traverse Resort

Springbrook in Maine was designed by a local golf pro over wonderfully rolling ground.

Best Public Courses

Gamble Sands
Lawsonia (Links)
Erin Hills
Harvester
Marquette (Greywalls)
Wild Horse
Wine Valley
Crumpin-Fox
Dakota Dunes
Springbrook

Best Municipal Courses

Bethpage State Park (Black) and (Red)
Chambers Bay
George Wright Municipal
Mark Twain GC
Vista Links

Least-Played Courses

Three Ponds Farm
Wawashkamo
Oakhurst
The Sheep Ranch
Canyata
Sanctuary
Dannebrog
Granliden on Sunapee
Yellowstone Club

Courses You Need a Guide to Play

Halifax GC (Old Ashburn)
North Haven
Eastward Ho!
Glens Falls
Uplands
White Bear Yacht Club
Blue Lakes
Whistling Straits (Irish)

Longest Courses

8,102 yds	French Lick (Dye)
7,889	3 Creek Ranch*
7,812	Erin Hills
7,790	Whistling Straits (Straits)
7,696	Castle Pines Golf Club*
7,690	Promontory (Dye)*
7,674	Hazeltine National
7,657	Medinah (No. 3)
7,653	Red Ledges*
7,650	The Monster GC, N.Y.

     * At least the starred courses are at altitude; but four of these are resorts, and four are housing-development courses!

Hardest Courses

Oakmont
Medinah #3
Butler National
French Lick (Dye)
Red Ledges
Sebonack
Wolf Run
Grand Traverse Resort (The Bear)
Whistling Straits (Straits)
Oakland Hills (South)

Windiest Courses

Harvester
Shooting Star
Bandon Dunes
Sankaty Head
Ballyneal
Crystal Downs
Prairie Dunes
Gamble Sands
Sand Hills
Tumble Creek

Widest Courses

Old Macdonald
Gamble Sands
Chambers Bay
North Haven
National Golf Links of America
Dismal River (Red)
Rock Creek
Pine Valley
Royal New Kent

Narrowest Courses

Uplands
Sanctuary
Shaughnessy
Grand Haven
Astoria

Most Ammo Required

Victoria National
Blue Lakes
Sanctuary
Muskoka Bay
Wolf Run
Sunday River
Indianwood (New)
Blackwolf Run (River)
Prairie Dunes
Grand Traverse Resort (The Bear)

Biggest Dunes

Astoria
Ballyneal
Pacific Dunes
Sand Hills
Dismal River
Prairie Dunes

Best Courses of Par Less Than 70

Wannamoisett
Cape Arundel
Plymouth CC
Northeast Harbor
Detroit Golf Club (South)
Halifax (Old Ashburn)

Best Par-3 Courses

Bandon Preserve
Ballyneal Short Course [under construction]
Pine Valley Short Course
The Horse Course @ The Prairie Club
Blue Rock Par-3

Best Use of Small Acreage

The Horse Course
Granliden on Sunapee
Three Ponds Farm
The Dunes Club
Whitinsville
Merion (West)
Coeur d'Alene Resort
Cape Arundel
Victoria, BC

Shortest Hole

77 yards - 7th at Pocono Manor
94 yards - 14A at Engineers
95 yards - 5th at Tan-Tar-A (Hidden Lake)

The Preserve at Bandon Dunes is the perfect late-afternoon jaunt for those who can't walk 36 holes.

Most Beautiful Courses

Fishers Island
Cabot Cliffs
Jasper Park
Pacific Dunes
Capilano
Gamble Sands
Banff Springs
Friar's Head
Victoria Golf Club, B.C.
Cape Breton Highlands

Best Trees

Country Club of Detroit
Old Elm
Manufacturers
Wannamoisett
Winged Foot
Capilano
Toronto Golf Club
Point O'Woods
Bandon Trails

Best Contour for Golf

Rock Creek
Cape Breton Highlands
National Golf Links of America
Sand Hills
St. George's, Ont.
Pacific Dunes
Sylvania
Oakland Hills (South)
Prairie Dunes
Dismal River (Red)

Best Wildlife Spotting

Jasper Park - elk and bears
Valley of the Eagles - bald eagles and bears
Banff Springs - elk
Rock Creek - bighorn sheep, buffalo
Bandon Trails - deer
Pikewood National - bears

Too Many Trees

Grand Haven
Cape Breton Highlands
Oak Hill (East)
Rochester G & CC, Minn.
Deepdale
Pine Valley
Hamilton G & CC
Sahalee
Capilano
Ozaukee

One of a Kind

Ladies' GC of Toronto
Forest Dunes (The Loop)
Wannamoisett
The Vineyard Club
Granliden on Sunapee
Garden City Golf Club
Myopia Hunt Club
Bethpage (Black)
Oakmont
Valley of the Eagles

The 16th at Bully Pulpit, North Dakota is dramatic, but makes the course impossible to walk.

Best Walk

Shoreacres
The Dunes Club, Mich.
Chicago Golf Club
Belvedere
Cape Breton Highlands
York Golf & Tennis
National Golf Links of America
Somerset Hills
Atlantic City CC

Most Artistic Routings

Cape Breton Highlands
Dismal River (Red)
Banff Springs
Jasper Park
Rock Creek
Forest Highlands (Canyon)
Fishers Island
Cascades (Upper)
Pacific Dunes
Friar's Head

Unwalkable Terrain

Sunday River
Stonehouse
Port Carling
Little Traverse Bay
Treetops (Jones)
Tan-Tar-A (Hidden Lake)
Bully Pulpit
Red Ledges
Sanctuary

Most Disjointed Routing

Lochenheath
Hudson National
Village Club of Sands Point
Stonehouse
Royal New Kent
Manitou Passage
Lost Dunes
Salt Lake CC
Victoria, B.C.
Chambers Bay

Best Nine-Hole Courses

Whitinsville
Hooper
The Dunes Club, Mich.
Culver Military Academy
Maxinkuckee
Pelican Beach
Wawashkamo
Phoenixville

Best 27-Hole Complexes

Ridgewood
The Country Club, Mass.
Huntingdon Valley
Banff Springs
Farmington
Firethorn
Hamilton G & CC

Best 36-Hole Complexes

Cabot Links / Cabot Cliffs
Winged Foot
Merion
Baltusrol
Olympia Fields
Dismal River
Whistling Straits
Stonewall
Oak Hill
Pronghorn

Top Multi-Course Complexes

Bandon Dunes Resort
Destination Kohler
Medinah CC
Bethpage State Park
Forest Dunes
Firestone CC
Saucon Valley
The Broadmoor Resort
260

Odd Numbers

10 holes - The Walton Club, Pine Valley Short Course, Farmington "3rd nine"
13 holes - Bandon Preserve
19 holes - Engineers, Forest Dunes, Kinloch, Knollwood, North Shore (NY), Sebonack, Blackthorn
20 holes - Double Eagle

Schizophrenic Courses

York Golf & Tennis Club
Misquamicut
The Creek Club
East Hampton
Maidstone
Forest Dunes (The Loop)
Brickyard Crossing
Bayside, Nebr.

Best "B Side" Course

Bandon Trails
Cabot Links
Baltusrol (Upper)
Forest Dunes (The Loop)
Winged Foot (East)
Olympia Fields (South)
Stonewall (North)
Oak Hill (West)
Medinah (#1)

Odd Couples - Distinctly Different Courses

Whistling Straits
Devil's Paintbrush / Devil's Pulpit
Indianwood
Black Forest / Wilderness Valley
Marquette / Greywalls
Dismal River
Old Channel Trail
Riverdale, CO

Best Par-3's

Merion (East)
Camargo
Somerset Hills
CC of Buffalo
Forsgate (East)
Pine Valley
Sand Hills
Manufacturers
Jasper Park
Banff Springs

Best Par-4's

Pine Valley
Shinnecock Hills
Oakmont
Cabot Links
Huntington CC
White Bear Yacht Club
Dismal River (Red)
St. George's, ON
Wykagyl
Rock Creek

The Devil's Cauldron at Banff.

Best Par-5's

Friar's Head
Cape Breton Highlands
Sand Hills
Roaring Gap
Beverly
Blackwolf Run (River)
Muirfield Village
Sebonack
Pine Valley
Butler National

Best Short Par-4's

Crystal Downs
Merion (East)
Pine Valley
National Golf Links of America
Pacific Dunes
Prairie Dunes
Shinnecock Hills
Ballyneal
Olympia Fields (South)

Best Front Nine

Pine Valley
Crystal Downs
Fishers Island
Pacific Dunes
National Golf Links of America
Sand Hills
Jasper Park
Gamble Sands
Prairie Dunes
Whitinsville

Best Starting Holes (1-2-3)

Hooper
Yale
Garden City Golf Club
Chicago Golf Club
National Golf Links of America
White Bear Yacht Club
Merion (East)
Pine Valley

Favorite Stretches of Holes

Cabot Links 10-16
National Golf Links 3-8
Pacific Dunes 6-11
Rock Creek 10-15
Shinnecock Hills 9-14
Shoreacres 10-15
Crystal Downs 5-9
Friar's Head 13-17
Whitinsville 5-9
Wykagyl 3-8
George Wright 4-8
Pine Valley 2-5
Bethpage Black 4-6
Tumble Creek 4-6
Yale 8-10

Best Back Nine

Essex County, Mass.
Shinnecock Hills
Somerset Hills
Pine Valley
Winged Foot (West)
Kirtland
Oakland Hills (South)
Cabot Cliffs
Ballyneal
Inverness

Best Finishing Holes (16-17-18)

National Golf Links of America
Sand Hills
Cabot Cliffs
Merion (East)
Jasper Park
Davenport CC
Dismal River (Red)
Inverness
Ballyneal
Capilano

Most Fun to Play

National Golf Links of America
Ballyneal
Roaring Gap
Jasper Park
Gamble Sands
Myopia Hunt Club
Pacific Dunes
Lawsonia
Cape Arundel
Sleepy Hollow

Best Bunkering

Banff Springs
Pacific Dunes
Yale
Oakmont
Garden City
Friar's Head
Hollywood
Myopia Hunt Club
The Prairie Club (Dunes)
Jasper Park

Wildest Greens

French Lick (Ross)
Engineers
Brookside, Ohio
Somerset Hills
Oakmont
Stonewall (North)
CC of Scranton
White Bear Yacht Club
Oakland Hills (South)
Lost Dunes

Best Courses With No Water Hazards

Sand Hills
Ballyneal
Friar's Head
Garden City Golf Club
Kingsley
Hooper
Chambers Bay
NCR (South)
The Loop at Forest Dunes

Best Bridges

Merion (East)
The Golf Club
Mayfield
Crooked Stick

Deepest Bunkers

Whippoorwill
Yale
Tamarack
Royal New Kent
Eastward Ho!
Lawsonia
Engineers
Forsgate
Fishers Island
French Lick (Dye)

Biggest Greens

Old Macdonald
Meadow Brook
The Sharon GC
National Golf Links of America
Wilmington CC (South)
Bedens Brook
Sagebrush
Devil's Paintbrush
Gamble Sands
Chicago Golf Club

Best Mounds

Myopia Hunt Club
Jasper Park
Moundbuilders
Somerset Hills
Harrison Hills
Garden City Golf Club

Fastest Fairways

Cabot Links
Old Macdonald
Chambers Bay
Ballyneal
The Kingsley Club

Sunday River looks north into miles of mountain wilderness.

Best Courses to Own a House On
[if you don't have to pay the property taxes]

Fishers Island
Roaring Gap
Oyster Harbors
Somerset Hills
Merion (East)
Bald Peak
Pine Valley
Wade Hampton
CC of Detroit
Flint Hills National

Too Many Houses

McGregor Links
Riverfront, Va.
Willowbend
Glenmoor, Colo.
Tallgrass, Kans.

Best Courses to Own a House On
[if you had to pay for it]

Crooked Stick
Prairie Dunes
Firethorn
Rock Creek
Tumble Creek
Crystal Downs
Biltmore Forest
Monroe, N.Y.
Northport Point
Forest Dunes

Best Spectator Courses

Muirfield Village
TPC at River Highlands
Oakmont
Glen Abbey
Oakland Hills (South)

"Dumb Blonde" Awards
  - Gorgeous but Lacking Substance

Sandpines
Sunday River
Bayonne
Caves Valley
Arrowhead

"Ends of the Earth"

Valley of the Eagles
Cape Breton Highlands
North Haven
Prouts Neck
Kittansett
Sakonnet
Gibson Island
Cabot Cliffs
Northport Point

"Sleeping Beauties"
  - More Than Meets the Eye

Springbrook, Maine
Bald Peak
Fenway
Mountain Ridge
Redtail
Teugega
The Broadmoor (East)
Belvedere
Warren Course at Notre Dame
Common Ground

Hardest to Find

Redtail
Newport
Tamarack
The Dunes Club
Halifax (Old Ashburn)
Roaring Gap

Even on a foggy morning, Prouts Neck is a beautiful corner of the world.

Upgrades from the Previous Edition

Old Elm
Lawsonia
Yale
Whippoorwill

Best Restorations

Sleepy Hollow
CC of Buffalo
Davenport
Waverley
Moraine
Hollywood
Roaring Gap
Indianwood (Old)
Culver
Wykagyl

Best Preserved Golf Courses

Myopia Hunt Club
Cape Arundel
Garden City Golf Club
Crystal Downs

Best Redesigns

TPC at River Highlands
Medinah #1
Olympia Fields (South)

Worst Redesigns

Timber Point
Shawnee on Delaware
Oak Hill (East)
Denison
Inverness

Courses That Would Most Benefit
From Restoration

Shawnee on Delaware
Hamilton
Kankakee Elks
Cascades (Upper)
Royal Colwood
McGregor Links
Baltusrol (Lower)
Rochester, MN
Newport
Veenker Memorial

Architects Whose Best Works
Are In Volume 3

Bill Coore
William Flynn
William Langford
Charles Blair Macdonald
Willie Park, Jr.
Seth Raynor
Donald Ross
Stanley Thompson
A.W. Tillinghast
Walter Travis

Best Courses That No Longer Exist

Lido Golf Club, NY
Mill Road Farm, IL
Sutton Bay, SD (Original 18)
The Links Golf Club, NY *
High Pointe, MI *
Wyandot, OH
Ithaca Country Club, NY
Beechtree, MD *
Annapolis Roads, MD

* courses I saw [or built] first-hand

ECLECTIC 18's

The Best 18 Holes in The Americas (Summer Destinations)
  (4 X 18 holes with no duplicates, and no more than one hole from any course on each list)

CONSENSUS LIST

#1	549	Sand Hills
#2	205	Somerset Hills
#3	451	The Country Club, MA
#4	517	Bethpage (Black)
#5	504	Merion (East)
#6	316	Pacific Dunes
#7	484	Inverness
#8	468	Prairie Dunes
#9	213	Yale
#10	632	Rock Creek
#11	175	Essex County, MA
#12	667	Oakmont
#13	486	Pine Valley
#14	440	Banff Springs
#15	588	Cabot Cliffs
#16	540	Shinnecock Hills
#17	375	National Golf Links of America
#18	190	Garden City Golf Club

The uphill par-3 11th at Essex County was one of just three holes nominated by all four of us.

Tom's nominees				Ran's nominees		
#1	549	Sand Hills		#1	302	Garden City Golf Club
#2	301	Gamble Sands		#2	205	Somerset Hills
#3	451	The Country Club, MA		#3	426	National Golf Links of America
#4	175	Banff Springs		#4	397	Fishers Island
#5	580	Pete Dye Golf Club, WV		#5	504	Merion (East)
#6	316	Pacific Dunes		#6	527	Piping Rock
#7	484	Inverness		#7	326	Moraine
#8	550	Crystal Downs		#8	400	Pacific Dunes
#9	231	Jasper Park		#9	213	Yale
#10	440	Highlands, NC		#10	632	Rock Creek
#11	158	Shinnecock Hills		#11	175	Essex County, MA
#12	375	Ballyneal		#12	449	Kirtland
#13	486	Pine Valley		#13	454	Friar's Head
#14	523	Friar's Head		#14	440	Olympia Fields (North)
#15	465	The Kingsley Club		#15	413	Cabot Links
#16	423	Davenport		#16	539	Roaring Gap
#17	246	Merion (East)		#17	122	St. George's, NY
#18	451	Stonewall (Old)		#18	358	Inverness

The short par-4 12th at Ballyneal features one of the great, wild greens in all of golf.

Friar's Head had three holes chosen for our eclectic 18's: here is Darius' pick, the par-4 9th.

Masa's nominees				Darius' nominees		
#1	350	Merion (East)		#1	382	Ballyneal
#2	401	Oak Hill (East)		#2	365	Pine Valley
#3	219	Chicago Golf Club		#3	428	Oakmont
#4	408	Bandon Trails		#4	517	Bethpage (Black)
#5	238	Pine Valley		#5	229	Fishers Island
#6	475	Sleepy Hollow		#6	470	The Golf Club, OH
#7	335	Crystal Downs		#7	484	Somerset Hills
#8	122	Victoria, BC		#8	468	Prairie Dunes
#9	402	Maidstone (West)		#9	400	Friar's Head
#10	452	Hazeltine National		#10	188	Winged Foot (West)
#11	496	Sebonack		#11	148	Pacific Dunes
#12	667	Oakmont		#12	383	White Bear Yacht Club
#13	444	Pacific Dunes		#13	344	Salem
#14	440	Banff Springs		#14	443	Shinnecock Hills
#15	529	Muirfield Village		#15	588	Cabot Cliffs
#16	540	Shinnecock Hills		#16	415	National Golf Links of America
#17	375	National Golf Links of America		#17	150	Sand Hills
#18	190	Garden City Golf Club		#18	521	Merion (East)

Perry Maxwell's short 2nd at Prairie Dunes (seen here from behind the green) is his most iconic par-3.

Honorable Mention - Par 3 Holes			Honorable Mention - Par 5 Holes		
#2	164	Prairie Dunes	#1	456	Hooper
#2	137	Garden City Golf Club	#2	565	Point O'Woods
#3	167	Kittansett	#3	549	Bandon Trails
#3	225	Rolling Rock	#3	499	Pacific Dunes
#4	195	National Golf Links of America	#4	611	Tumble Creek
#4	225	Friar's Head	#7	570	Cape Breton Highlands
#6	187	CC of Buffalo	#7	592	Ekwanok
#6	146	Roaring Gap	#7	636	Pine Valley
#7	207	Chicago Golf Club	#8	515	Ballyneal
#9	136	Myopia Hunt Club	#9	530	Interlachen
#10	161	Pine Valley	#10	481	Chevy Chase
#10	139	Chicago Golf Club	#11	620	Cabot Links
#11	148	Plainfield	#14	508	Sand Hills
#11	164	Fishers Island	#14	603	Baltimore CC (East)
#14	148	Maidstone (West)	#14	576	Quaker Ridge
#15	192	Camargo	#15	521	Shoreacres
#15	139	Chambers Bay	#16	612	Sand Hills
#15	138	Jasper Park	#17	523	Prairie Dunes
#16	155	Sleepy Hollow	#18	570	Sebonack

Honorable Mention - Par 4 Holes

#1	460	Crystal Downs	#10	525	Kirtland
#1	450	Winged Foot (West)	#10	414	Garden City Golf Club
#1	341	Old Macdonald	#11	428	Lost Dunes
#2	401	Cabot Cliffs	#11	378	Shoreacres
#3	330	Cabot Links	#12	445	Chicago Golf Club
#4	388	Dismal River (Red)	#13	332	Shoreacres
#4	392	Myopia Hunt Club	#14	334	Ekwanok
#5	353	Crystal Downs	#14	360	Cedar Rapids
#5	441	White Bear Yacht Club	#15	406	Bandon Trails
#6	353	Olympia Fields (South)	#15	327	Crystal Downs
#6	450	The Creek	#15	431	Gozzer Ranch
#6	465	Cabot Links	#15	352	Rock Creek
#7	352	Ballyneal	#16	363	Bandon Dunes
#7	486	Rock Creek	#16	430	Merion (East)
#8	400	National Golf Links of America	#16	457	Cabot Links
#8	326	Pine Valley	#17	387	The Country Club, OH
#8	445	Wykagyl	#17	331	Cabot Cliffs
#9	443	Shinnecock Hills	#18	427	Davenport
			#18	484	Oakmont
			#18	467	Sand Hills

The uphill 4th at Tumble Creek is one of my best-ever par-5 holes.

COURSES IN ORDER OF DOAK SCALE RATING

I have included this feature in the book because so many readers have asked for it. We do not intend it as a "ranking" of courses in any way. Courses are listed in order of the highest grade given by one of us.

While the book gives the impression that the four of us think alike, you will see below that about half of the time, my co-authors disagree with my rating for a course, but seldom by more than one point. In many of those cases, a lower rating is outdated after the renovation of a course; in the rest, just assume they're wrong!

10 10 10 10	Pine Valley
10 10 10 10	Sand Hills
10 10 10 10	Shinnecock Hills
10 10 10 9	National Golf Links of America
10 10 10 9	Merion (East)
9 10 9 9	Oakmont
10 9 10 9	Pacific Dunes
10 8 9 8	Crystal Downs
9 9 9 9	Ballyneal
9 9 8 9	Friar's Head
9 9 8 8	Prairie Dunes
9 9 - 7	Rock Creek Cattle Company
8 9 8 8	Bandon Trails
8 9 - 8	Cabot Links
8 8 9 8	Chicago Golf Club
8 9 8 8	Fishers Island
9 8 8 8	Winged Foot (West)
8 9 8 7	Garden City Golf Club
9 8 - 7	Oakland Hills (South)
8 9 7 7	The Country Club, MA
8 8 8 8	Old Macdonald
8 8 8 8	St. George's, ON
8 8 8 8	Somerset Hills

8 8 8 7	Banff Springs
8 8 - 8	Cabot Cliffs
7 8 8 8	Essex County, MA
8 8 8 7	Highlands Links, NS
8 8 8 7	Quaker Ridge
8 8 7 7	Bethpage (Black)
7 8 8 7	Camargo
7 8 8 7	Capilano
8 8 - 7	Dismal River (Red)
7 8 7 8	Eastward Ho!
8 8 7 7	Inverness
8 8 7 7	Jasper Park
7 8 8 7	Maidstone
7 8 8 7	Old Sandwich
8 7 8 7	Shoreacres
8 7 8 7	The Golf Club, OH
8 6 8 7	Sebonack
8 8 - 6	Yale
7 8 7 7	Chambers Bay
8 7 - 7	Gamble Sands
8 - - -	Forest Highlands (Canyons)
8 7 - -	Glens Falls
- 8 7 -	Kirtland
- 8 - -	Moraine
8 7 7 7	Muirfield Village
7 7 8 7	Myopia Hunt Club
8 7 7 7	Plainfield
7 8 7 7	Ridgewood
7 7 8 7	Sleepy Hollow
7 8 7 7	Wade Hampton
7 7 8 7	Whistling Straits (Straits)
7 6 8 7	Baltusrol (Lower)
5 8 - -	Culver
7 6 8 7	Hamilton
8 7 7 6	Lancaster
7 8 7 6	Milwaukee CC
7 8 6 6	Olympia Fields (North)
7 8 7 6	Salem
6 8 6 -	Whippoorwill
7 - 6 8	White Bear Yacht C
8 - 6 -	Whitinsville

7 7 7 7	Aronimink	
7 7 7 7	Baltimore CC (East)	
7 7 7 7	Bandon Dunes	
7 7 7 7	The Creek Club	
7 7 7 6	Baltusrol (Upper)	
7 7 - 7	The Dunes, MI	
7 7 - 7	Franklin Hills	
- 7 7 7	Hidden Creek	
7 7 6 7	Kingsley	
7 7 7 6	Kittansett	
6 7 7 7	Oak Hill (East)	
7 7 6 7	Pete Dye Golf Club, WV	
7 7 7 6	Scioto	
7 - 7 7	Stonewall (Old)	
7 7 7 6	Wannamoisett	
7 7 7 6	Winged Foot (East)	
7 7 6 6	Blackwolf Run (River)	
- 6 7 7	Boston Golf Club	
7 6 7 6	Cascades	
6 7 7 6	Canterbury	
7 6 6 7	Colorado Golf Club	
6 - 7 7	East Hampton	
7 6 - 7	Ekwanok	
7 7 6 6	Fenway	
7 7 - -	Forest Dunes (The Loop)	
7 7 6 6	Huntingdon Valley	
6 - 7 7	Interlachen	
7 7 - 6	Lawsonia (Links)	
7 7 6 6	Lehigh	
7 6 7 6	Lost Dunes	
6 7 7 -	Newport	
- 7 - 7	Olde Farm	
7 - 7 6	Philadelphia Country Club	
6 7 7 6	Piping Rock	
7 7 - 6	Roaring Gap	
7 7 - 6	Rolling Green	
7 6 6 7	Tumble Creek	
6 7 6 7	Victoria National	
7 7 - -	Waverley, OR	
6 7 7 -	Winchester	
6 7 6 7	Wolf Run	
7 7 5 -	Beverly	
6 7 7 5	Congressional (Blue)	

7 7 5 5	Hollywood, NJ
7 7 5 -	Olympia Fields (South)
7 - - -	Bald Peak
- 7 - 6	Ballyhack
7 - - -	Barton Hills
6 7 - -	Blue Mound
6 6 7 6	Broadmoor, IN
- 7 6 -	Charles River
7 - 6 6	Cherry Hills
- 7 - 6	Clear Creek Tahoe
7 6 6 6	Crooked Stick
7 - - -	Davenport
- 7 6 6	Devil's Paintbrush
6 7 6 6	Erin Hills
7 - - -	Forest Dunes
- 7 - -	Flossmoor
6 7 6 -	Forsgate (East)
6 - 7 -	Fox Chapel
- 7 - -	French Lick (Ross)
- - 6 7	Galloway National
- 7 - -	George Wright
- - 6 7	Gozzer Ranch
7 - - -	Harvester
7 - - -	Hooper
6 7 6 -	Indianwood (Old)
7 - - -	Manufacturers
7 - - 6	Marquette (Greywalls)
6 7 6 -	Meadow Brook
7 - - -	Monroe
7 - - -	Mount Bruno
6 7 6 6	Mountain Ridge
6 - 7 -	Nantucket
7 - - -	Northland
- 7 - 6	Orchard Lake
7 - 6 -	Oyster Harbors
7 - - -	Pikewood National
7 - 6 -	Pronghorn (Fazio)
6 7 6 -	St. Louis CC
6 7 - -	Scranton, CC of
- - - 7	Shelter Harbor
7 - - -	Shooting Star
6 7 6 -	Skokie
6 6 7 6	Stonewall (North)
6 7 - -	Taconic

6 7 6 -	The Country Club, OH	
6 - 6 7	Toronto GC	
6 7 - 6	Wild Horse	
6 - 7 -	Wine Valley	
- 7 - -	Wykagyl	
5 7 - -	Black Forest	
5 - 7 -	Century	
5 6 6 7	Essex County, NJ	
5 7 6 5	CC of Fairfield	
- 7 5 -	Farmington	
- 7 6 5	Grandfather	
6 7 5 -	NCR (South)	
6 - 7 5	Royal Montreal (Blue)	
7 6 6 5	Redtail	
6 7 4 -	St. George's, NY	
5 7 - 5	Dismal River (White)	
6 6 6 6	National G & CC, ON	
6 6 6 5	Atlantic	
6 - 6 6	Butler National	
6 - 6 6	Castle Pines GC	
6 - 6 6	Double Eagle	
- 6 6 6	French Lick (Dye)	
6 6 6 -	The Greenbrier (Old White)	
6 6 6 -	Highlands, NC	
- 6 6 6	Kinloch, VA	
6 6 6 5	Saucon Valley (Old)	
6 6 - 6	Warren Course at Notre Dame	
6 - 6 -	Atlantic City	
6 6 - -	Bidermann	
6 - 6 -	Bob O'Link	
- - 6 6	The Bridge	
6 - 6 -	CC at Castle Pines	
6 - - 6	Cataraqui	
6 - 6 5	Cog Hill (No. 4)	
6 6 5 -	Common Ground	
6 - 6 5	Crosswater	
6 6 - -	Crumpin-Fox	
6 6 - -	Deepdale	
6 - 6 -	CC of Detroit	
- 6 - 6	Diamond Creek	
6 6 - -	Engineers	
6 - 6 5	Firestone (North)	
6 6 - -	Firethorn	

6 - 6 5	Glen Abbey
- - 6 6	Hazeltine National
5 - 6 6	Hudson National
6 - 6 5	Laurel Valley
6 6 - -	Mayfield
6 - 5 6	Oak Hill (West)
6 - 6 -	Orchards, MA
6 - 5 6	Philadelphia Cricket C
6 6 - 5	Pilgrim's Run
6 - 6 -	Point O'Woods
6 - 6 -	Pronghorn (Nicklaus)
6 - 6 -	Pumpkin Ridge (Witch Hollow)
6 - 6 -	Rochester, MN
6 - - 6	Teugega
6 6 - -	Treetops (Fazio)
5 - 6 6	Victoria, BC
5 6 6 -	Westhampton
6 - 6 -	Weston
- - 6 6	Wolf Creek, AB (North/South)
5 6 6 4	Ohio State (Scarlet)
- 6 - -	Alpine, NJ
6 - - -	Astoria
6 - - -	Bandon Preserve
6 - - -	Battle Creek
6 - - -	Bethpage (Red)
- 6 - -	Biltmore Forest
- 6 - -	Black Rock, MA
6 - - -	Blue Lakes
- 6 - -	Boonesboro
6 - - -	Brae Burn
6 - - -	Brookside, OH
6 - - -	Buffalo, CC of
6 - - -	Burning Tree
6 - - -	Calgary
6 - - -	Cape Arundel
6 - - -	Cedar Rapids
- - 6 -	Dakota Dunes, SK
6 - - -	Des Moines (North)
- - - 6	Flint Hills National
- 6 - -	The Fort
- 6 - -	Full Cry
6 - - -	Giant's Ridge (Quarry)
6 - - -	Glenwild
- - - 6	Greywolf

6 - - -	Harrison Hills	
6 - - -	Headwaters	
6 - - -	Huntington CC	
6 - - -	Huntsman Springs	
6 - - -	Idle Hour	
6 - - -	Kahkwa	
6 - - -	Kawartha	
6 - - -	Laval (Blue)	
6 - - -	Leatherstocking	
6 - - -	Longmeadow	
6 - - -	Lookout Point	
- - - 6	Mahopac	
6 - - -	Medford Village	
6 - - -	Medinah (No. 1)	
6 - - -	Moselem Springs	
- - 6 -	Muskoka Bay	
6 - - -	North Shore, NY	
- - 6 -	Olympic View	
- - - 6	Omaha CC	
- - - 6	Oviinbyrd	
- 6 - -	Paramount	
6 - - -	Penobscot Valley	
6 - - -	Prouts Neck	
- - - 6	The Prairie Club (Dunes)	
- - - 6	The Prairie Club (Pines)	
6 - - -	Red Ledges	
6 - - -	Redlands Mesa	
6 - - -	Rhode Island CC	
6 - - -	Robert Trent Jones, VA	
6 - - -	Rolling Rock	
6 - - -	Rutland	
- 6 - -	Saratoga	
6 - - -	Snake River Sporting Club	
- - - 6	Summit	
- - - 6	Sutton Bay	
- 6 - -	Sylvania	
- - - 6	Taboo	
6 - - -	Troy, CC of	
- - - 6	Wilderness Club	
6 - - -	Wilmington, DE (South)	

6 - 5 5	Arcadia Bluffs	
6 - 5 5	Bayonne	
- - 6 5	Beacon Hall	
- - 6 5	Bellerive	

6 - 5 -	Belvedere	
- - 6 5	Bigwin Island	
- - 5 6	Black Sheep	
5 - 6 5	Blackwolf Run (Meadow Valleys)	
- - 5 6	Chevy Chase	
5 - 6 -	Denver CC	
6 - 5 -	Detroit GC (South)	
5 6 5 5	Devil's Pulpit	
5 - 6 -	Edgewood Tahoe	
6 5 5 -	Essex, ON	
5 5 6 5 -	Golden Horseshoe (Gold)	
6 5 5 -	Linville	
6 - 5 5	Medinah (No. 3)	
5 5 6 -	Merion (West)	
6 5 - -	Metacomet	
5 - 6 -	Oak Hill, MA	
5 6 - -	Pine Valley (Short)	
6 - 5 -	Plymouth	
6 - 5 -	Portland, ME	
- - 6 5	Rocky Crest	
6 - - 5	St. Thomas	
- 6 5 5	Sand Ridge	
5 6 - -	Sands Point	
6 - - 5	Stanwich	
- - 6 5	Tetherow	
6 - - 5	Trump Ferry Point	
- - 5 6	Trump National Bedminster (Old)	
5 - 6 5	Westmount	
- - 5 6	Wolf Creek, AB (East/West)	
4 6 - -	Birmingham, MI	
- - 4 6	Blackhawk	
5 6 4 -	Indianwood (New)	
6 - 4 -	Old Elm	
5 6 4 4	Saucon Valley (Grace)	
5 - 5 5	Caves Valley	
5 - 5 5	Columbia, MD	
5 - 5 5	Eugene	
5 - 5 5	Sahalee	
5 - 5 5	University of Michigan	
5 - 5 5	Valhalla	
5 - 5 5	Whistling Straits (Irish)	
5 - 5 -	Arrowhead	
5 - 5 -	Bay Harbor	
5 - 5 -	Boyne Highlands (Ross Memorial)	

5 - 5 -	Brickyard Crossing		5 - - -	Denison
5 5 - -	Crag Burn		- - - 5	Dundarave
5 - 5 -	Detroit GC (North)		5 - - -	Dunmaglas
- 5 - 5	The Foundry		- - - 5	Eagle's Nest
5 5 - -	Gulph Mills		5 - - -	Edina
5 5 - -	Inwood		- - 5 -	Emerald Hills
5 5 - -	Kansas City CC		- - - 5	Forest Highlands (Meadow)
5 - 5 -	Knollwood		- - - 5	Fountain Head
5 - 5 -	London Hunt C		5 - - -	French Creek
5 - - 5	The Mines, MI		5 - - -	The Greenbrier (Greenbrier)
5 - 5 -	North Shore, IL		5 - - -	The Glen Club
5 5 - -	Onwentsia		5 - - -	Glen View, IL
5 - 5 -	Port Ludlow		5 - - -	Golden Valley
- 5 - 5	Pound Ridge		5 - - -	Hawktree
5 5 - -	Quail Crossing		- - 5 -	Kananaskis
5 5 - -	Riverfront, VA		5 - - -	Kanawaki
5 5 - -	Royal New Kent		5 - - -	Kankakee Elks
5 - 5 -	Pumpkin Ridge (Ghost Creek)		5 - - -	Kebo Valley
5 - 5 -	Riverdale (Dunes), CO		5 - - -	Kenosha
5 4 5 -	The Sheep Ranch		5 - - -	Keystone Ranch
- 5 5 -	CC of Virginia		5 - - -	Knoll (West)
4 5 5 -	Wampanoag		5 - - -	Lake Sunapee
5 - 5 -	Westchester (West)		5 - - -	Laval (Green)
5 - 5 -	Worcester, MA		5 - - -	Mark Twain
5 - - -	Amana Colonies		5 - - -	Metedeconk National
5 - - -	Barrington Hills		5 - - -	Minikahda
5 - - -	Bayside, NE		5 - - -	Misquamicut
5 - - -	Bully Pulpit		5 - - -	Mohawk, OH
- 5 - -	Bedens Brook		5 - - -	Morris County
5 - - -	Belgrade Lakes		- 5 - -	NCR (North)
- - - 5	Blackthorn, IN		5 - - -	New Haven CC
- - - 5	Canyata		- 5 - -	New Seabury (Ocean)
5 - 5 -	Broadmoor (East), CO		- 5 - -	Nicklaus North
5 - - -	Brooklawn, CT		5 - - -	Links of North Dakota
5 - - -	Bulle Rock		5 - - -	North Jersey
- - 5 -	Camelot		5 - - -	Northeast Harbor
5 - - -	Canyon Springs		5 - - -	Oakhurst, WV
5 - - -	The Connecticut Golf Club		5 - - -	Old Warson
5 - - -	Chagrin Valley		5 - - -	Old Works
5 - - -	The Champions, KY		5 - - -	Olde Kinderhook
- - - 5	Crowbush Cove		5 - - 5	Oneida
5 - - -	Colbert Hills		5 - - -	Onondaga
5 - - -	Coldstream		5 - - -	Ozaukee
5 - - -	Columbia Edgewater		5 - - -	Palouse Ridge
5 - - -	TPC at Deere Run		5 - - -	Park CC, NY

- 5 - -	Pete Dye River Course, VA	
5 - - -	Philmont (North)	
5 - - -	Pine Hills, WI	
5 - - -	Pinehurst, CO	
5 - - -	Plum Creek	
5 - - -	Plum Hollow	
- - - 5	Port Carling	
5 - - -	Prairie View, IN	
5 - - -	Promontory (Dye Canyons)	
5 - - -	Radrick Farms	
5 - - -	Ravisloe	
5 - - -	Red Rock, SD	
5 - - -	Rockaway Hunting C	
5 - - -	Round Hill	
- - - 5	Royal Colwood	
5 - - -	Royal Montreal (Red)	
5 - - -	The Sagamore	
- - 5 -	St. Andrew's East	
5 - - -	Sakonnet	
5 - - -	Salt Lake CC	
5 - - -	Sand Creek, IN	
5 - - -	Sankaty Head	
5 - - -	Scarboro	
5 - - -	Shanty Creek (Legend)	
5 - - -	The Sharon GC	
- - - 5	Shaughnessy	
- - - 5	Siwanoy	
5 - - -	Somerset	
5 - - -	Sonnenalp	
5 - - -	Southampton	
5 - - -	Southwind	
- - - 5	Spanish Peaks	
5 - - -	Spirit Hollow	
5 - - -	Springbrook	
5 - - -	Staley Farms	
5 - - -	Sunday River	
- - - 5	Sunningdale, NY	
- - - 5	Sycamore Hills	
5 - - -	Tamarack	
5 - - -	3 Creek Ranch	
- - - 5	Tobiano	
5 - - -	Treetops (Jones)	
5 - - -	Veenker Memorial	
- - - 5	Vermont National	
- 5 - -	Vista Links	

5 - - -	Wakonda	
5 - - -	Washington G & CC, VA	
5 - - -	Wawashkamo	
5 - - -	Waynesborough	
5 - - -	Wolf Creek, KS	
5 - - -	Woodhill, MN	
- - - 5	Woodmont (South)	
5 - - -	York G & Tennis	
5 - - -	Wyndance	
5 - - -	Yahnundasis	
- - - 5	Yellowstone Club	
4 - 5 -	Algonquin Hotel	
4 - 5 -	Beaver Creek	
5 - 4 -	Boyne Highlands (Heather)	
- - 4 5	Brantford	
4 - 5 -	Briarwood	
4 - 5 -	The Broadmoor (West), CO	
5 - 4 -	Coeur d'Alene	
- - 5 4	Firestone (South)	
4 - 5 -	Hartford	
5 - 4 -	Kemper Lakes	
4 - 5 -	King Valley, ON	
4 - 5 -	Pinehills, MA	
4 - 5 -	Rochester, NY, CC of	
4 - 5 -	Rockies, CC of the	
- - 5 4	Sanctuary	
4 - 5 -	Sandpines	
5 - 4 4	Saucon Valley (Weyhill)	
4 - 5 -	Tallgrass, KS	
4 - 5 -	Timber Point	
5 - 3 -	Green Bay	
5 - 3 -	McGregor Links	
0 - 5 -	Stonehouse	
- 4 3 4	Bell Bay	
4 - 4 -	Boyne Highlands (Moor)	
4 - 4 4	Congressional (Gold)	
4 - 4 -	Colorado, CC of	
4 - 4 -	Fresh Meadow	
4 4 - -	Halifax (Old Ashburn)	
4 4 - -	Maxinkuckee	
4 - 4 -	Melrose, PA	
4 - 4 -	Midland Hills	
4 - 4 -	Millbrook	
4 - 4 -	Monster GC, NY	

4 - 4 -	New Albany	
4 3 4 -	Ohio State (Grey)	
4 - - -	Agawam Hunt	
4 - - -	Alvamar	
4 - - -	Apawamis	
4 - - -	Audubon, KY	
4 - - -	Bellewood	
4 - - -	Big Spring	
4 - - -	Blind Brook	
4 - - -	Blue Rock Par-3	
4 - - -	Blythefield	
4 - - -	Bonneville	
4 - - -	Boyne Mountain (Alpine)	
4 - - -	Canoe Brook (East)	
4 - - -	Chenequa	
4 - - -	Cold Spring	
4 - - -	Cornell University	
4 - - -	Digby Pines	
4 - - -	Egypt Valley	
4 - - -	Elizabeth Manor	
4 - - -	Elk Ridge	
4 - - -	Fairview, CT	
4 - - -	Garland	
4 - - -	Garrison, NY	
4 - - -	Gearhart GL	
4 - - -	Glen Head	
4 - - -	Grand Haven	
4 - - -	Grand Traverse (The Bear)	
4 - - -	Hanover, NH	
4 - - -	Heartland Crossing	
4 - - -	Hell's Point	
4 - - -	Heritage Hills	
4 - - -	Hiawatha Landing	
4 - - -	Hinsdale	
4 - - -	Hulman Links	
4 - - -	Hurstbourne	
4 - - -	Indian Canyon	
4 - - -	Ladies' GC of Toronto	
- - - 4	Lake Shore, PA	
4 - - -	Little Traverse Bay	
4 - - -	Lochenheath	
4 - - -	Long Island National	
4 - - -	Maple Downs	
4 - - -	Marquette (Heritage)	
4 - - -	Medinah (#2)	

4 - - -	Metropolis	
4 - - -	Montauk Downs	
- 4 - -	Montclair GC	
4 - - -	Muirfield Village, CC of	
4 - - -	New Canaan, CC of	
4 - - -	Nissequogue	
4 - - -	North Haven	
4 - - -	North Hempstead	
4 - - -	Northport Point	
4 - - -	Ocean Dunes	
4 - - -	Old Silo	
4 - - -	Patterson Club	
4 - - -	Pelican Beach	
4 - - -	Perry Park	
4 - - -	Philmont (South)	
4 - - -	Phoenixville	
4 - - -	Pine Meadow	
4 - - -	Richter Park	
4 - - -	Royal Mayfair	
- - 4 -	Royal Ottawa	
4 - - -	St. David's, PA	
4 - - -	Sand Barrens	
4 - - -	Sand Creek, ID	
4 - - -	Shawnee	
4 - - -	Sleepy Hole	
4 - - -	Split Rock	
4 - - -	SunCadia (Prospector)	
4 - - -	Teton Reserve	
4 - - -	Three Ponds Farm	
4 - - -	Trump National Philadelphia	
- - - 4	Tullymore	
4 - - -	Twisted Dune	
4 - - -	Uplands	
4 - - -	Upper Montclair	
4 - - -	Urbana, OH	
4 - - -	Valley of the Eagles	
4 - - -	Village C of Sands Point	
4 - - -	Warwick Hills	
4 - - -	Waveland	
4 - - -	Westmoreland	
4 - - -	Whitemarsh Valley	
4 - - -	Wichita	
- - - 4	Willow Oaks	
4 - - -	Willowbend	
4 - - -	Wilmington (North), DE	

4 - - -	Wolferts Roost	
- - - 4	Woodmont (North)	
4 - - -	Woodway	
3 - 4 -	Baltimore CC (West)	
3 - 4 -	Kernwood	
4 - 3 -	Nassau	
- - 4 3	Rich Harvest	
0 - 3 4	Black Rock, ID	
4 - 2 -	Glenmoor, CO	
3 - - -	Antrim Dells	
3 - - -	Bedford	
3 - - -	Boyne Mountain (Monument)	
3 - - -	Blackfoot	
3 - - -	Calverton Links	
3 - - -	Cardinal Hills	
3 - - -	Cincinnati CC	
3 - - -	Crestview	
3 - - -	Crystal Mountain (Betsie Valley)	
3 - - -	Crystal Mountain (Mtn. Ridge)	
3 - - -	Dannebrog	
3 - - -	Darien, CC of	
3 - - -	Elmbrook	
3 - - -	Granliden on Sunapee	
3 - - -	Harbor Point	
3 - - -	Hidden River	
3 - - -	Highland Links, MA	
3 - - -	Highlands, KS	
3 - - -	Ithaca, CC of	
- 3 - -	Kingsmill (River)	
3 - - -	Lake Success	
3 - - -	Macdonald Park	
3 - - -	Maggie Valley	
3 - - -	Manistee	
3 - - -	Manitou Passage	
3 - - -	Mistwood	
3 - - -	Mt. Kineo	
3 - - -	Old Channel Trail	
3 - - -	Pinecrest, ID	
3 - - -	Polo Fields	
3 - - -	Royal Oaks	
3 - - -	Schuss Mountain	
3 - - -	South Suburban	
3 - - 3	Springville	
3 - - -	Sterling Farms	

3 - - -	Traverse City G & CC
3 - - -	Twin Birch
3 - - -	Walton Club
3 - - -	Wequetonsing
3 - - -	Wentworth by the Sea
3 - - -	White Beeches
3 - - -	Wray
2 - - -	American Legion, IA
2 - - -	Black Mountain
2 - - -	Brandybrook, Legend at
2 - - -	E. Gaynor Brennan
2 - - -	The Briar
2 - - -	Clearview, NY
2 - - -	Don Valley
2 - - -	Essex, IA
2 - - -	Grand Hotel
2 - - -	Hillendale
2 - - -	Jackson Park
2 - - -	Kennedy Municipal
2 - - -	Lake Arbor
2 - - -	Lakeview Par-3
2 - - -	Lawrenceville School
2 - - -	Lido, Town of Hempstead
2 - - -	Meadowink
2 - - -	Mullen
2 - - -	Pocono Manor (East)
2 - - -	Riverdale (Knolls), CO
2 - - -	Rolling Hills, IL
2 - - -	Scalawags
2 - - -	Sugarloaf
2 - - -	South Shore
2 - - -	Tam O'Shanter
2 - - -	Tan-Tar-A (Hidden Lake)
2 - - -	Wilderness Valley
1 - - -	Drummond Island
1 - - -	Fresh Pond
1 - - -	D. Fairchild Wheeler
1 - - -	Gibson Island
1 - - -	Heatherridge
1 - - -	Pine Bay
0 - - -	Kiln Creek
0 - - -	Stone Harbor
0 - - -	Terradyne

INDEX OF GOLF COURSES

284

PHOTO CREDITS

On the cover is a painting by Josh Smith of the 10th at Rock Creek Cattle Company, from a photograph taken by Ran Morrissett.

Unless noted below, all photographs were taken by Tom Doak. Copyrights to each of the images are retained by the photographer.

MOST WANTED LISTS - The Courses We Look Forward to Seeing Someday

Tom's Ten Most Wanted

George Wright Municipal, MA
Kirtland, OH
Knickerbocker, NJ
Martis Camp, Truckee, CA
Mountaintop, NC
Olde Farm, VA
Pepper Pike Club, OH
The Prairie Club (Dunes), NE
Sagebrush Sporting Club, BC
Silvies Valley Ranch, OR

Masa's Ten Most Wanted

Burning Tree, MD
Cabot Cliffs, NS
Davenport, IA
Dismal River (Red), NE
The Dunes Club, MI
Forest Dunes (The Loop), MI
Gamble Sands, WA
Mt. Bruno, QC
Pikewood National, WV
Yale, CT

Ran's Ten Most Wanted

Bedford, NY
Brookside, OH
Century, NY
Forest Highlands, AZ
Harvester, IA
Mt. Bruno, QC
The Prairie Club, NE
Toronto Golf Club, ON
The Vineyard Club, MA
White Bear Yacht Club, MN

Darius' Ten Most Wanted

Beverly, IL
Engineers, NY
Flossmoor, IL
Forest Dunes (The Loop), MI
French Lick (Ross course), IN
Manufacturers, PA
St. Louis CC, MO
The Sheep Ranch, OR
Waverley, OR
Whitinsville, MA

Three Courses We Hope To See Built Someday

Lido Golf Course replica, somewhere or other!
The Prairie Club [Hanse course], NE
Sand Valley [Doak course], WI